The Interfaith Manual

The Interfaith Manual

Rev. Dr. Stephen L. Albert

Waterside Productions

Copyright © 2023 by Rev. Dr. Steve Albert

www.allfaithcenter.org

All rights reserved. This book or any portion thereof may not be reproduced or used in any manner whatsoever without the express written permission of the publisher except for the use of brief quotations in articles and book reviews.

ISBN-13: 978-1-960583-24-6 print edition
ISBN-13: 978-1-960583-25-3 e-book edition

Waterside Productions
2055 Oxford Ave
Cardiff, CA 92007
www.waterside.com

Dedication

*This manual is dedicated to the merging of Souls
and our acceptance and Love of ALL people
no matter how they worship.*

*To my love, my best friend and wife Abigail,
who is the most beautiful example of God's Grace on Earth.*

Thank you God.

*"There are no religions which are false.
All are true in their own fashion;
all answer, though in different ways,
to the given condition of human existence."*
Emile Durkheim

TABLE OF CONTENTS

I. **INTRODUCTION**	1
II. **OVERVIEW**	9
Part 1 - General History About the Faiths	11
Bahá'í	13
Buddhism	14
Christianity	16
Confucianism	20
Hinduism	22
Islam	24
Jainism	25
Judaism	27
Native American	29
New Thought	31
Sikhism	33
Taoism	35
Faith History Time Line	37
Part 2 – WHERE WE CAME FROM (Alphabetically by Faith)	39
Our "Creation Story"	39
Part 3 – OUR DIVISIONS (Alphabetically by Faiths)	57
The Step <u>BEFORE</u> Interfaith	61
Faith Divisions	65
The Laws of Science	
Evolution versus Creationism	99
The Names We Use for "God"	103

Part 4 – WHAT WE STRIVE TO ACHIEVE IN LIFE
    (Alphabetically by Faith) ·119
Our Search for Meaning ·119
Suffering · 127
Original Sin & Salvation · 135
Prayer ·141
Healing · 149
Material Wealth · 157

Part 5 – WHERE WE ARE GOING (Alphabetically by Faith) · · · 165
Death and Dying
    Our Rituals & Prayers · 165
The Soul · 185
Karmic Law · 187

Part 6 – HOW WE CONSIDER OTHER FAITHS
    (Alphabetically by Faith) ·191
Predestination vs. Free Will · 193
Prophets · 201
Conversion · 209

Part 7 – THE TABOOS TO KNOW (Alphabetically by Faith) · · ·215
How NOT To Insult · 215
    Drugs and Alcohol · 222
    General Greeting · 222
Required Rituals & Observances · · · · · · · · · · · · · · · · · · · 225
The Role of Men versus Women · 239

III. HOW TO "DO" INTERFAITH · · · · · · · · · · · · · · · · · · **247**
Part 1 - THE Interfaith Environment · · · · · · · · · · · · · · 249
Holidays & Observances
    The Calendar · 251

Part 2 - Materials for Interfaith Services · · · · · · · · · · · 263
Interfaith Quotes · 263
Miscellaneous Quotes · 271

Part 3 - Interfaith Worship Lessons (Alphabetically by Faiths) · · · 275
On Creativity · 277
On The Environment · 285
On Forgiveness · 291
On Gratitude · 297
On Love · 301
On Marriage and Divorce · 307
On Miracles · 315
On Mysticism · 321
On Peace · 335
On Prosperity · 339
On Spiritual Growth · 345
On Unhappiness/Renewal · 351
On Violence · 357
On Wisdom · 363

Part 4 - INTERFAITH Songs · 369
Weave · 369
No Man Is an Island · 375
One Voice · 371
One God · 372
What a Wonderful World · 372
Simple Gifts · 373
Day By Day, Oh dear Lord · 374
I Believe · 374
On Holy Ground · 375
Surely The Presence · 375
In This Very Room · 376
Let There Be Peace on Earth · 377

REFERENCES · 379
Interfaith Groups Around The World · · · · · · · · · · · · · · · · · · · 391
About The Author · 393

*"I appreciate any organization or individual people
who sincerely make an effort
to promote harmony between humanity,
and particularly harmony between
the various religions.*

I consider it very sacred work and very important work."
His Holiness, The Dalai Lama

I. INTRODUCTION

Since the late 1970s I have advocated peace and understanding between people and, for the most part, until 1990 I had only touched the surface regarding my knowledge about what world peace actually means and how it can be accomplished. I left the discussions about world religions for the researchers and philosophers; I stayed in my comfortable position of helping people to know themselves better and then to learn how to increase their effectiveness with other people who were like themselves. Christians should learn to appreciate themselves, members of their own congregations and then other Christians; Jews should learn to appreciate themselves and then other Jews and so on. I believed, and still do, if you could not learn to really like yourself first, you would have a hard time liking someone else even if they came from your own faith? And if you did see the good in yourself, and in those who were like you, how could you take your acceptance a step farther? Which methods would you use to begin liking someone who was NOT like you or NOT from your own faith? How would you even begin to know which questions to ask people who were different from you so as not to insult the other person or embarrass yourself?

I stayed in my safe world, developing my counseling and ministering abilities, and I slowly drew even further away from the Jewish religious upbringing which I had abandoned in my teens. Throughout the late 1970s through the 1980s I taught meditation and a variety of metaphysical subjects and thought I had reached the high point of my career. In 1990 I found the New Thought Faith which had begun in America in the mid to late 1800s. Thus began my next step into learning how better to define who I was as a person, a spirit and a soul on this planet. It opened the doors for me to explore what I wanted to become in my role as a more enlightened being. In 2000 I found myself writing and talking about world peace and still not completely knowing if the man in the turban sitting in the next row actually wanted the same peace I did.

In December of 2005, my wife Rev. Abigail and I and others from different Faith groups were asked to participate in the Bahá'í's World Religion Day event in Poway, California. From that experience we became the Poway Interfaith Council now called the Poway Interfaith Team. In the summers of 2006 and 2007 we organized eight-week educational and fun seminars where spiritual leaders from eight to ten different faiths spoke about their faith's beliefs. This activity exposed the community and surrounding neighborhoods to a myriad of new understandings, which were geared to helping each person live more contented by and peacefully with each other. Every interfaith speaker I have ever heard has made me believe there are many more similarities than differences between their faith and mine. The longer I became immersed in who THEY were, the more I began to look forward to the wonderful learning and times I spent with my interfaith friends. I more deeply learned about who they were and so often found myself exclaiming, "I believe that also!"

In 2006 I published my first Interfaith book, __REBOOT the SOUL__, which researched what each of the world's religions believed about the existence of the Soul, Death and Dying and the concepts of Karma and Reincarnation. I compared the spiritual beliefs with scientific evidence about the existence of the Soul. Doing all the research and getting answers from my interfaith colleagues, I was learning much more than I had ever expected. It was amazing how similar the beliefs of the different faiths were. My book, __REBOOT to PEACE__ came out in 2007, and I explored the many ways we could create peace within ourselves, our family, others in our community and in our workplace. I also presented the concept of TALK ZONES as designated places in which people from all different backgrounds and faiths could "talk" to one another and get to know how similar they were. I imagined sitting under a "TALK ZONE" sign at an airline boarding gate or restaurant and interacting with travelers from around the world.

The more I interacted with people from different faiths, the more I chose to do further research about Interfaith. I quickly discovered how strong the interest about Interfaith was and I was amazed to learn the Interfaith movement was a wonderful epidemic spreading almost everywhere throughout the globe! People around the world were gathering in interfaith groups and various churches, mosques and temples were offering a variety of interfaith classes, seminars and programs to help bring a deeper understanding of each faith to others. Those who took the time to understand, learned that no one specific religious group had the only "correct" franchise to God. Abigail and I came to the conclusion that our weekly New Thought worship service needed to include the beliefs of many faiths in each weekly worship sermon. To that end in 2007 we began to include multi-faith beliefs in all our weekly New Thought services. At the same time we began working with other faith leaders on OUR DREAM which is to create what will be called The Universal Center or All-Faiths Center This will be a regional gathering place somewhere in or near San Diego which will hold various faiths' services and interfaith services as well as providing community programs about world religions, peace and the integration of subjects like meditation and prayer into daily life. The only two areas I found missing as I began to research Interfaith was a "one place to shop" for all my interfaith questions, and information which would allow me as a minister to integrate more easily other faith beliefs into my own. So... I began to see if I could satisfy my own desires.

As much as I would have liked this Interfaith Manual to have every answer for every question for anyone who might be researching into Interfaith, it does not. Yet it has a myriad of wonderful surprises which you will find very transforming as you read through it. If you have been interested in and studied interfaith before, much of the material in this manual might be familiar to you, and perhaps you may have even aided in the distribution of similar information in your own circles. I applaud you for your actions and I ask that you continue to spread the word.

In order to cover the most ground and to more easily compare the faiths, as well as to have a book with fewer than a thousand pages, I have chosen to present the beliefs of twelve major faiths out of the 1500 or so in the world today suggested by Rev. Hal A. Lingerman, Professor at Palomar College in San Marcos, California. As we compare the faiths' major beliefs and attitudes about life, we will delve into how to grow a little closer to each other in our thinking. The unfortunate part about researching only twelve faiths in depth is that we pass over the special qualities of other important faiths. Certainly, the fantastic, non-violent tenets of Zoroastrianism which are not covered in this manual, positively affected many other faiths and, although the adherents of this faith are very small in number today, they have influenced deeply other religions and individuals who have sought peace or who are today helping to create peace in the world. The Zoroastrian Faith, which some have dated as the world's oldest monotheism, has had a large influence on Judaism, Christianity and Islam, especially relating to the aspects of dualism, judgement at death, heave and hell, a savior born of a virgin, a day of judgement, apocalypse and resurrection. (The Influence of Zoroastrianism, everything2.com)

This manual will also not cover the development of The Axial Age (a term coined by German philosopher Karl Jaspers) which is the period between 800 BCE and 200 BCE during which time the early religious traditions of Iran, South Asia, and China arose and changed views about how people dealt with metaphysics and human development. These changes Jasper says contributed to contemporary Judaism, Christianity, and Islam and together indicate a dynamic jump in consciousness, which changed "Faith" throughout the entire world. (*Religions of the Axial Age*, Mark Muesse, teach 12.com)

There is a consistent structure throughout the Manual which will make it easy to read through and search for information. Each area of discussion will be titled and then the beliefs of the twelve faiths will follow in alphabetical order.

A manual of this magnitude is obviously not the work of one person. Endless hours were spent seeking out the most accurate websites and references for unbiased information. Hours were spent with members of each faith to be sure the material presented here was as fair as it could be. And yet, as we know, different people interpret the same material differently; we recognize others may feel there might be a wrong depiction or description in a particular passage here or there in this manual. Very Orthodox members of a faith may have very different beliefs about life than someone who follows the (extreme) Reform segment of the same faith. To this end we humbly apologize to anyone who may feel offended by any of the material here within. Our goal is to educate and I assure you the people who contributed to this Interfaith Manual are interested only in all faiths coming together in greater love, peace, and understanding.

PLEASE NOTE: We do not want to convert any faith believer away from their faith's beliefs; rather we wish you to find the beauty in what you believe, and we respect you for honoring the best of your faith. At the same time we want to make you aware of how, in the same way, others feel as passionate about their faith as you do about yours and that it is all good. As someone said, "If you are going to be a Christian, be the best Christian you can be; If you are going to be a Jew, be the best Jew you can be; If you are going to be a Sikh, be the best Sikh you can be," and so forth.

Thank you to all my interfaith friends and to those who helped me with editing this manual with special thanks to Rev. Hal A. Lingerman for his detailed editing of the manual for the second printing. Those friends include: Deidre Merrill and Rick Patton from the Bahá'í Faith and Lynne Yancy from the Review Office at the Bahá'í National Center, Sondra Bushman, Rinpoche Zhai Xhuoma, and Melodie Chang from the Buddhist Faith, Rev. Glen Larsen,

Janet Williams, and Elma Harmston from the Christian Faith, Rev. Dr. John Berthrong from the Confucian Faith, Lakshmi and Srinivas Sukumar from the Hindu Faith and Panditji Rajagopalan, Sri Kathachr T. Rangachar and Panditji Ravi Kumar Trivedi from The Hindu Mandir Society of San Diego, Iman Baseem Syed and Carol Esfahanizadeh from the Islamic Faith, Rohak Vora Past President of the Jain Society of San Diego, Marilyn Clement and Phyllis and Jay Mehlman from the Jewish Faith, Evans Craig and Rev. Adelia Sandoval from the Native American Faith, Gagandeep Kaur and Ramandip Singh from the Sikh Faith, Atma Advani from the Sufi Faith and Dr. Michael Arnold from the Taoist Faith. From the New Thought Faith I have learned so much about interfaith from so many people including Sandi Angotti, Revs. Audrey and Les Turner, Judy Blonski and so many other Ministers and people from the Affiliated New Thought Alliance (ANTN) and of course the number one person who influences my life so positively every day and from whom I derive such incredible learning and joy, my wife Rev. Abigail Albert.

The Dalai Lama has said, "My religion is Kindness" and he has instructed people from throughout the world to, "Do no harm." I would ask you to follow these wise words every day. I would also ask one more thing. Do what you can to spread the word that **WE CAN** live together in peace, WE CAN show compassion for people who are not like us, and WE CAN show respect to all the other Faith-based representatives by acknowledging their right to be who they are in this world.

The Interfaith Manual

Poway Interfaith Team (POINT)
17762 Sat. Andrews Drive
Poway, CA 92064
www.powayinterfaithteam.org

"Lord, make me an instrument of your peace: where there is hatred, let me sow love: where there is injury, pardon; where there is doubt, faith; where there is despair, hope; where there is darkness, light; and where there is sadness, joy."
Saint Francis of Assisi

II. OVERVIEW

PART 1
GENERAL HISTORY
ABOUT THE FAITHS

(The material in this section, and throughout this manual, was gathered from the books, <u>Bridging Our Faiths</u>, The Interreligious Council of San Diego, Paulist Press 1997, <u>How to Be a Perfect Stranger</u>, Stuart Matlins, Sunlight Paths Publishing, 2006, <u>The Spiritual Seeker's Guide,</u> Steven Sadlier, Allwon Publishing, 1992, scores of internet sites plus interviews with representatives from each faith and material gathered from seminars, classes and from each faith's holy books.)

One underlying goal of this manual is to attempt to define more deeply what people have had a difficult time defining for centuries, that is, what is the difference between a "Religion" and a "Faith?" Furthermore, can one Religion or Faith have the only "right answers" as to how each person should behave and live his or her life. As the root of the word "religion" is usually traced to the Latin *religare* (*re*: back, and *ligare*: to bind), so the term is associated with "being bound" by choice or by commitment to the tenets of a particular faith system. Religion may embrace a conception of "faith." The reference is generally that which individuals or groups are loyal to, believe in, and place their trust in. So the offerings of a religion are geared to the setting down of liturgical tenets or rules for people to follow concerning how to live life and interact with everything and everyone in their environment. Religion has been called, "reverence for the Holy."

Faith however, is based upon the person's personal interpretation of or feelings about the "intangible parts" of life, such as the feelings and emotions they have regarding the liturgical tenets of a particular religious organization. Faith is a trust you place in your belief in God and your religion. When you say, "I believe this or that about my religion," how do you feel inside when you state you have that belief? Saying, "I believe in" can be very different that saying, "I have faith in." When you participate in a religious rite, chant a spiritual song or read a particular verse or passage from a religious book, do you resonate with what you are doing? For me it can be as simple as holding the hands of people who are encircling a room and loudly singing "Let There Be Peace on Earth" and who are obviously meaning the words they are singing. Many times I well up with tears and have a hard time getting the words out as I am "feeling" the experience of everyone else's Faith. It all depends on what you value in the experiences of your chosen religion. Having faith brings you closer to having a relationship with God rather than only observing certain rituals of that faith.

"Whereas a theist may express such a faith in a god, an atheist or a humanist may also claim to have such a value-center that gives meaning and direction to life. This value-center could be a faith in the possibilities and potentials of "humanity." Inasmuch as many religions have humanistic concerns and dimensions, there will be overlaps in outreach to those in need and in the interpretation of meaningful response. Whereas the religious person may respond to human need because his or her faith system demands such response, the humanist will respond out of the well-springs of compassion. The responses may be the same or paralleled, but the motivations will emerge from different value-centers." (What Is "Religion?" Gerald A. Larue)

Perhaps the easiest analogy to use to discuss "Faith" and "Interfaith" is to picture a crowded room of strangers from all different parts of the world; on every wall is a scrolling projection of slides depicting magnificent pictures of sunsets & sunrises, children smiling and playing together, colorful flowers and plants, seascapes and similar beautiful pictures. Without needing words, each person in the room will most likely have the same reactions with oohs and aahs and even applause. "Faith" is not generated by words but by the feelings one has inside about something. When that Faith is about something good the reaction is intensified. "Interfaith" is the coming together of those wonderful common feelings of good shared by all different types of religious and non-religious people for the good of all. It is all about us finding the commonalities between us regarding our feelings and how we can appreciate and enjoy each other's being human.

Bahá'í – The Bahá'í Faith sprang out of the Islamic movement in Persia (Iran) on May 23, 1844. The Báb (meaning the Gate or Doorway) was a Siyyid, an actual descendant of Prophet Muhammad. The Báb was the forerunner to the One He called "Him Whom God shall make manifest," a Messenger of God to come after Him. In 1863 Baha'u'llah (disciple of The Báb) announced he was the messianic figure predicted. The Bahá'ís believe he is the second coming of Jesus the Christ. The Religious Authority is Baha'u'llah's teachings.

The Nineteenth Day (Spiritual) Feast is the centerpiece of their services. It is held on the first day of each of the 19 months in the Bahá'í calendar. The Bahá'í Faith calendar has 19 months of 19 days with 4 extra days (5 days in a leap year). The year begins on March 21, which is the first day of Spring. These services are the local community's regular worship gathering. Devotions and selections are read from the writings of the Bahá'í Faith and other faiths. Then there is a general discussion. This lasts about 90 minutes. The Nineteen Day "Spiritual" Feast can fall on any day of the week.

A local area may have regular devotional services scheduled for a particular day, but that is not universally the case. Also, while some communities may hold Sunday schools, not all do. Readings at these events include numerous Bahá'í scriptures published under several titles. Also, readings from other sacred texts (the Bible, Koran, etc.) may form part of the devotional programs. On Sunday mornings Bahá'ís offer Sunday school for youth. In the service, a Chairperson or host conducts the service and makes the announcements. The Bahá'í Faith has no clergy, ministers or priests. Their meetings are for worship and spiritual education; elected bodies known as Spiritual Assemblies direct their activities. They meet in homes, community centers and/or in a local Bahá'í Center on a property purchased for the purpose of having a central meeting location. Every Bahá'í is instructed to pray daily and study the sacred writings. (Lynne Yancy, Bahá'í National Center)

The Baha'i Faith scriptures constitute the books, essays and letters composed by Baha'u'llah, `Abdu'l-Baha, and Shoghi Effendi. Together they comprise nearly 60,000 letters, a significant portion of which are available in English; the content of this scriptural corpus is encyclopedic in nature. The Bahá'í teachings are those principles and values promulgated in the Bahá'í scriptures, and touch on nearly every aspect of human life. (*The Bahá'í Faith*, United Communities of Spirit, Dr. Robert Stockman)

Buddhism – Buddhism began in the 6th Century BCE in Northern India (now southern Nepal) with Siddhartha Gautama. He was the son of a King, who was brought up in a very wealthy environment, not knowing about the ills of the common man. At the age of twenty-nine Siddhartha, without his wife and child, left the palace because he had seen the old, weak, sick, and diseased people outside in the city. He practiced austerities until He starved himself almost to death. He then realized he needed a healthy body to continue. Then he sat under the Bodhi tree until the age of 35 when he became the Buddha, the Enlightened One. He taught the Noble Eightfold Path through the 4 Noble Truths, which are discussed later in this manual. The truths discovered by the Buddha might be called "religious authority," but there really is no dogma in Buddhism. The Buddha said, "You should take these principles and test them for yourself and do not accept them just because I said so." Buddhists take refuge in or rely on the Three Jewels—The Buddha, The Dharma (what the Buddha taught), and the Sangha (The holy followers of the Buddha which became the spiritual community). These are like "role models" that the practitioner relies on to guide him/her in one's quest to become a holy being. (Sondra Buschmann & Rinpoche Zhai Xhuoma)

Tripitaka or "Three Baskets" is a collection of sacred books including the teachings of Buddha which discuss methods of moral standards (The Vinaya), methods of concentration (The Sutras), and metaphysics and the philosophy of Buddhism (The Abhidharma). The worship service is usually on Sunday and lasts from one to two hours. In the service there is the ringing of the Kansho, chanting sutras, singing gathas (hymnals), meditation and messages from the priest, monk or nun. Most temples offer classes for children and adults to learn about the Dharma (Buddhist teachings). In the Sanctuary the altar contains a statue of the main Buddha. Side altars contain statues or pictures of the founder of the particular lineage of the temple. There may also be Dharma Protectors or Dharmapalas, holy beings who watch over the practitioner and protect the teachings. Congregants sit on floor pillows although some temples have pews. The congregation acknowledges the Clergy as "Reverend, Venerable, Lama, or Roshi." Ritual Objects in the service include: incense burner, Ouzo. which are used to burn incense in offerings to Buddha or Mala, a string of beads use to count recitations of a mantra, and a bell to announce the beginning or end of meditation.

Buddhist scriptures are essential to the understanding of Buddhism. The Pali Canon, for example, is the closest to what the Buddha did and said. As mentioned above, the Tripitaka [Sanskrit] [Pali: Tipitaka] is the Canon of the Buddhists, both Theravada and Mahayana. Thus it is possible to speak of several Canons such as the Sthaviravada, Sarvastivada and Mahayana as well as in term of languages like Pali, Chinese and Tibetan. The word is used basically to refer to the literature, the authorship of which is directly or indirectly ascribed to the Buddha himself.

Christianity – Christianity began after the death and resurrection of Jesus of Nazareth approximately 32 C.E. Led by the Apostles who followed Jesus, the Jews and gentiles (Roman and Greek people of the times) gathered in the homes of followers who believed Jesus was the foretold Messiah of the Jews and the savior of those who were waiting for the "Christ" (the anointed one) to heal the world. The "Christian" faith was birthed and the gospel of grace began being preached from 70-312 C.E. although the Jewish, Greek and Roman people who attended meetings and became the Jesus Movement, were far from being a strong one-minded congregation.

The major shift came in the year 325 when under the rule of the Emperor Constantine, the Nicene Creed was written to unify the Christian church and declare Christianity the official religion of the Roman Empire. Under this core set of beliefs, a blueprint was constructed detailing what one could believe and what would be considered heresy. The Creed read:

"We believe in one God the Father Almighty, Maker of heaven and earth, and of all things visible and invisible. And in one Lord Jesus Christ, the only-begotten Son of God, begotten of the Father before all worlds, God of God, Light of Light, Very God of Very God, begotten, not made, being of one substance with the Father by whom all things were made; who for us men, and for our salvation, came down from heaven, and was incarnate by the Holy Spirit of the Virgin Mary, and was made man, and was crucified also for us under Pontius Pilate. He suffered and was buried, and the third day he rose again according to the Scriptures, and ascended into heaven, and sitteth on the right hand of the Father. And he shall come again with glory to judge both the quick and the dead, whose kingdom shall have no end. And we believe in the Holy Spirit, the Lord and Giver of Life, who proceedeth from the Father and the Son, who with the Father and the Son together is worshipped and glorified, who spoke by the prophets. And we believe one holy catholic and apostolic Church. We acknowledge one baptism for the remission of sins. And we look for the resurrection of the dead, and the life of the world to come. Amen." (The Nicene Creed)

The age of Catholic Christianity followed with the spread of the Christian faith formally establishing Jesus' incarnation as God in human form. Those early believers who chose not to follow this belief were considered heretics and became martyrs. A heretic was someone who practiced or believed in something which was labeled as unorthodox by one or more of the Christian churches. The first church councils canonizing the scriptures were formed between 325 and 590, and Christianity then became a faith for the masses. Between 367 and 327 the books of the New Testament were canonized and made the standard. It was also the start of Monasticism which was the religious practice in which one renounced worldly pursuits in order to fully devote one's life to spiritual work. (Rev. Glen Larsen) Note: Monasticism of the Essenes in the time of Jesus became the monks and nuns of the Roman Church and the Eastern Orthodox church.

Although each of the different "Christian" divisions today has its own style of church service, the scriptures for most Christian faiths are the New Testament Bible. Those who follow the Catholic Church [Apostolic succession (Peter)] are very different from many others in the various Protestant churches. Of the many different Protestant churches, Southern Baptists are very different than those who attend The United Church of Christ, and both of them are very different from others such as the Mormon church called Church of Jesus Christ of Latter Day Saints. In general, there are reported to be 39,000 different denominations and groups in Christianity which would be very difficult to compare in one book or manual. (Rev. Hal Lingerman)

The Roman Catholic Church clergy members wear a zucchetto on their head which is based on a very old *kippah* design similar to the Jewish yarmulka. The color of their zucchetto denotes the rank of the wearer. Worship tends to have two major parts: the Word and the Sacraments (a sacrament is "an outward and visible sign of an inward and spiritual grace" (from the Anglican Book of Common Prayer)). Services often begin with a combination of prayer, responsive readings and music, all of which simply celebrate being in God's presence. This is adoration. Catholic worship also includes readings from the Bible and some exposition. This is normally referred to as a "homily," rather than a sermon. The center of worship in the Catholic church, as well as other "liturgical" churches, is the Eucharist or sacrament of Holy Communion. Holy Communion is very important in the Christian faith and can be traced back to "The Last Supper" with Jesus on Maundy Thursday before his crucifixion. Maundy Thursday stands for a 'New Mandate' during which time Jesus and his Disciples, all Jews, were celebrating the Passover. The New Mandate gave a new commandment which said, "Love one another as I have loved you." The meal which included Jesus breaking the bread and telling his disciples, "this is (represents) my body" and pouring the wine saying, "this is (represents) my blood" then became the communion event which is celebrated in remembrance of Him. The Holy Communion created a New Covenant between the Christ and all Christians who followed. (Rev. Glen Larsen)

The Protestant churches tend to emphasize the proclamation of the Word. This includes readings from the Bible, and a sermon, which will normally help the congregation understand the reading and apply it to their lives. In addition to believing: 1). Jesus is the only way to God, 2). through the Holy Spirit of God, a sinner can be regenerated and given a new heart, 3). the scriptures are the inspired word of God, 4). that Jesus Christ is God, Man and Lord, Southern Baptists also believe in historic Christian confessions and creeds. In Baptist life each and every church is autonomous. The term "Baptist" refers to a person who believes in the adult "baptism of believers" in Jesus. In other words, Baptists are those who claim a personal faith in Christ alone for salvation and who also reject the baptism of infants, believing that only adult believers in Jesus, (or those at least old enough to actually understand about trusting in Christ), should be baptized. (*Baptist vs. Roman Catholic*, baptist-catholic.com)

Unlike Roman Catholicism which is overseen by the Vatican, neither bishop nor hierarchical body can tell any local church how to conduct its business. There is no manual of discipline. Local churches themselves select their pastors and staff. Baptism is performed by immersion only. The doctrine of a believer's church is a key belief in Baptist life. Members come into the church personally, individually, and freely; no one is "born into the church." Baptists are also evangelicals. (*The Baptist Start Page*, baptiststart.com)

Each congregation of the United Church of Christ is self-governing and sets its own standards for membership, mode of worship, etc. As part of that, each congregation determines the frequency of the celebration of communion. A number of churches now have communion at all services on the first Sunday of the month, and at the first service on all Sundays of the month. They do not have creeds, but they do have statements of faith which they use as affirmations, but not as tests of faith. (ucc.org)

Regular **Mormon worship** takes place on Sundays in buildings called churches or chapels. Unlike in **Mormon temples** which are set aside for special rituals, visitors are always welcome to attend these services. The dress code is generally formal - dresses or skirts are considered appropriate for women, while men generally wear dress slacks and dress shirts, usually with a tie. The service begins with hymns and prayers, followed by the Sacrament Meeting, the main part of a Mormon service. This lasts a little over an hour and involves the whole community together. During the service the members receive a sacramental communion of bread and water, during which they remember the Last Supper, the Atonement of Jesus Christ, and their own baptismal promises to serve the Lord and keep his commandments. A Mormon service also includes several short talks or sermons given by members of the congregation (ranging in age from young to old) chosen by the bishop. These talks range from quite formal doctrinal lectures to more informal chats about the application of faith to family life. The Mormon Church has 4 Standard Works that are authoritative: The Bible (in so far as it is translated correctly) is fourth in order of authority after the Book of Mormon, Doctrine & Covenants, and Pearl of Great Price. Speeches and writings of the current president of the church are also authoritative. (Mormon.org)

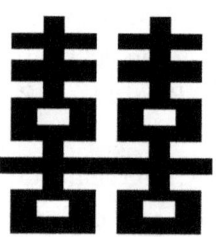

Confucianism - Confucianism is a "Code of conduct" used to live on Earth, and it has had a tremendous impact on how the Chinese live their lives...with a great influence in Chinese government, education, and attitudes toward correct personal behavior and the individual's duties to society. The word "Confucianism," represents the complex system of moral, social, political, and religious teaching built up by Confucius based on the ancient Chinese traditions and perpetuated as the State (ideology) religion down to the present day. Confucianism aims at developing a person of virtue, as well as a scholar of learning and good manners. The perfect person must combine the qualities of saints, scholars, gentlemen and gentlewomen. Furthermore, Confucianism is a religion without positive revelation, with a minimum of dogmatic teachings. Its popular worship is centered in offerings to the dead, where the notion of duty is extended beyond the sphere of proper morals so as to embrace the details of daily life. (religion-cults.com) It is a philosophy that in its most basic form deals with human relationships. All relationships must be approached with virtue which comes from having *li* (decorum and etiquette) and *jen* (humanity and love). (712educators.about.com) (Rev. Dr. John Berthrong)

Confucius was the most influential and respected philosopher in Chinese history. His ideas were the single strongest influence on Chinese society from around 100 B.C. to the A.D. 1900's. The Chinese government made his ideas the official state philosophy, and many nearby countries honored his beliefs. Confucius was believed to have been born in 551 BC., in the state of Lu, known today as the Shandong province. His father, who died while he was a child, named him Kong Qui. (cyberessays.com/History/7)

Confucius taught five fundamental relationships or ideals. The first is *Jen* or the ideal relationship between individuals. It is here that Confucius asked the individual to measure the feelings of others by one's own feelings for them. Second is *Chun tzu* which represents the mature person who can say to someone, "How can I help you" rather than, "What can I get from you." Third was Li or propriety about the way things should be done. Confucius believed in moderation with nothing to the extreme. Fourth is *Te* which is the power by example. Here Confucius asked people to respect their leaders especially those who are older according to their life experience. The fifth and last ideal is *Wen* which is the arts of peace. Confucius felt all the arts like music, painting, or poetry which express beauty and harmony, ennoble the human spirit. Confucius stated that if everyone did their part in these relationships, life would be better. (Rev. Hal Lingerman)

Confucian scriptures include: 1). The *Analects* which were originally compiled by Confucius' students seventy years after his death,

2). The *Mencius* meaning 'a philosopher' which were stories of living, 3). *The Great Learning* alternatively known as Education for Adults, written to illustrate illustrious virtue so as to elevate people to their highest level of excellence, and 4). *The Doctrine of The Means* which was more mystical than the other texts.

Hinduism – Hinduism does not have a founder: there is not one text, there is no elite priesthood and there is incredible variety of thought in the Faith. The word Hindu comes from the river Indus, and it just means the people who live near the Indus River. *Sanatana Dharma*, meaning "Eternal or Universal Righteousness" is the original name of what is now popularly called Hinduism. Sanatana Dharma comprises spiritual laws which govern the human existence. Sanatana Dharma is to human life what natural laws are to the physical world. Just as the phenomena of gravitation existed before it was discovered, the spiritual laws of life are eternal laws which existed before they were discovered by the ancient *rishis* (sages) for the present age during the Vedic period. Sanatana Dharma declares that something cannot come out of nothing and, therefore, the universe itself is the manifestation of the Divine being. This truth forms the invocation of the *Isa Upanishad* (a Hindu scripture):

> *Poornam-adah, poornam-idam, poor-nath poornam-udachyate.*
> *Poor-nasya poornam-adaya, poornam-eva-va-sishyate.*
> That is full; this is full. The full comes out of the full.
> Taking the full from the full, the full itself remains.

This verse expresses the mystery of creation. This universe comes forth from the Divine, yet the universe takes nothing from the Divine and adds nothing to It. Divinity remains ever the same. Since the universe has come forth from the Divine, all things and beings are sacred and must be treated as such in human thought and action. This panentheism view says God is all and all are in God and the whole of God is greater than the sum of its parts. The Divine sleeps in minerals, awakens in plants, walks in animals and thinks in humans. Sanatana Dharma looks upon a person as a part and parcel of the mighty Whole, but never regards him as "the Measure of all things." In the West, "person" is a supreme and final value, while Sanatana Dharma regards person as a part of the Whole, having the same vital essence as all other human and subhuman creatures of the universe. This cosmic view of Hinduism transcends the sectarian or group dogmas and paves a way for the coexistence of all creatures under the Vedic principle of Vasudev Kutumbhkam, meaning "The Universe is One Family." This principle guides humankind towards universal harmony through acceptance and tolerance. *Slokas* are like affirmations and are spoken in the language the speaker understands. The essence of Sanatana Dharma is set in this *sloka* which is acceptable to every human being:

> "*Udarah Sarva Evaite, Jnani Tvatmaiva Me Matam
> Asthitah Sa Hi Yuktatma Mamevanuttamam Gatim*"
> This Sloka states that all those who worship God are
> commendable. But the outstanding devotees, who worship God
> with the single motive to merge in the God,
> are the true devotees who have achieved the highest aim of life.

Sanatana Dharma recognizes that the Ultimate Reality, which is the ground of infinite potentiality and actualization, cannot be limited by any name or concept. The potential for human wholeness (or in other frames of reference, enlightenment, salvation, liberation, transformation, blessedness, nirvana, moksha) is present in every human being. No race or religion is superior, and no color or creed is inferior. All humans are spiritually united like the drops of water in an ocean. (Sanatana Dharma, ansatana-dharma.tripod.com)

Hinduism is a personal, not church-centered faith. There is a basic tie between a teacher, (guru) and his or her students (disciples). A Hindu household has 5 debts to repay daily which are: 1). Debt to God – repaid by prayer, worship, meditation, 2). Debt to the ancient sages – repaid by study of the scriptures, 3). Debt to one's ancestors, -repaid by living honorably and carrying on the family line, 4). Debt to other people – repaid by charity and 5). Debt to lower beings, - repaid by acts of kindness like feeding.

Hindu scriptures include The Four Vedas which are the primary text of Hinduism, The Vedas contain hymns, incantations, and rituals from ancient India. Along with the Book of the Dead, the Enuma Elish, the I Ching, and the Avesta, they are among the most ancient religious texts still in existence. Besides their spiritual value, they also give a unique view of everyday life in India four thousand years ago. The Vedas are also the most ancient extensive texts in an Indo-European language, and as such are invaluable in the study of comparative linguistics. (*Hinduism*, Internet Sacred Text Archive, sacred-texts.com)

Islam - Islam began in 570 CE. The founder, Muhammad, was born in Mecca (Saudi Arabia) and is regarded as the last and final prophet of Allah. In solitude, in a cave he received a revelation from God. Muhammad taught there is one God in heaven, and He demands morality and monotheistic devotion from those he has created. By 632 CE most of Arabia had embraced Islam. The Religious Authority is the Qur'an (Literal Speech of God).

Muslims are required to pray 5 times a day: daybreak, noon, mid-afternoon, sunset and evening wherever they are. Beforehand, they must wash their hands, mouth, face and feet to purify themselves and cleanse the body and spirit and then they also perform 2-4 prostrations with the declaration, "God is most great" and other fixed prayers. At the end of the prayers, the peace greeting (*taslim*) is repeated twice, "Peace be upon all of you and the mercy and the blessings of God." The leader at the worship service, The Imam, delivers the sermon. The *Muezzin* is the man who calls the faithful to prayer and gives the announcements. At Friday noon (*jumma*), a congregational prayer, is said at a mosque for thirty to sixty minutes. Men and women form separate lines for prayer, extending from one side to the other. Women sit and pray behind the men. The tight ranks symbolize unity and equality. Each gender has its own line to maintain modesty and concentration during the physical movements of standing, bowing and prostration. This does not indicate superiority or inferiority.

The principal scriptures of Islam are the Qur'an and the Hadith. The Qur'an is the source of Allah's revelations to humanity, transmitted through his messenger, Muhammad. The Hadith is not considered a direct source of revelation; instead, it is supposed to contain the records of the traditions, practices and decision of the very earliest Muslim community.

Jainism – Jainism is one of the most ancient religious traditions of not just India, but the world. Some scholars trace its antiquity to the Indus Valley civilization dating back to 4000 BC. Jainism is much older than Buddhism and can be truly considered as one of the most ancient and living religions of the world. Jainism is also the most difficult religion to practice because of its uncompromising emphasis on austerities and self-mortification. Jainism was made into a popular religion by Mahavira (599 BC), the 24th Thirthankara (enlightened one) of Jainism. Unlike Buddhism, Jainism remained mostly confined to the Indian subcontinent, and there, too, unlike Buddhism, its influence remained confined to certain sections of society. While Buddhism almost vanished from the subcontinent, Jainism maintained its influence and importance in the religious milieu of India. Today, Jainism is still practiced by eight to ten million Jains all over the world, especially in India. (hinduwebsite.com/Jainism)

The Jain faith has three main beliefs which help set the pulse of everything a Jain may encounter in life. The first is non-violence at a level far beyond any other faith. They believe EVERYTHING has life (a soul; jiva) and nothing should be treated violently. This includes every person, animal, blade of grass, microbe, etc. on the planet. Even the death of a microbe, which cannot be seen is considered violent by a Jain, which is why many Jains cover their mouths when walking in fear that they may inhale and kill a flying bug. They cover their mouth to also guard speech and regulate the temperature of their breath. The second belief is reincarnation and transmigration (returning to a different kingdom of life after death) and every Jain believes they continue to come back life after life until they have completed their sacred journey. This brings us to the third major belief, that of the Fear of Karma which to a Jain is called Karmic Burn or Stains. The Jains believe their reincarnation will not end until they have balanced out, burned, their karmic metal which is accumulated by doing violent acts. They believe we have layers of negative karma around us which develops from hurting another person, stepping on and killing an ant or insect, or killing microbes on your body when we wash. To offset the negative Karma, which usually cannot be helped, and which comes from normal daily life activities, they spend the rest of their day/life doing good for others in one way or another as well as meditating and asking forgiveness every morning and in the evening. (Rohak Vora)

Jain worship provides individuals with a discipline that helps them concentrate on the Jain ideals and cultivate detachment. The worshiper concentrates on the virtues of the tirthankaras and other pure souls, in order to help them follow their example. So for Jains, worship is a means to an end and not just a spiritual end in itself. And worship is not a sufficient means to that end. "Some religions preach that an individual can be saved by devotion to God, the saviour, or to God's incarnations and intermediaries. Jainism teaches we can attain true peace and happiness only through behaving and thinking rightly." (Acharya Kundakunda) A key difference between Jain and Hindu worship, which seems similar on the surface, is that although Jains appear to worship the tirthankaras in particular they don't worship them as persons; what they worship is the ideal of perfection that the tirthankaras have achieved (bbc.co.uk/religion/religions/jainism). Jains reject the Vedas and caste system in Hinduism and recognize higher beings of light: gods of the house, intermediaries, luminaries and astral gods (in the next dimension of life).

The sacred texts of Jainism include the original canon of 71 works from the council of Valabhi (312 B.C.E.), the Angas ("parts") which are made up of 11 books which were dialogues of Mahavira and followers, Upangas which are 12 books complementing the doctrine, Prakirnakas which are 10 assorted books, Cheda Sutras which are 6 books with rules for ascetic life, Culika which are 2 sutras and Mula Sutras which include 4 miscellaneous works. (Jain Society of San Diego)

Judaism - Judaism is a Way Of Life which includes religious rituals and beliefs along with a code of ethical behavior. It incorporates and reflects the history of the Jews as a nation in its ancient rituals, ceremonies and celebrations. The Religious Authority is The Torah, which are the first five books of the Old Testament. "As well as being a religious faith community, Judaism is also called a *Peoplehood*, for all Jews share a history, languages, a literature, a land, a culture and a future." (Yossi Abramowitz.) One becomes a Jew by being born to a Jewish mother or by converting to Judaism. The Reform movement has added Patrilineal descent also for being considered a Jew. There are five Major Jewish Movements: Reform, Reconstructionist, Humanistic, Conservative and Orthodox which includes the fundamental Hasidim. Kabbalistic groups also meet which adhere to the metaphysical/spiritual side of Judaism.

For Orthodox Jews, there is communal or personal prayer done for 15-30 minutes three times daily in the early morning, afternoon, and evening. At least ten people over the age of 13 must be present at each public meeting. Orthodox & Conservative congregations count only the males in attendance for these prayer times. Small private gatherings do not have to have ten people present. The celebration of *Shabbat* (the Jewish Sabbath) begins at sunset on Friday and ends at nightfall on Saturday, or when Jews can see three stars. The major service led by the Rabbi on Friday evening lasts from 30-90 minutes. The service on Saturday morning, also led by the Rabbi and accompanied by a Cantor who sings the Hebrew verses and prayers, is 90 minutes to 3 hours long because it includes the reading of the Torah. The amount of HEBREW used will vary with each congregation. Reform congregations have the least, Orthodox the most. The books used are The Siddur (prayer book), and Torah (Scroll).

The Jewish scriptures include the Torah, the Nevi'im, and the Kethuvim which together is referred to as Tanakh. The Torah, which includes Genesis, Exodus, Leviticus, Numbers and Deuteronomy, is used for teaching and instruction, the Nevi'im discusses the Hebrew Prophets and the Kethuvim contains eleven writings including Psalms and Proverbs. The other scripture book is the Talmud, composed of the Mishnah which is a body of legal and theological material supposedly delivered by God to Moses at the same time as the Torah.

Native American – Long before the white man set foot on American soil, the American Indians, or rather the *Native Americans*, had been living in America. When the Europeans came here, approximately 10 million Indians populated America north of present-day Mexico, and they had been living in America for quite some time. It is believed the first *Native Americans* arrived during the last ice-age, approximately 20,000 - 30,000 years ago through a land-bridge across the Bering Sound, from northeastern Siberia into Alaska. The oldest documented Indian cultures in North America are Sandia (15000 BC), Clovis (12000 BC) and Folsom (8000 BC). Although it is believed that the Indians originated in Asia, few if any of them came from India. The name "Indian" was first applied to them by Christopher Columbus, who believed mistakenly that the mainland and islands of America were part of the Indies, in Asia. (nativeamericans.com)

The Native American faith is considered a Way of Life to the people who follow the various divisions/ tribes. The First Nations religion does not exist as a single, readily identifiable faith and few use the word "religion." There are over 500 Tribal Nations, including 200 dialects in the U.S. and over the last 500 years the Native People have endured constant mistreatment, exploitation and disrespect. The people are wary about sharing their important ceremonies. Both Canadian and U.S. governments tried to eradicate the Indians (the name given by governments) as well as their religious and spiritual traditions in order to "educate" and "civilize" them.

Rev. Dr. Stephen L. Albert

Although there is no one Native American faith, there have been attempts by groups of people to create such a thing. There are those who have been acculturated into a mainstream religion coming from the missionary proselytizing of various denominations. Some have adapted different traditional ways with Christianity. The Bahá'í faith has a large Native American population, as well many Native Americans choosing the Mormon Church. Because of the 1954 Termination and Relocation Act of the US government, many people were separated from their traditional homelands. Many ended up in California while many of the recent generations born in California and descendants of those relocated from other parts of the country have NEVER been on the traditional homelands of their grandparents. Because of this, various groups have formed gatherings, and this is why the Pow Wow has become so popular. Some people have even formed their own clans and bands and dance groups with their own spiritual teachings and rituals, all out of need to be with like-minded people and to identify as Indian. Culturally, the Native American people overall are in an extremely unfortunate place due to the genocidal tendencies of the dominant paradigm. So much tradition has been lost. Bits and pieces still remain. Much has died along with the Elders who had no one to sit at their feet and learn. Many have died with few to carry on the ancient ways that carried the true spiritual power.

The safest thing to say is the Native American experience is based on the relationship they have had on the land they were born on, laughed and cried on, did ceremony on and buried their dead within. Because of this relationship with the land, a deep spiritual message ultimately comes forth. It has to do with gratitude, and it has to do with every act being rendered for those coming and not for those living right now except to teach the children even the little bit that is still alive. The spiritual fire must be kept burning. This is the only hope of the indigenous people of this land. (Rev. Adelia Sandoval, Cultural Liaison, Juaneno Band of Mission Indians/Acjachemen Nation)

The Native American/First Nations religion is primarily about experience, not about theology or doctrine. Ceremonies, customs and cultural traditions (exercising spirituality) at their core are community activities for community members. Native spirituality perceives the entire natural world as deeply endowed with the sacred power of the Creator and always surrounded by It and imbued with one small part of It. Humans are but one part of the natural world, not the privileged or even the only. There are the four-legged, water or winged persons. They are also part of the moral, political and spiritual community. Their job is to recognize Earth as sacred and recognize all members are sacred. They acknowledge the existence of unseen powers. (Evans Craig, Navaho)

There is no one set of scriptures for the Native American faith. The strong spiritual faith of the members of each tribe has, in many ways, a stronger connection to God than other faiths. This bond of kinship comes from them believing every gust of wind, everything which moves and all which they cannot see, is part of God, and thereby they are in continual contact with Spirit. (Rev. Adelia Sandoval)

New Thought – New Thought, not to be confused with New Age, is more than a century-old, practically-oriented spiritual faith which promotes fullness of all aspects of living. It embraces positive thinking, listening to one's inner voice, affirmative prayer, meditation, and other ways of realizing the presence of God within. It began in the mid-1800's with Ralph Waldo Emerson and Phineas P. Quimby who both came to believe the mind can create good health or disease. Many of their beliefs came from Emanuel Swedenborg, who gave metaphysical interpretations of religious scriptures 100 years before. Followers of New Thought believe disease is a belief and can be changed by affirmations and denials and an inward realization of the presence of Spirit. Emerson said, "The measure of mental health is the disposition to find good everywhere." Quimby believed our minds are controlled by a Supreme Wisdom which we can call upon. Following the Apostle Paul's message, "The Christ in you, the hope of glory," (Col:1:27) Quimby was the first to present the idea of the "Christ Principle" in every man. Mary Baker Eddy, a cured patient of Quimby and founder of Christian Science, believed Spirit triumphed over matter. Other New Thought leaders were Thomas Troward, Ralph Waldo Emerson, Emma Curtis Hopkins and Emmet Fox. These people influenced Malinda Cramer, founder of Divine Science, Ralph Waldo Trine and Albert Greel, founders of Church of truth, Myrtle and Charles Filmore, founders of Unity and Ernest Holmes, founder of Religious Science. New Thought was recognized as "The Religion of Healthy-Mindedness" by William James in *The Varieties of Religious Experience.* It involves habitual God-good-aligned mental self-discipline. (Sandi Angotti, New Thought)

Except for Christian Science, which has an outlined set of beliefs defining the organization, New Thought has no dogma or creed but has affinities to idealistic philosophical traditions of all ages and places. (*Phineas Parkhurst Quimby: The Complete Writings,* Science of Mind by Ernest Holmes, Spirits in Rebellion by Braden) Its roots are in Christianity, but it is not limited or bound by it. (Rev. Wendy Craig-Purcell, Unity) William Hornaday, Dr. of Divinity says, "It is a practical and spiritual approach to life." New Thought is not a static or fixed belief system. Ernest Holmes in the Science of Mind says, "Religious Science is a correlation of laws of science, opinions of philosophy and revelations from all religions. It is the wisdom of the ages, with the essence of the world's great spiritual traditions offering a universal key to well-being, which can be used by anyone, anywhere, at any time."

New Thought believers believe, "God is in all, as all and is all" and "There is one life, that Life is God, and that Life is our life now.

There is a Power in the universe greater than you are, and you can use it." New Thought believes this power was present in Jesus the Christ. Jesus embodied the "Christ Principle" and used his God-given power to teach, heal and do only good. Each person has the Christ potential within and continues to grow spiritually. Jesus is the Great Example, not the Great Exception. New Thought believes "Jesus is the Son, begotten of the only Father, not the only begotten Son of God. We are all sons and daughters of God with the potential to embody the Christ on Earth as we raise our consciousness. New Thought continues to develop conceptually, educationally, and organizationally because New Thought affirms freedom of belief of each person. (*Science of Mind*, Ernest Holmes)

New Thought has no one set of scriptures it adheres to. <u>The Science of Mind</u> text by Ernest Holms is the major guideline for all groups of Religious Science followers and <u>The Quest</u> by Richard Jafolla and Mary-Alice Jafolla and <u>Lessons in Truth</u> by Emily Cady are considered guidelines for Unity. In classes and spiritual worship, New Thought churches will refer to the Old and New Testaments, and teachings from Buddhist and Hindu faiths. New Thought believes there is Truth in all religions. (Rev. Abigail Albert)

Sikhism – Sikhism originated in the late 15th century in India through the life and teachings of Guru Nanak (1469-1539 CE), the first Sikh guru. He taught that ALL creation is part of the One Creator. He passed his light to 9 other gurus, who further evolved his teachings. Each guru denounced India's caste system and the oppression of anyone based on class, creed, color or sex. 1708 Guru Gobind Singh (10th and last human guru) "gave" the eternal guruship to the Sikh scriptures known as the Siri Guru Granth Sahib. The Guru Granth Sahib was compiled by the 5th guru, GuruArjan Dev and contains sacred writing by Sikh gurus, several Sikh, Hindu and Moslem saints and bards. The Sikhs bow before the Siri Guru Granth Sahib and consult it as their only guru and treat it with reverence. Guru Gobind Singh also initiated the Khalsa (the Pure Ones). The Khalsa are men and women who have undergone the Sikh baptism ceremony and who follow the Sikh Code of Conduct and Conventions and wear the prescribed five articles of the faith. One of the more noticeable is the uncut hair (required to be covered with a turban for men).

The Sikh place of worship is the *Gurdwara* (Doorway to the Guru). When entering the Gurdwara, everyone is required to remove their shoes and wear a head covering. Often, there are bowls for washing hands and feet. In the main room, the Guru Granth Sahib is elevated at the front of the room under a canopy. Sikhs bow to it, which symbolizes the Infinite Word of God, as an act of humility and acknowledges an Infinite Power pervading all life. All people, regardless of their status, sit on the floor as a sign of equality. Men and women do not generally sit together but on separate sides of the room, both at an equal distance from the Guru Granth Sahib. Gurdwaras are open to all people of all religions and are generally open 24 hours a day. Some Gurdwaras also provide temporary accommodations for visitors or pilgrims. The service consists of *Kirtan* -songs of praise to God, *Ardas* – community prayer lead by any one person, and *Hukam* – the Guru Command, which is read from the SGGS, randomly chosen by the reader. Once the service is over, Sikhs and visitors to the Gurdwara partake of *Langar* (Community Kitchen). In the Langar, all sit on the floor and food is cooked and served by volunteers; this food is available at all times. During Langar, only vegetarian food is served so no person may be offended, and all people of all religions can sit together to share a common meal free of any dietary restrictions. (Gangadeep Kapur) The Sikh's scripture is the Guru Granth Sahib (also known as the Adi Granth) which is truly unique among the world's great scriptures. It is considered the Supreme Spiritual Authority and Head of the Sikh religion, rather than any living person. It is also the only scripture of its kind which contains not only the works of its own religious founders but also writings of people from other faiths.

Taoism—Tao (pronounced "*Dow*") can be roughly translated into English as *path,* or *the way*. It is basically indefinable; it has to be experienced. It "refers to a power which envelops, surrounds and flows through all things, living and non-living." The Tao regulates polarity of natural processes and nourishes balance in the Universe. It embodies the harmony of opposites (i.e. there would be no love without hate, no light without dark, no male without female.)" The founder of Taoism is believed by many to be Lao-Tse (604-531 BCE), a contemporary of Confucius. (Alternative spellings: Lao Tze, Lao Tsu, Lao Tzu, Laozi, Laotze, etc.). He was searching for a way that would avoid the constant feudal warfare and other conflicts that disrupted society during his lifetime. The result was his book *Tao-te-Ching (a.k.a. Daodejing)*. Others believe he is a mythical character. (*Our Beliefs,* Reform Taoist Congregation)

Taoism started as a combination of psychology and philosophy but evolved into a religious faith in 440 CE when it was adopted as a state religion. At that time Lao-Tse became popularly venerated as a deity. Taoism, along with Buddhism and Confucianism, became one of the three great religions of China. With the end of the Ch'ing Dynasty in 1911, state support for Taoism ended. Much of the Taoist heritage was destroyed during the next period of warlordism. Since the Communist victory in 1949, religious freedom has been severely restricted. (*Gods, Ghosts, and Ancestors*, Arthur P. Wolf, Pages 131-182)

The Tao-te-Ching (*The Way of Power*, or "*The Book of the Way*") is the major religious book of Taoism and is believed to have been written by Lao-Tse. It describes the nature of life, the way to peace and how a ruler should lead his life. Religious or esoteric Taoism, as a movement of organized religious communities, developed only in the 2nd century AD, appropriating a variety of themes and spiritual techniques associated with the common objective of immortality. "Religious" services are not held regularly as in other faiths. Members get together for specific holidays and live their faith every day.

Philosophical Daoism's main scriptures are the Dao De Jing [Tao Te Ching], which speaks about the rhythms and flow of life and the power of good, the Zhuang Zi, [Chuang Tzu], which is a composite of writings from various sources and sometimes the Huahu jing [Hua Hu Ching], which discusses the Conversion of the Barbarians, Lie Zi [Lieh Tzu], which discusses the prince and sage Lie Zi, and Wen Zi [Wen Tzu] about Taoist government. Religious Daoism and some other branches use the Daoist Canon (Daozang), which is made up of Three Grottoes and Four Supplements. These consist of almost 5000 individual texts about Taoism collected by Daoist monks.

FAITH HISTORY TIME LINE REVIEW

Native American
North America—15000 B.C.E
Jainism
India—4000 B.C.E
Hinduism
India—1400 B.C.E
Judaism
Mesopotamia—1224 B.C.E
Taoism
China—600 B.C.E
Buddhism
Northern India—560 B.C.E
Confucianism
China—100 B.C.E
Christianity
Judea—29-35 C.E.
Islam
Mecca—622 C.E.
Sikhism
India -1469 C.E.
Baha'i'
Persia (Iran) – 1844 C.E.
New Thought
United States -1879 C.E.

REV. DR. STEPHEN L. ALBERT

*"It is well to remember that the enlightened in every age
have taught that back of all things there is
One Unseen Cause.
In studying the teachings of the great thinkers
we find that a common thread runs through all –
the thread of Unity.
There is no record of any great thinker,
of any age, who taught duality."*
(Ernest Holmes, The Science of Mind, page 44)

PART 2

WHERE WE CAME FROM

Our "Creation Story"

Many of us have been brought up with some religious belief which may have made sense to us as children and young adults, and we have continued with those Faith practices because they were comfortable, or we chose a different path because that new path offered more of the answers we were seeking. A third choice is that we accepted what our parents told us we had to believe and continued to practice the Faith in a piece-meal way until we were on our own. A fourth alternative might have been our choosing not to engage in any Faith practice at all. None of these is wrong as long as whatever we chose to pursue, we work at with conviction and intent. Unfortunately for many people, their early Faith education seemed to be full of holes and made no sense for various reasons. Some people pulled away, while others blindly accepted a Faith leader's word for what actions they were supposed to carry on in life and what a life of Faith was all about.

My wife, Abigail, and I were leaving a movie theatre a few years ago after seeing the movie, "The Nativity Story." In the lobby two boys, perhaps brothers, ages about 11 and 13 were discussing the film and commenting about the absence of "Christian people" in the movie. Since this movie was the story about the birth of Jesus and how his Jewish Mother Mary and Jewish Father Joseph learned of and dealt with Mary's pregnancy and the eventual birth of Jesus in the manger, the period which the movie focused on preceded the start of Christianity by over sixty years. The boys were confused about the basics of their Christian religion. Since no parents were with the boys, I chose not to engage them about the fact that Christians did not exist at that time, and Jesus was Jewish.

I spent years researching and teaching the metaphysical interpretation of the Old and New Testament, and I was told by New Thought people who had begun their Faith journey years before in another Faith, how surprised they were when they actually read the words they had been taught in their church only to find the words meant something else when we explored what was happening at that time in history. I have been in discussion with people who tried to convert me to their beliefs, yet when I questioned them about the meaning of certain chapters and verses which their beliefs were founded on, they could not defend their interpretation of the words.

As was said in the introduction, this Interfaith Manual does not exist to tell you your beliefs might be inaccurate. It exists to allow you to learn what others believe about their faith and to identify how similar you may be from others of a faith you know little about. That said, let's begin to go over the basics of the other major Faiths around the world contemplating about how life began on Earth.

Bahá'í - First of all, we should be clear about what God is for Bahá'ís. Since Bahá'ís do not accept a "literal" interpretation of the Bible, they do not believe the world was created in seven days and that the Earth is only five thousand years old. As Abdu'l-Bahá. (1844-1921), who was the eldest son of Baha'u'llah and who was appointed in Bahá'u'lláh's Will and Testament as His successor and the authorized interpreter of His teachings said of the Old Testament stories, "The divine Words are not to be taken according to their outer sense. They are symbolical and contain realities of spiritual meaning." (Abdu'l-Baha, PUP, p. 458). The Bahá'í conception of God therefore accepts the beliefs of modern science, which expands our understanding of the universe beyond the creationists' beliefs.

Bahá'ís also turn to philosophy when it is guided by spiritual values. Indeed, they believe God works through the sciences and arts to inspire and educate humanity. As Bahá'u'lláh wrote, "Verily We love those men of knowledge who have brought to light such things as promote the best interests of humanity, and We aided them through the potency of Our behest, for well are We able to achieve Our purpose." (Tablets of Bahá'u'lláh, p. 150)

Whether the Lord created this universe through a Big Bang or some other event, or whether the universe has always existed, Bahá'ís believe God is the ultimate Source of the universe and there is great intention and purpose behind its creation. And Bahá'u'lláh wrote, "Having created the world and all that lives and moves therein, He, through the direct operation of His unconstrained and sovereign Will, chose to confer upon man the unique distinction and capacity to know Him and to love Him, a capacity that needs to be regarded as the generating impulse and the primary purpose underlying the whole of creation." (Gleanings From The Writings Of Bahá'u'lláh pg. 65). (dailybahai.com/archives/category/spiritual-growth)

Buddhism - There is no creation story in the Buddhist scriptures. The Buddha said we should not concern ourselves with questions to which there are no answers but concentrate rather on seeking enlightenment and escape from suffering. The key elements in Buddhism are the teachings on the inter-dependence and interconnectedness of all living things. To harm one part is to impact all parts. This teaching links directly with the practice of non-injury or non-violence (the first precept).

The Buddha actually poked fun at the idea of a Creator God, according to The Sutra of Hundred Parables. In this Sutra, he told approximately one hundred humorous stories to his disciples during a sermon. One of the stories told by the Lord Buddha is as follows (Chapter 61): Other religions said, "The Brahma ('God' in Sanskrit) is the Father of all sentient beings. He created everything in the Universe and therefore He is the Lord of everything." Thus, one of His disciples went to see God and said, "I can also create things in the Universe because I am your student." God replied, "This is stupid. Don't even think of it! You cannot create anything at all!" God's disciple did not listen and went ahead to create something. When God saw what his disciple had created, He burst into laughter, "HA! HA! See what you had created? The head is too big! The neck is too small! The hand is too big and the arm too short! And look at the feet: big feet with a very short leg! What you had created is a terrible monster." <u>NOTE</u>: you are free to interpret this story told by Buddha in any way you want. (geocities.com/Tokyo/Courtyard/1652/God) (ngfl.ac.uk/docs/DraftTeachingMaterial/2KS1-OurWorld)

Christianity – (Taken from The Christian Bible): The Christian creation story was taken from the Jewish text and goes as such: In the beginning, God created the universe. At first the earth was shapeless and covered in darkness, and God's spirit hovered over the waters. God said, "Let there be light." And there was light. God divided the day from the night, naming them ' day' and 'night.' This was the first day, and God saw that it was good. On the second day God made the heavens to separate the water from the earth and on the third day He raised the dry land up from the waters below the heavens and commanded the earth to bring forth all plants. God saw that it was good. God then made the greater light for the day and the lesser light for the night, and He saw it was good. This was the fourth day. On the fifth day God commanded the waters to fill with living creatures and the air to fill with birds. And He was pleased with what he saw. On the sixth day God commanded the earth to bring forth all kinds of living creatures and He saw that it was good. God then said, "Let us make man in our own image." So God created man and woman in his own likeness and gave them authority over all living things. God looked at everything He had made and was very pleased; it was very good. On the seventh day, God rested.

Now the first man, Adam, was created by God out of soil and given life by God's breath. Adam named all the animals and birds that God had made, but Adam had no companion of his own so God caused him to fall into a deep sleep and created woman, Eve, from one of Adam's ribs. God told them that together they could live in the Garden of Eden eating whatever they wished except the fruit of the tree of knowledge of good and evil. But the most cunning animal, which God had made, the serpent, tempted Eve to eat the forbidden fruit. So Adam and Eve both ate and suddenly saw what they had done and that they were naked. Covering themselves with fig leaves they tried to hide from God. But God knew of their sin and called out to them. Then he cursed the serpent and Adam and Eve, and in shame they were driven from the beautiful Garden. God told Adam he would now have to toil and sweat to work the very soil from which he had been created. Then God blocked the entrance to the Garden with a great fiery sword so no one could enter in. (Christian Bible)

In Genesis 1, the words state we are individual breaths, emerging from One Breath. The words, "You are the Light of the World," indicates we are an ever awakening expression of our Source and Creator. (Rev. Hal Lingerman) In Genesis 2, the concept of Creation supposes God made something/everything out of nothing. This is different from an artisan or potter who reshapes his clay into something more beautiful or useful. Unlike God, the potter did not originally create the clay, he only reshaped it. The concept then is, God creates things and we reshape them. God created paradise and, according to the Bible, man and woman whom God created to have a relationship with, felt that paradise was not enough, so they reshaped their relationship with God to what they wanted versus what God had provided. William Paley's *Natural Theology*, published in 1800 speaks to the concept of, "if there is a watch, there must be a watchmaker." Something (God) created everything and mankind reshaped it in his image. (Rev Glen Larsen)

Confucianism - Three rivers of thought and practice flow into making traditional Chinese belief. These are Taoism, based on the teachings of the book *'Tao Te Ching*, Confucianism, springing from the ethics of Confucius, and Buddhism, which first appeared in China during the 1st century CE. All three speak of the yin and yang, the dark and the light, as being the creative power, which sustains all life and being. Yin and yang are not to be seen as gods or deities in any sense. They are the natural forces behind nature and even the gods, such as P'an Ku, are creations of the yin and yang.

"Let it be told of a time when there was nothing but chaos, and that chaos was like a mist and full of emptiness. Suddenly, into the midst of this mist came a great colorful light and from this light all things that exist came to be. The mist shook and separated, that which was light rose up to form heaven and that which was heavy sank. It became solid and formed the earth. Now from heaven and earth came forth strong forces and these two forces combined to produce yin and yang. Picture this yang like a dragon - hot, fiery, male, full of energy. Imagine this yin as a cloud - moist, cool, female, drifting slowly. Each of these forces is full of great power. Left alone they would destroy the world with their might and chaos would return. Together they balance each other and keep the world in harmony. This then is yin and yang and from them came forth everything. The sun is of yang and the moon, yin. The four seasons - winter, spring, summer and autumn - and the five elements - water, earth, metal, fire and wood - sprang from them; so did all kinds of living creatures.

So there was the earth, floating like a jellyfish on water. But the earth was just a ball without features. Then the forces of yin and yang created the giant figure P'an Ku, the Ancient One. P'an Ku, who never stopped growing every year of his great long life, set to work to put the earth in order. He dug the river valleys and piled up the mountains. Over many thousands of years, he shaped and created the flow and folds of our earth. But such work took its toll. Even mighty P'an Ku could not escape death and, worn out by his struggle, he collapsed and died. His body was so vast that when he fell to the ground his body became the five sacred mountains, his hair the plants and his blood the rivers. From his sweat came the rain and from the parasites living on his body came forth human beings.

The people at first lived in caves but soon Heavenly Emperors came to teach them how to make tools and houses. The people also learned how to build boats, to fish, to plow and plant, and to prepare food. This is how it all began.' (innovationslearning.co.uk/subjects/re/information/creation/chinese_creation)

Hinduism - There are several creation stories in Hinduism. Hinduism believes there are times when the universe takes form and times when it dissolves back into nothing. The in-between times are known as the days and nights of Brahma, who is the Hindu god of creation.

Before time began there was no heaven, no earth and no space between. A vast dark ocean washed upon the shores of nothingness and licked the edges of night. A giant cobra floated on the waters. Asleep within its endless coils lay the Lord Vishnu. He was watched over by the mighty serpent. Everything was so peaceful and silent that Vishnu slept undisturbed by dreams or motion.

From the depths a humming sound began to tremble: Om. It grew and spread, filling the emptiness and throbbing with energy. The night had ended. Vishnu awoke. As the dawn began to break, from Vishnu's navel grew a magnificent lotus flower. In the middle of the blossom sat Vishnu's servant, Brahma. He awaited the Lord's command. Vishnu spoke to his servant, "It is time to begin." Brahma bowed. Vishnu commanded: 'Create the world.' A wind swept up the waters. Vishnu and the serpent vanished. Brahma remained in the lotus flower, floating and tossing on the sea. He lifted up his arms and calmed the wind and the ocean. Then Brahma split the lotus flower into three. He stretched one part into the heavens. He made another part into the earth. With the third part of the flower he created the skies. The earth was bare. Brahma set to work. He created grass, flowers, trees and plants of all kinds. To these he gave feeling. Next he created the animals and the insects to live on the land. He made birds to fly in the air and many fish to swim in the sea. To all these creatures, he gave the senses of touch and smell. He gave them power to see, hear and move. The world was soon bristling with life and the air was filled with the sounds of Brahma's creation. (painsley.org.uk/re/signposts/y8/1-1creationandenvironment/c-hindu)

Islam – Prophet Muhammad said, "The world was created for man, but man was created for the *Hadeeth*, the hereafter." The Muslim creation story is found in the Qur'an, and further explained in various teachings given by Muhammad, which were collected and are known as the *Hadath*. At the heart of the creation story is something which Muslims all over the world hear every day in their Call to Prayer - God is great. Muslims believe there is only one God who created everything. God's world is a good world, and when people obey or submit to God then life is good. The word 'Islam' means submission. Although God made humans superior to the rest of creation, Muslims believe this means humans have been given everything on earth to care for and look after. The world is not ours to do with as we want. The Qur'an teaches that Muslims should be thankful for all living things, for God is the creator of all life.

In the time before time, God was. And when God wants to create something, all he needs to say is "Be", and it becomes. So it was that God created the world and the heavens. He made all the creatures, which walk, swim, crawl and fly on the face of the earth. He made the angels, and the sun, moon and the stars to dwell in the universe. And consider, as the Qur'an says, how God poured down the rain in torrents, and broke up the soil to bring forth the corn, the grapes and other vegetation; the olive and the palm, the fruit trees and the grass.

God created Adam (from the clay) and breathed into him something from his Spirit, called *"Rooh."* And the first man was called Adam. Then God called the Jinns and the Angels to bow down to Adam. The Angels (from the light) and the Jinns (from the fire) obeyed. But Iblis, one amongst the Jinns, (later called Satan) refused to do this because of arrogance and thus became the outcast from God's grace. The Angels could not disobey God however the Jinns and man could. God took Adam to live in Paradise. In Paradise, God created Eve, the first woman, from out of Adam's side. God taught Adam the names of all the creatures, and then commanded them to bow down before Adam. Then God commanded Adam and Eve to go to the world and live there for awhile. He told them, "I will send you guidance, you should follow it and do not follow Satan." (Imam Baseem Syed)

God placed the couple in a beautiful garden in Paradise, telling them they could eat whatever they wanted except the fruit of a forbidden tree. But Satan tempted them to disobey God, and eat the fruit. Adam and Eve were ashamed of their mistake and God taught them how to ask for forgiveness. They were forgiven by God upon asking for forgiveness. God is merciful. The earth was created to give food, drink and shelter to the human race. The sun, moon and stars give light. It is a good world, where everything has been created to serve people. And people, the Qur'an teaches, should serve God and obey his will. For those who submit to the will of God will be saved, and taken to live forever in Paradise and those who do not submit to the will of God will be punished in this world and the next. (innovationslearning.co.uk/subjects/re/information/creation/muslim_creation)

Jainism – The Jains believe the universe was never created nor will it ever be destroyed. Time, to them, is separated into unequal periods of *Utsarpinis* (progress) and *Avsarpinis* (decline) in morality, ethics, culture, religion, health, happiness, et cetera. Each period of progress or decline is sectioned into 6 unequal sections called *Aras*. The Jains believe we are currently in the 5th Ara of the decline period Avsarpinis. The 6th Ara of Avsarpinis should start around 19,000 years from now and will last for an unknown amount of time until Utsarpinis can begin. Jains also believe that existence is split into two groups. The first group, *jiva*, is the spiritual side of existence and the other group is *ajiva* which is non-life. Jiva would be anything (spirits, souls, ghosts) that apparently make up life and ajiva is everything else. Ajiva is specifically grouped into five categories: space, time, matter and energy (grouped together as interchangeable entities well before science caught up), movement, and rest. They also predated modern science in saying that ajiva (as well as jiva) cannot be created or destroyed. (Rev. Reed Braden)

Judaism – The Jewish calendar is dated from the supposed year of the Creation. This is indicated by the letter 'AM' after each year - meaning 'Anno Mundi', Year of the World. For Judaism sees its origins in the Act of Creation and its own inceptions as being part of the Divine plan. In the Torah (which became the first five books of the Christian Bible) and later in the Talmud (a collection of commentaries on the Torah), the pattern and purpose of Creation is revealed and the important role assigned to humans is spelled out. There are actually two creation stories in Jewish literature, one from a nomadic viewpoint and the other from an agricultural viewpoint. The nomads looked at the world much differently than the settled farmers and therefore the content of the stories are somewhat different. (Marilyn Clement)

In the beginning, God created the heavens and the earth. Some say God also created the Torah at this time, and a mighty voice crying, "Return, you children of men." God said, "Let there be light." And there was light. And God saw it was good, God divided the light from the darkness, naming them ' day' and 'night.' Evening and morning came - the first day. God said, "Let the waters be divided." And God made the arch of the sky to hold back the waters from the earth. He placed some above the arch and some below. Some tell of the waters arguing about this division, and thus disagreement entered the universe. Of this day God did not say, "It is good." Evening and morning came- the second day. God said, "Let the waters under heaven come together, and dry land appear." Thus the earth arose, and plants and trees grew, and God saw is was good. Evening came and morning came - the third day. God said, "Let the great light and the small light appear in heaven to govern day and night. God saw it was good. Evening came and morning came - the fourth day. God said. "Let the waters fill with creatures and the sky with birds." God saw it was good and blessed them. Evening came and morning came - the fifth day.

God said "Let the earth bring forth every kind of living creature." God saw it was good. Then, last of all when the earth was ready God said. "Let us take dust and create man, Adam, to be master over all creatures." So Adam was created in God's own image. God saw that Adam needed a friend - woman. Some say the earth was worried and asked, "How shall I feed all her children?" God replied, "Fear not, together we shall find food." So God made a woman before Adam's eyes, but Adam turned from her. Finally, putting Adam in a deep sleep, God took one of Adam's ribs and made Eve, and placed the couple in Paradise.

On the seventh day, God finished his work and rested. And Paradise was blissful, until Adam and Eve ate fruit from the tree of knowledge of good and evil, which God had forbidden them to do. God punished them, and cast them out of Paradise to struggle in this earthly life.

The Break in the relationship between God and first humans is however not seen as a final one. Through the Covenants with Abraham and Moses, the Jewish people have a close relationship with God; they are to act as a model of the way God wishes people to live and to use the world. The world is a larder full of good things, but it is ours on trust, and we must care for it as well as use it. (The Tanach)

Native American – Native American creation stories are passed down orally from generation to generation and there are as many creation stories as there are Native American tribes. Writings are published from the oral script and explain the origin of the world as well as establish how people were to live and worship. The Navajo creation story involves three underworlds where important events happened to shape the Fourth World where we now live. The Navajo were given the name Ni'hookaa Diyan Diné by their creators. It means "Holy Earth People" or "Lords of the Earth." Navajos today simply call themselves "Diné," meaning "The People." The

Tewa Indians were the first to call them "Navahu," which means "the large area of cultivated land." The Mexicans knew them as "Apaches Du Nabahu" (Apaches of the Cultivated Fields), where "Apache" (Enemy) was picked up from the Zuni Indian language. The "Apaches Du Nabahu" were known as a special group somewhat distinct from the rest of the Apaches. Alonso de Benavides changed the name to "Navaho" in a book written in 1630. The English name the Diné officially use for themselves is "Navajo." Recently, Navajos have been referring to themselves by their original name, "Diné."

According to the Diné, they emerged from three previous underworlds into this, the fourth, or "Glittering World," through a magic reed. The first people from the other three worlds were not like the people of today. They were animals, insects or masked spirits as depicted in Navajo ceremonies. First Man ('Altsé Hastiin), and First Woman ('Altsé 'Asdzáá), were two of the beings from the First or Black World. First Man was made in the east from the meeting of the white and black clouds. First Woman was made in the west from the joining of the yellow and blue clouds. Spider Woman (Na ashje'ii 'Asdzáá), who taught Navajo women how to weave, was also from the first world. Once in the Glittering World, the first thing the people did was build a sweat house and sing the Blessing Song. Then they met in the first house (hogan) made exactly as Talking God (Haashch'eelti'i) had prescribed. In this hogan, the people began to arrange their world, naming the four sacred mountains surrounding the land and designating the four sacred stones that would become the boundaries of their homeland. In actuality, these mountains do not contain the symbolic sacred stones. The San Francisco Peaks (Dook'o'osliid), represents the Abalone and Coral stones. It is located just north of Flagstaff, Arizona and is the Navajo's religious western boundary. Mt. Blanco (Tsisnaasjini'), in Colorado, represents the White Shell stone, and represents the Navajo's religious eastern boundary. Mt. Taylor (Tsoodzil), east of Grants, New Mexico, represents the Turquoise stone, and represents the Navajo's religious southern boundary. Mt. Hesperus (Dibe Nitsaa), in Colorado, represents the Black Jet stone, and represents the Navajo's religious northern boundary. After setting the mountains down where they should go, the Navajo deities, or "Holy People," put the sun and the moon into the sky and were in the process of carefully placing the stars in an orderly way. But the Coyote, known as the trickster, grew impatient from the long deliberations being held, and seized the corner of the blanket where it lay and flung the remaining stars into the sky. The Holy People continued to make the necessities of life, like clouds, trees and rain. Everything was as it should be when the evil monsters appeared and began to kill the new Earth People. But a miracle happened to save them, by the birth of Ever Changing Woman (Asdzaa Nadleehe) at Gobernador Knob (Ch'ool'ii), New Mexico.

Changing Woman grew up around El Huerfano Mesa (Dzil Na'oodilii), in northern New Mexico. She married the Sun and bore two son, twins, and heroes to the Navajo people. They were known as "Monster Slayer" and "Child-Born-of-Water." The twins traveled to their father the Sun who gave them weapons of lighting bolts to fight the dreaded monsters. Every place the Hero Twins killed a monster it turned to stone. An example of this is the lave flows near Mt. Taylor in New Mexico, believed to be the blood from the death of Ye'iitsoh, or the "Monster who Sucked in People." All of the angular rock formations on the reservation, such as the immense Black Mesa (Dzil Yijiin), are seen as the turned-to-stone bodies of the monsters. With all of the monsters dead, the Navajo deities, or "Holy People", turned their attention to the making of the four original clans. Kiiyaa aanii, or Tall House People, was the first clan. They were made of yellow and white corn. Eventually other clans traveled to the area round the San Juan River, bring their important contributions to the tribe. Some were Paiutes who brought their beautiful baskets. Others were Pueblos who shared their farming and weaving skills. Still others were Utes and Apaches.

For her husband, the "Sun," to visit her every evening, Changing Woman went to live in the western sea on an island made of rock crystal. Her home was made of the four sacred stones: Abalone, White Shell, Turquoise, and Black Jet. During the day she became lonely and decided to make her own people. She made four clans from the flakes of her skin. These were known as the Near Water People, Mud People, Salt Water People, and Bitter Water People. When these newly formed clans heard there were humans to the east who shared their heritage, they wanted to go meet them. Changing Woman gave her permission for them to travel from the western sea to the San Francisco Peaks. They then traveled through the Hopi mesas where they left porcupine, still commonly found there today. Then they traveled toward the Chuska Mountains and on to Mt. Taylor. Finally, the people arrived at Dinetah, the Diné traditional homeland, and joined the other clans already living there. Dinetah is located in the many canyons that drain the San Juan River about 30 miles east of Farmington, New Mexico. (The Navajo Creation Story, lapahie.com)

New Thought – The creation story, for those who follow the New Thought faith, is a metaphysical, non-literal interpretation combining the Christian and Jewish Bibles as well as factoring in well-accepted scientific evidence. New Thought believers feel all Bibles and holy books are a product of Divine inspiration and man's consciousness with his understanding of God at that time, as well as someone's interpretation of various beliefs and historic facts. No one really knows what happened on the first days of creation or for millions of years thereafter. "Spirit governs the universe through the power of His WORD; hence when He speaks His word becomes Law. The Law must obey. The Law is mechanical, the word is spontaneous. God cannot speak a word which contradicts His own nature." (*Science of Mind*, Holmes, pg. 64) New Thought followers believe God created everything and everyone and that, "...it was good." Ernest Holmes writes, "God in the beginning was conscious of Himself and desired to manifest in form. He did so by the power of His Word. He created by the power of His Word, plant and animal life. He created a being who could respond to and understand Him. He could do this only by imparting His own nature to this being whom He called man. Humanity must partake of the nature of Divinity to have real life." (*Science of Mind*, Holmes) In that belief they believe everything including mankind is a part of God and therefore, each one of us is part of the God-essence and thereby good. They believe from the very onset, billions of Souls were created, "Let us make man in Our own image..." all which exist today in the form of humans and spirits which go back and forth from one form to another as their infinite learning process dictates.

Sikhism – Sikhs believe God existed alone before God created the whole universe. According to the Guru Granth Sahib, there was darkness and chaos for millions of years. There were mists and clouds, then in deep meditation God willed the creation of the universe and it was created. God then diffused Himself/Herself in nature. According to Sikhism, when the world was created is a mystery. Was this process of creation a sudden and impulsive one or was it one of evolution and growth? Only God who created it knows. Like a spider, God spun Himself into a web. A day will come when God will destroy that web once again and begin to become His/Her sole self. (Gangadeep Kapur)

Taoism – Ge Hong, the famous accomplished Taoist and reputed astronomer of the Jin dynasty, made an important contribution to Taoist Cosmogony. In his *Inner Book of the Master Who Embraces Simplicity*, he considered the concept of 'xuan/mystery', and its effect on the formation of Heaven and Earth because he felt like Dao had been used so much it didn't mean much to people anymore at that time. (Michael Arnold, Taoist) In his later years as a hermit on Mt. Luohu, he wrote the important work *The Book of Pillow Secrets* in which he discussed the 'most sublime root' and pointed out that before the formation of the world, the original chaos was like an egg, inside which was Perfect Man Pangu who called himself the King of Primeval Heaven. As the universal egg grew larger in its initial stages, he grew larger inside it. At the formation of the world, the light elements rose upwards to form Heaven and the heavy elements descended to form Earth, while the King of Primordial Heaven resided on Jade Capital Mountain in the center of Heaven. Later on, other spirits, men and animals were formed. (The Book of Pillow Secrets, Ge Hong) Ge Hong's theory was later developed into a systematic Cosmogony. At about the same time, the Highest Clarity sect also reflected on the question of the origin and structure of the universe. Around the end of the Eastern Jin, the grandson of Ge Hong's brother, Ge Caofu, wrote a large number of scriptures, amongst which the *Numinous Treasure's Lofty and Sublime Book of the Limitless Salvation of Mankind* and other writings fully described the process of the formation of the world. Subsequently, the *Book of the Supreme Venerable Sovereign's Opening of the Heavens* appeared, which also discussed the question of the creation of Heaven and Earth.

The thing to remember when reading Daoist passages with lots of images is that often the images are metaphors for specific things. For example, if you were to read "guard the valley breath in the yellow court," the meaning would be much clearer if we knew the "valley breath" is the energy we get from food and the "yellow court" is the epigastrium. Then the phrase might mean to give yourself a little time to digest after you eat. A lot of times when someone is seriously practicing Taoism with an eye to realization they use the word which is translated "cultivation." Then they would meditate and use certain diets, practice various moving meditations like qi gong and so on. (Michael Arnold, Taoist)

There is no fixed way in Taoism, so rules, etiquette and moral codes are only guidelines. In this sense Taoism sets itself somewhat against Confucianism, which believed that social order is based on the rules. Taoists were more willing to break out from the social expectations, but only with the understanding that if we act in accord with the mystery, with the Dao, then our actions will be right and good, however they might appear to others. (Michael Arnold, Taoist)

The Interfaith Manual

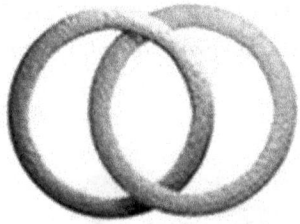

The rings represent members of an interfaith family
joining together to celebrate their traditions while
respecting the distinctiveness of each faith.
Inter–Faith Family Project P.O. Box 5413 Takoma Park, MD 20913

Rev. Dr. Stephen L. Albert

*"I believe all suffering is caused by ignorance.
People inflict pain on others
in the selfish pursuit of their happiness or satisfaction.
Yet true happiness comes
from a sense of brotherhood and sisterhood.
We need to cultivate a universal responsibility
for one another and the planet we share."*
Dalai Lama

Part 3
Our Divisions

Cults - Different Within Ourselves

It seems no matter how perfect a religion may be to the people who believe its tenets, there will come a time when some of the congregation will break away from the teachings for any variety of reasons. When they do, they are called "cults." Initially exclusive and secretive at first, every religion first developed as a cult because of the definition of the word itself which according to Webster's Dictionary means, "a system of religious beliefs and rituals regarded as unorthodox or spurious by the people." The people of course were the ones who had created the previous system from where the new cult arose. When the first caveman chose to live his life differently than the rest of the cavemen and got others to join him, he had created a cult. So it was with each religion and the changes each faith experienced over the years.

Why is it so difficult for people outside a faith to understand how that faith operates? Perhaps the problem stems from the in-fighting of the people in the faith itself. For example in the Christian faith there are sixteen different sects which believe their way is the right way to practice Christianity. There are six different Jewish divisions including Kabbala and four major New Thought divisions and so on and so on. If we have a hard time understanding what we believe about our own faith, imagine how difficult it might be to understand a different faith which also has many divisions and so many contrasting beliefs. There are over 500 different American Indian tribes (24 are described in this manual), each with their own rites and rituals. Yet even with this diversity, the American Indian Faith is possibly the most consistent regarding what they believe from tribe to tribe.

Note: all figures regarding the percentage of the faith's population compared to the world's population was taken from Religious Tolerance.com. It is estimated over 12% of the world's population say they have no religion and 2% say they are Atheists.

The Interfaith Manual

West Virginia Interfaith
P.O. Box 226
Talcott, WV 24981

The Step Before Interfaith

'INTRA-FAITH'

"Why do you look at the speck of sawdust in your brother's eye and pay no attention to the plank in your own eye?"
Jesus, Christian Bible, Luke: 6:41

Before we can begin to accept the full rights of people to have a different way of worshipping God through their own faith, we must first begin to accept the full rights of people FROM OUR OWN FAITH to have a different way of worshipping God. To do otherwise is working backwards. One of the definitions of "tolerance" in the dictionary is "a willingness to recognize and respect the beliefs and practices of others." Many religious people agree if we can more fully understand different faiths' beliefs and practices, we would be a step closer to helping the world to realize peace. That is what this interfaith manual is about. However, if for example, a Christian from the Catholic Faith will accept a Jew from the Jewish Orthodox faith, yet will not accept a Christian from the Mormon faith, there cannot be world peace. The same would be true of a Buddhist from the Mahayana faith accepting a Sikh from the Sikh faith yet not accepting a Buddhist from the Hinayana faith. So before we can call for "Interfaith peace," we must first have "Intra-faith" peace.

Calling for Intra-faith peace means allowing each other in each subdivision of our own faith to worship how they want assuming no person is hurt in the process. It is allowing the equal rights we give to people of other faiths, to exist also for those who are practicing our own faith differently. Catholics and Protestants have been at war with each other in Ireland since the 1960's (and before) due to political issues, yet the basics of their religious beliefs come from the same background. Their ability to accept Hindu, Buddhist, Bahá'í, and other faiths BEFORE they accept each other is baffling. Religious Science International in the New Thought faith uses the same text books and basic tenents and worship parameters as the United Church of Religious Science and yet each does not accept the other's ministers in their churches. Since all of New Thought is very pro-interfaith and each division of New Thought sponsors world religion classes to help bring about peace between faiths, the non-acceptance of those from their own faith seems misguided.

On and on we can look at religious people being tolerant of those who are most *unlike* themselves yet shun their brothers in faith. Probably every country in the world has had some sort of civil war in which one side of the country fought against the other side because of not agreeing with the other side's political stance or border decisions. The civil war in the United States had brothers fighting brothers and cousins fighting cousins for four years in the mid 1800's based solely on which state of the union each inhabited. War between South Korea and North Korea took the lives of hundreds of thousands of relatives. Sunni and Shi'ite Islamic groups (all Muslim) fight each other and are more apt to speak and be friends with a Christian than with one of their Muslim neighbors. So again, understanding the need for "Interfaith peace," we must also strive to have "Intra-faith" peace.

THE INTERFAITH MANUAL

North American Interfaith Network
1426 9th Street NW, Second Floor
Washington, DC 20001-3330
Phone: 202-234-6300

Rev. Dr. Stephen L. Albert

*"When we lose the right to be different,
we lose the privilege to be free."*
Charles Evans Hughes

Faith Divisions

Bahá'í
This Faith represents less than 1.0% of the world population. (Religious Tolerance.org) There are no subdivisions in the Bahá'í faith.

Buddhism
This Faith represents approximately 6.0% of the world population. (Religious Tolerance.org)

Hinayana – (Theravada) A Hinayana Buddhist focuses primarily on meditation and concentration; a person centers on a monastic life and an extreme expenditure of time in meditating.

Mahayana - The Mahayana Buddhists claimed their canon of scriptures represented the final teachings of Buddha; they account for the non-presence of these teachings in over five hundred years by claiming these were secret teachings entrusted only to the most faithful followers.

Christianity
This Faith represents approximately 32% of the world population. (Religious Tolerance.org)

Roman Catholicism – The Roman Catholic Church or Catholic Church is the Christian church in full communion with the Bishop of Rome. The Catholic Church is the largest Christian church, representing around half of all Christians, and is the largest organized body of any world religion. Many people around the world feel that being "Catholic" is, for the most part, in a separate category as being called "Christian."

Eastern Orthodoxy - The Eastern Orthodox Church is the modern name commonly applied to the ancient, theologically unified, multinational Christian Communion that views itself as the historical, unbroken continuation of the original Christian community established by Jesus the Christ and the twelve Apostles. It says it has preserved the apostolic traditions handed down to them, and maintained an unbroken link between its clergy and the Apostles by means of Apostolic Succession and ecclesial communion, which has never fallen into error nor deviated from the beliefs and traditions of the original Christian body, but rather has gone to great lengths to preserve them for future generations. All theological concepts, all explanations and expansions are compared to and validated by the original core beliefs; no deviation is allowed. (Religionfacts.com)

Protestantism - Protestantism originated in the 16th century Reformation, and most modern Protestant denominations can trace their heritage to one of the major movements that sprang up in the 16th century. Martin Luther is considered to be its founder when he challenged the authority of the papacy by holding that the Bible is the sole source of religious authority and that all baptized Christians are a general priesthood. His actions divided Christianity into two separate churches, which led the way for further divisions in the years to come. Martin Luther developed his own personal theology, which erupted into outright blasphemy when he protested the use of indulgences in his 95 Theses. (Luther, Martin. *Concerning the Ministry* 40:18 ff.) Presbyterians are indebted to John Calvin and Reformed theology, as well as to John Knox and the Church of Scotland. Anglicans and Episcopalians trace their heritage to the Church of England that resulted from King Henry VIII's break from the authority of Rome. Evangelicalism (and to a slightly lesser degree, Methodism) is indebted to Pietism, a 17th century Protestant movement emphasizing a holy life, individual study of the scriptures, and better training of ministers. Protestant denominations differ in the degree to which they reject Catholic belief and practice. Some churches, such as Anglicans and Lutherans, tend to resemble Catholicism in their formal liturgy, while others, like Baptists and Presbyterians, retain very little of the liturgy and tradition associated with the Catholic church. In common with Catholic and Orthodox Christians, Protestants adhere to the authority of the Bible and the doctrines of the early creeds. Protestants are distinguished by their emphasis on the doctrines of "justification by grace alone through faith, the priesthood of all believers, and the supremacy of Holy Scripture in matters of faith and order." Most Protestant churches recognize only two sacraments directly commanded by the Lord - baptism and communion - as opposed to the seven sacraments accepted by the Catholic Church. (Orange Pages, Protestantism) All the other divisions sprang from Protestantism, but since this manual is not discussing which group has more "correct" tenets, they will be presented in alphabetical order.

Adventists - Seventh-day Adventists are a faith community rooted in the beliefs described by the Holy Scriptures. Named for the seventh day in the Bible, (Saturday), as the one day God has set aside for focused fellowship with His people. Adventists believe God has named that day "Sabbath" and asks us to spend it with Him. "Remember the Sabbath day," He says, "to keep it holy." The Sabbath is a whole day to deepen our friendship with the Creator of the universe! Adventists describe these beliefs in the following ways: God's greatest desire is for you to see a clear picture of His character. When you see Him clearly, you will find His love irresistible. For many, "seeing God clearly" requires they see God's face. However, how He looks is not the issue. Seeing and understanding His character is what's most important. The more clearly we understand Him, the more we will find His love irresistible. As we begin to experience His love, our own lives will begin to make more sense. They believe God most clearly reveals His character in three great events. The first is His creation of man and woman and His giving them the freedom of choice. He created humans with the ability to choose to love Him or to hate Him! They believe the death of Jesus Christ, God's only Son, on the cross as our substitute is the second great event. In that act He paid the penalty we deserve for our hateful choices toward God and His ways. Jesus' death guarantees forgiveness for those choices and allows us to spend eternity with Him. The third event confirms the first two and fills every heart with hope: Christ's tomb is empty! He is alive, living to fill us with His love! (Seventh Day Adventist Church)

Anabaptists - The Anabaptist disciples center their faith in Jesus. An Anabaptist Christian is a follower of Jesus the Christ, not merely a believer in Jesus. He or she has a personal relationship with Jesus. He or she reads the Bible from a Jesus point of view. Jesus is his or her master-teacher, savior from sin and Lord of Lords. A very powerful and Living Jesus is at the center of their faith. Being a community is also at the center of their life and building a belief together, as a community, is paramount to healing relationships in the community and the world. (New Advent Encyclopedia)

Anglicans – The Church of England is part of the worldwide Anglican church which includes the church in Wales, the church in South Africa, the church of India as well as many other state or National churches. The Episcopal Church is the official name of the Province of the Anglican Communion in the United States. Each of the Anglican churches has an archbishop at its head, but the figurehead of all the Anglican churches is the Archbishop of Canterbury. Most Anglican churches were established by missionaries from England, who went out to the colonies to spread the gospel chiefly between 1600 and 1900, though there are still many missionaries in the world today. The Anglican church is found mainly in countries that were part of the British Empire in African, India,

Canada, Australia, New Zealand, South Africa and parts of the far East. Most Anglican churches are governed by a synod or committee which decides how the church should respond to events in the world. These authorities consist of three groups: the bishops, the clergy (priests and ministers) and the laity (ordinary churchgoers). (The Anglican Church, re-xs.ucsm.ac.uk/)

Baptists - The first Baptist congregation was founded in 1609. Whereas other Christian churches allowed the baptism of infants, Baptists believed baptism should be confined to adults after a personal confession of faith. (spartacus.schoolnet.co.uk)

Baptists believe quite a bit of authority is given to the congregation when it comes to church affairs. There is a significant emphasis put on the importance of freedom of speech. Baptists often consult the Scripture when it comes to matters of faith and morality. Baptists believe their members are people who have been born again by the Holy Spirit. They therefore attempt to live life in direct contact with Jesus. Baptists believe the church is ultimately governed by the Holy Spirit brought forth through each member of the church instead of being governed by a company of priests. Baptists believe each person is responsible for relating to God. Authority in matters of religion rests first with the individual believer and second with the local congregation of believers. (American Baptist Churches)

Congregationalists - A Congregational Christian Church is a church of self-governing Christian believers organized on a democratic basis. Congregationalists believe in a free church, one unfettered by established creeds and outside control and under the sole authority and leadership of Jesus the Christ represented by the Holy Spirit. The Free Church insures true freedom of the individual before God, liberty of conscience, the autonomy of the local church, and the free fellowship of churches. A Congregational Church acknowledges Jesus the Christ as its head and finds in the Holy Scriptures, interpreted by the Divine Spirit through faith, conscience, and reason, its guidance in all matters of faith and practice. The government of the Church shall be vested in its members, who exercise the right of control in all its affairs. While Congregational Churches recognize no superior denominational law, they accept all the obligations of mutual council, courtesy, and cooperation involved in the free fellowship of the Congregational Christian Church, and pledge themselves to share in the common aims and work of the Congregational Christian Churches in state associations or fellowships and in the national association. (The Victorian Web, The Congregationalists)

Jehovah's Witnesses - Jehovah's Witnesses, also known as the Watch Tower Bible and Tract Society (with headquarters in Brooklyn, New York), was officially founded in 1884 as the Zion's Watch Tower and Tract Society (originally the Zion's Watch Tower in 1879), officially adopting the name of Jehovah's Witnesses in 1931], by Charles Taze Russell (1852-1916). In 1870, Russell was exposed to the teachings of William Miller, one of the founders of the Second Adventist Movement and acquired an interest in end-time prophecies. Russell originally denied the doctrine of Hell, and would go on to reject nearly every other Christian doctrine, as well as add many physical and spiritual doctrines of his own making. Many of these unique teachings were to be found in his six volume series titled, *Studies in the Scriptures*. Jehovah's Witnesses' leadership claims to be the sole Christian religion and authority on the Earth today, as well as God's mouthpiece or prophet. (Watchtower.org)

Lutherans - The Lutheran tradition arose during the European Reformation times of the 16th Century c.e.. Martin Luther (1483-1546), in stating differences with the dominant Catholic tradition, based his opinions on the Bible. Rejected by the Catholic Church, Luther promoted beliefs such as the "priesthood of all believers" and "salvation by faith alone in the life, death, and resurrection of Jesus the Christ." The tradition eventually spread across northern Europe and across the globe. The Lutheran World Federation represents unique forms of the church worldwide and coordinates education, interfaith cooperation, relief and outreach ministries. (New Advent Encyclopedia, Lutherans)

Methodists - The Methodist (Wesleyan) tradition arose out of Reformation times in 18th century Great Britain. John Wesley (1703-1791) and Charles Wesley (1707-1788) found that the Anglican tradition limited their call to ministry. Transforming personal religious experiences led them to minister to the poor and dominated people who were seeking religious consolation and teaching. Scripture, tradition, experience, and reason are accepted as the basis for spiritual belief and daily living. Vital piety and social action are to be joined in faithfulness to Jesus Christ. Wesleyan tradition churches are now present in most countries of the world. John Wesley describes the core values of the Methodist tradition in "The Character of a Methodist." 1. Rejoicing over the goodness of God. 2. Belief in the power of prayer. 3. Belief in purity of heart and holiness. 4. Keeping the commandments of God. 5. Glorifying God in all that is done. 6. Doing good, for the body and soul. 7. Belief in the unity of the church. (New Advent Encyclopedia, Methodists)

Mormons - Mormons do not follow or believe in the historic Jesus Christ of the Bible, but rather in a different Jesus. This is why most Biblical Christians emphatically insist that Mormons are not Christians. The god of the Mormons is not the God of the Bible. To the Mormons, Jesus is the firstborn son of an exalted "man" who became the god of this world. The man-god of Mormonism was made the god of this world because of his good works on another planet somewhere out in the universe. He "earned" godhood and was thus appointed by a council of gods in the heavens to his high position as the god of planet Earth. The Mormon god of this world was a man, like all men, who became a god. This is what the celestial marriage and the temple vows are all about. LDS men, by doing their temple work, are striving for exaltation by which they, too, shall one day become gods. Their wives will be the mother goddesses of "their" world and with their husband will produce the population of their world. This is the Mormon doctrine of "eternal progression." (lds.org)

Orientals – Oriental Christianity followers believe Christianity began in Asia. They believe Jesus spent all of his earthly life in Palestine, on the continent of Asia, and the early church had its strongest congregations in Asia Minor, (which, conquered by Islam, has become modern Turkey.) When the church began on the day of Pentecost, there were many Asians there, people from Persia, Medea, and Mesopotamia (modern Iran and Iraq), Cappadocia, Pontus, Phrygia and Pamphylia (modern Turkey). See Acts 2:9-10. Some of these Asians were undoubtedly among the three thousand who were baptized that day. They returned to their homes with much to tell about Jesus. The apostle Paul went first to the cities of Asia Minor. Galatians, Ephesians, and Colossians were epistles written to Asian churches. The churches of Revelation 2-3 (Ephesus, Smyrna, Pergamum, etc.) were all in Asia Minor. (Christian History Institute)

Pentecostals - The Pentecostal Church is a conservative Protestant Christian denomination which has had significant influence on American politics and the growth of America's radical Christian Right. Pentecostal Christianity is not the same as fundamentalist or even conservative evangelical Christianity. Indeed, many fundamentalist and evangelical Christians can be very critical of Pentecostal theology. Unfortunately, too many atheists simply equate "Christian Right" with "fundamentalism." Pentecostal Christianity grew out of the Holiness movement of the 20th century; this, in turn, was a product of traditional Methodism. The two beliefs which most characterize Pentecostal churches and differentiate them from other Protestant groups are the belief in a "Baptism of the Spirit" and in resultant *charismata* ("Gifts of the Spirit," like speaking in tongues). Belief in Gifts of the Spirit and *charismata* is based on Acts 2 when the apostles were visited by the Holy Spirit. Holiness groups emphasized what they called the "second blessing" which was bestowed upon those who underwent an ecstatic conversion experience. Some manifested this blessing through Gifts of the Spirit, like prophesies. Others regarded such activities as a form of heresy, and this is where Pentecostals diverged from the Methodist and Holiness churches (though early on, many wanted to remain part of their original churches). Today, unusual practices like speaking in tongues, faith healing and ecstatic experiences are characteristic of Pentecostal services. Pentecostals focus upon the importance of personal religious experiences rather than upon specific doctrines; indeed, there is little consensus among Pentecostals with regards to most Christian doctrines except those of Baptism of the Spirit and *charismata*. (Pentecostalism and the Christian Right in America, About.com)

Presbyterians - Presbyterianism was inspired by the teachings of the Swiss Protestant reformer John Calvin (1509-1564), who started a movement that spread to France, Germany, and other parts of Europe. On the Continent, the Reformed
Church came into being in response to his message. The fiery John Knox (1505?-1572), a friend of Calvin, brought his doctrines to Scotland. When Puritanism took power in 17th-century England, the Presbyterians were the largest faction within it. Presbyterianism was first introduced to America by the Dutch Reformed in New Amsterdam and by the English Puritans in New England. Large numbers of Scottish immigrants spread the faith throughout the Colonies; by the time of the Revolution, Presbyterians were an important element in America. The Westminster Confession (1645-1647), the most famous statement of English Calvinism, is the basis of the Presbyterian creed. Presbyterians believe the Scriptures are "the only infallible rule of faith and practice." They also believe in the Trinity and the existence of heaven and hell. A once important Calvinist tenet, predestination (holding that God, not the individual, determines the individual's fate) is no longer emphasized. Church rule is democratic. The individual church is governed by the "session," consisting of a "teaching elder" (an

ordained minister) and "ruling elders" (members elected from the congregation). The world membership of the Presbyterian Church has been estimated at 40 million, including over 4 million members in the U.S. In Scotland, Presbyterianism is the established religion. (Presbyterian Church USA)

Reformed Churches - The Christian Reformed Church in North America (CRCNA or CRC) is a Protestant Christian denomination which follows Reformed Calvinist theology. The church promotes the belief that Christians do not earn their salvation, but that it is a gift from God despite one's failings and that good works are the Christian response to that gift. The denomination is considered evangelical and Calvinistic in its theology. It places high value on theological study and the application of theology to current issues. It emphasizes the importance of careful "Biblical hermeneutics" and has traditionally respected the personal conscience of individual members who feel they are led by the Holy Spirit. Church-authorized committees generally study contemporary societal and religious issues in-depth, and the CRC is cautious about changes. Reformed theology as practiced in the CRC is founded in Calvinism and influenced by the other great reformers, such as John Calvin. (Christian Reformed Church)

Confucianism

This religious community represents less than 1.0% of the world population. There are no known subdivisions in the Confucian faith. (Religious Tolerance.org)

Hinduism

This Faith represents approximately 13.4% of the world population. (Religious Tolerance.org)

Brahmins – Hindus believe Brahmins were created from the mouth of Brahma so they might instruct mankind. This is why they are considered the highest of the four castes, as they have the most to do with intellect. Since it was recognized that knowledge is the only thing that remains with a person throughout life, Brahmins, as teachers, are duly respected. (gurjari.net)

Kshatriyas - Kshatriya literally means "protector of gentle people." Second in the social hierarchy of the caste system, the Kshatriyas were kings and warriors. They are said to have evolved from the arms of Brahma, signifying their role in society was the protection of people and livestock. The Hindus maintain that only a Kshatriya had the right to rule, though Brahmin rulers are not unknown. They were supposed to be brave and fearless, and to live and die by a code of honor and loyalty. They could eat meat and drink liquor, and their most exalted death was to die in battle. (gurjari.net)

Vaishyas - Third in the caste system, Vaishyas supposedly evolved from Brahma's thighs. The Vaishya's duty was to ensure the community's prosperity through agriculture, cattle rearing and trade. Later, the Sudras took over agriculture and cattle rearing while the Vaishyas became traders and merchants. (gurjari.net)

Sudras - Sudra is the fourth Hindu social category. The origin of the term is uncertain, but it is mentioned in the *Rig Veda*. The Sudras included the menials who were assumed already present, at least within the Vedic community, but were not "twice-born" or totally integrated into the Hindu society. Their emergence from under the feet of Purusa summarized their social position. (gurjari.net)

Islamic

This Faith represents approximately 19.0% of the world population. (Religious Tolerance.org)

Sunnis – Sunnis are the largest group in Islam, making up 90% of the religion's adherents. They have been dominant almost continuously since 661, when the Shi'is departed from the main fold in 658. Sunni Islam claims to be the continuation of the Islam as it was defined through the revelations given to Muhammad and his life, a claim which is substantiated through the fact that Shi'i Islam for a number of decades had a very small following and had no real, formal organization. As for the theology, Sunni Islam represents no more of a continuation of Islam than the other orientations. (Encyclopedia of The Orient, Sunni)

Shi'ites - Shiites, in contrast, believe only the heirs of the fourth caliph, Ali, are the legitimate successors of Mohammed. In 931 the Twelfth Imam disappeared. This was a seminal event in the history of Shiite Muslims. According to R. Scott Appleby, a professor of history at the University of Notre Dame, "Shiite Muslims, who are concentrated in Iran, Iraq, and Lebanon, believe they had suffered the loss of divinely guided political leadership" at the time of the Imam's disappearance. Not "until the ascendancy of Ayatollah Ruhollah Khomeini in 1978" did they believe they had once again begun to live under the authority of a legitimate religious figure. Another difference between Sunnis and Shiites has to do with the Mahdi who are called "the rightly-guided ones." Their role is to bring a just global caliphate into being. (What Is the Difference Between Sunni and Shiite Muslims, History News Network)

Sufis - The word Sufi comes from the Arabic word "suf" meaning wool or cloth and the Arabic meaning of 'Sufi' is purity or wisdom. From the original root many derivations can be traced; among them the Greek word Sophia is one of the most interesting. Wisdom is the ultimate power. In wisdom is rooted religion, which connotes law and inspiration. But the point of view of the wise differs from that of the simple followers of a religion. The wise, whatever their faith, have always been able to meet each other beyond those boundaries of external forms and conventions, which are natural and necessary to human life, but which none the less separate humanity. Sufism, which is without any religious obligations, regards spirituality as the religion of the heart. "During the time

Prophet Muhammad was preaching Islam, history says there was a group of very religious and poised people who came from outside to Arabia, and Prophet Muhammad liked them very much. He used to meet them often on his own private prayer platform. He called them Ahl-e-Suffa; obviously they were not Muslims. "Since then all the poised and very religious Muslims have been called Sufis. The idea of Sufism has existed from the beginning of creation. Sufism has no connection with any one religion. Dr Mohan Gurnani in his book says, "Worship with intense Love for God, has been practiced by Hindus for very long time. Lord Shri Krishna, The Hindu Prophet reintroduced it in the Hindu Holy book, <u>Gita</u>. At that time India had many connections with many countries in the world and was considered a spiritual center." In India Sufis were then called Yogis. (Atma Advani)

That religion is one wherein the unity of religious ideals is followed unconditionally in search of truth. In Sufism there is no place for comparisons or preferences. All Messengers are regarded with the same respect and their messages are worshiped with the same veneration, knowing that Buddha was not a Buddhist, Christ was not a Christian, and Mohammed was not a Mohammedan. They were bringers of new impulses of the Divine Message. (Hazrat Inayat Khan)

Prof. Dr. Philosopher, Poet, Great Sufi Saint Sakhi Qabool Muhammad IV, the present Sufi Master of Sachal Sarmast Dargah, Shah Daraza, Sindh, Pakistan, said in a small portion of his speech: "Sufism is the source of unity and brotherhood through human tolerance and love. Sufism's unique characteristic is that it has respect for all religions, including its orthodox opponents. A true Sufi longs for equality, and he never discriminates. Rigveda has rightly proclaimed 'Eternal Truth is one: Sages call it by different names.' Mysticism is wide spread in Hinduism, Christianity, Buddhism, Islam, Taoism and all other religions. The aim of a mystic is the union of the soul with God. A Sufi can be in any religion. Sufism is the basic root of all religions. It has nothing to do with any particular cast, creed or culture. Sufism can exist without any religion. But no religion can exist without Sufism. Religion is the body, and Sufism is its soul. Sufism is true love affair with God." (Atma Advani)

Swami Chinmayananda once said that Sufism is "The Cream of all Religions." Sufism is "A Reality of Religions" and another name for Tasauf is Aatum Gyan in Vedas.

In one of the poems made famous by Sufi Saint Rumi, he says:

"What can I do, Moslems? I do not know myself.
I am no Christian, no Jew, no Magian, no Musulman
Not of the East, not of the West,
Not of the land, not of the sea."

Idries Shah says in his book "The Way of The Sufi": "Muslim Rumi had Christian, Zoroastrian and other disciples. The great Sufi teacher Khidr was a Jew. And Dara Shikoh of the Qadiri Order identified Sufi teachings in the Hindu Vedas."

In the book <u>The Sufi Path to Seeking Wisdom</u> Rumi says:

"I have again and again grown like grass,
I have experienced seven hundred and seventy moulds.
I died from minerality and became vegetable,
And from vegetativeness I died and became animal.
I died from animality and became man."
(Here Rumi is talking about reincarnation.)

Great Sufi Saint Poet shah Abdul Latif says in his poetry:
"Fasting and namaz are alright,
But you need something else to reach God."

Kharijite - The Kharijites [meaning "those that seceded"] were members of the earliest sect in Islam who left the followers of Ali [cousin and son-in-law of Muhammad]. The third Caliph, Uthman, was killed by mutineers in 656 AD, and a struggle for succession ensued between Ali, and Mu'awiya, the governor of Damascus. The Kharijites left the followers of Ali [the Shia] because of

Shia willingness to allow human arbitration of Ali's dispute with Mu'awiya in 657, rather than accepting divine judgment. The Kharijites believed the Imam should be elected for his moral qualities. The Kharijites considered Ali made a mistake in looking for a compromise with Mu'awiya. For this reason they are not considered as properly as Shiite by some commentators. Ali defeated their rebellion, but the Kharijites survived and an adherent of the movement murdered Ali in 661. Kharijites rejected primogeniture succession of the Quraysh, the tribe of Muhammad, and asserts that leadership of Islam, the caliphate, should be designated by an Imam elected by the community from candidates who possess spiritual and personal qualities. (Kharijite, Encyclopedia Britannica)

Jainism

This Faith represents less than 1.0% of the world population. (Religious Tolerance.org) Jainism has two major divisions both of which have exactly the same religious and philosophical beliefs and practically the same mythology (jainstudy.org):

Digambaras – Digambaras are those monks who give up all material possessions including clothing; the Digambaras are also divided into two or three groups. Some Digambaras think it is not possible for a woman to achieve salvation.

Shwetambaras – Shwetambaras are those monks who also give up all material possessions but they are clad in white cotton. Shwetambers have been further divided into Deraavaasi (temple goers who worship idols of Jins), and Sthaanakvaasi who do not worship idols. There is another group among Shwetambers called Teraapanthi who do not worship idols and emphasize thirteen virtues.

Judaism

This Faith represents less than 1.0% of the world population. (Religious Tolerance.org)

Orthodox – Orthodox Judaism is not a unified movement with a single governing body, but many different movements adhering to common principles. All of the Orthodox movements are very similar in their observance and beliefs, differing only in the details that are emphasized. They also differ in their attitudes toward modern culture and the state of Israel. They all share one key feature: a dedication to Torah, both written and oral. All forms of Judaism view themselves as the continuation of the beliefs and practices of normative Judaism, as accepted by the Jewish people at Mt. Sinai and codified in successive generations in an ongoing process that continues to this day. Orthodox Judaism believes that both the Written and Oral Torah, *the Talmud*, are of divine origin, and represent the exact word of God and does not represent any human creativity or influence. (Orthodox Judaism, Jewish Virtual Library)

Conservative - In Conservative Judaism, the central halachic authority of the movement, the Committee on Jewish Law and Standards (CJLS), will often set out more than one acceptable position. In such a case, the rabbi of the congregation (*mara d'atra*) is free to choose from the range of acceptable positions (or none of them), and his congregation is expected to abide by his choice. The CJLS speaks for the Conservative movement and offers parameters to guide local rabbis who turn to it for assistance. Local rabbis will make use of traditional sources and, when available, the *teshuvot* which was written for the CJLS. Although rabbis mostly adhere to the CJLS, they have the ability to make their own *halachic* (decisions) when appropriate. (Conservative Judaism, Jewish Virtual Library)

Reconstructionist – According to the Jewish Virtual Library, Reconstructionists define Judaism as the evolving religious civilization of the Jewish people. By "evolving," they mean Judaism has changed over the centuries of its existence. A Reconstructionist Jew has strong commitments both to tradition and to the search for contemporary meaning. Reconstructionists encourage all Jews to enhance their own lives by reclaiming their shared heritage and becoming active participants in the building of the Jewish future. They believe all peoples are called to the service of righteousness, and welcome dialogue with people of good will from all traditions. (Reconstructioist, Jewish Virtual Library)

Reform - Reform Judaism affirms the central tenets of Judaism: God, Torah and Israel, even as it acknowledges the diversity of Reform Jewish beliefs and practices. They believe all human beings are created in the image of God, and we are God's partners in improving the world. *Tikkun olam*, repairing the world, is a hallmark of Reform Judaism as we strive to bring peace, freedom, and justice to all people. Reform Jews accept the Torah as the foundation of Jewish life containing God's ongoing revelation to their people and the record of their people's ongoing relationship with God. They see the Torah as God inspired, a living document that enables them to confront the timeless and timely challenges of our everyday lives. In addition to their belief that Judaism must change and adapt to the needs of the day to survive and their firm commitment to *Tikkun Olam*, the following principles distinguish Reform Jews from other streams of Judaism in North America: Reform Jews are committed to the principle of inclusion, not exclusion, they are committed to the absolute equality of women in all areas of Jewish life, including as Rabbis, and they are also committed to the full participation of gays and lesbians in synagogue life as well as society at large. (What Reform Jews Believe, Beliefnet)

Humanistic - Humanistic Judaism has existed since the early 19th century as an intellectual tradition. It was first formally organized in 1969 as the *Society for Humanistic Judaism* — founded by Rabbi Sherwin T. Wine in Detroit, MI. The Society currently has about 50 affiliated communities in the U.S. and about 35,000 members worldwide. According to their official web site, "Humanistic Judaism embraces a human-centered philosophy that combines rational thinking with a celebration of Jewish culture and identity.

Humanistic Jews value their Jewish identity and the aspects of Jewish culture that offer a genuine expression of their contemporary way of life. Humanistic Jewish communities celebrate Jewish holidays and life cycle events (such as weddings and bar and bat mitzvah) with inspirational ceremonies that draw upon but go beyond traditional literature." (The Society for Humanistic Judaism, shj.org)

Kabbalistic – The word "Kabbalah" is derived from the root "to receive, to accept", and in many cases is used synonymously with "tradition." Kabbalah is an aspect of Jewish mysticism and it consists of a large body of research on the nature of divinity, the creation, the origin and fate of the soul, and the role of human beings. It consists also of meditative, devotional, mystical and, what some people would call magical practices which were taught only to a select few and for this reason Kabbalah is regarded as an esoteric offshoot of Judaism. When Moses received the written law from God, tradition has it he also received the oral law, which was not written down, but passed from generation to generation. At times the oral law, the *Talmud*, has been referred to as "Kabbalah" - the oral tradition. Some aspects of Kabbalah have been studied and used by non-Jews for several hundred years. It is believed Jesus was a Kabbalistic master learning from his travels in the Far East and around the Asian Peninsula (Kabbalah: The Misunderstood Doctrine, Judaism 101)

Hasidic – Hasidic Jews are called *Hasidim* in Hebrew. This word derived from the Hebrew word for loving kindness (*chesed*). The Hasidic movement is unique in its focus on the joyful observance of God's commandments (*mitzvot*), heartfelt prayer and boundless love for God and the world He created. Many ideas for Hasidism derived from Jewish mysticism (*Kabbalah*). The movement originated in Eastern Europe in the 18th century, at a time when Jews were experiencing great persecution. While the Jewish elite focused on and found comfort in Talmud study, the impoverished and uneducated Jewish masses hungered for a new approach. Fortunately for the Jewish masses, Rabbi Israel ben Eliezer

(1700-1760) found a way to democratize Judaism. He was a poor orphan from the Ukraine. As a young man, he traveled around Jewish villages, healing the sick and helping the poor. After he married, he went into seclusion in the mountains and focused on mysticism. As his following grew, he became known as the Baal Shem Tov (abbreviated as Besht) which means "Master of the Good Name." (Ultra-Orthodox Judaism, about.com)

Native American
This Faith represents less than 4.0% of the world population. (Religious Tolerance.org)

The Native American people have endured their own long journey throughout time as their original homelands gave way to the development of North America, Canada and the United States. Though much of the original freedoms associated with the Native American way of life have been lost in time, much of their culture, traditions, and legends remains in tact. Indigenous people within the area that is now the U.S. such as the Native American people, encompass descendants of many distinct tribes and Indian nations. Though there were once many more, today there are just over 500 federally recognized Native American tribes. Native American culture is deep-rooted, tracing back thousands of years, some to 15,000 B.C., and it is a culture of tradition, ceremony, spiritual significance, loyalty to tribe and family as well as a respect for each other and for earth.

Native American culture also believed and espoused the value of the spiritual side of life, many of those beliefs also rooted in nature, such as spiritual animal guides and a more religious and metaphysical connection to Mother Nature and the earth itself. Native American Culture valued this spirituality, celebrating it in dance, looking to the spiritual to assist them in hunting and crop harvesting and farming and to protect them and their families. While Native American culture differs from tribe to tribe, these similarities paint a beautiful portrait of a people who are deep-rooted in tradition, at one with the earth and their spiritual being, and whose devotion to tribe and family makes Native American culture so significant in the history of the United States. (native-languages.org)

Alaskan - Today, there are more than 500 federally recognized American Indian and Alaskan Native tribes. Each tribe maintains a spiritual and cultural heritage that identifies its members as a unique part of a larger group of Native Americans. (MarcoGram, marcopolo.mci.com)

Apache - There are at least seven Apache reservations that are in existence today. These reservations are not only functional, but they are also highly prosperous. The reservations are Camp Verde, San Carlos, Jicarilla, White Mountain, Fort Sill, Anadarko, and Mescalero. Today, the residents of these reservations are the direct descendents of the many Apache tribes that were the first original settlers of this land. (Apache tribes, native languages.com)

Athabaskans - The story of the Navajo and Apache tribes begins with the Athabaskan (*Ghunanaa*) people of interior Alaska and western Canada, a land of lakes and rivers, of birch and spruce forests, and the moose and caribou. Life in this continental climate is harsh, with bitterly cold winters and hot summers. One year the people had a particularly poor harvest over a summer, and it was obvious the winter would bring with it many deaths from starvation. The elders gathered together and decided that people would be sent out to find a land which was rumored to be rich in food, a place where one did not even have to hunt for something to eat. A group of people was selected and sent out to find this new place; they were to come back to tell the elders where this land could be found. They were never heard from again. However, we now know these people were the Navajo and Apache, for they left the Athabaskan lands for a different place far south of their home, and yet retain a close relationship with their Athabaskan ancestors. (Educational Cyber Playground, edu-cyberpg.com)

Blackfoot 2 - Today the Blackfoot tribes reside on four reservations. More than 6000 Indians, mostly of Piegan decent, live on the Blackfeet Indian Reservation in Montana. Spiritual beliefs and ceremonies are an important part of the Blackfoot culture. Their religious life centered upon medicine bundles, which were individually owned and originated from a supernatural experience. It was the adolescent warrior who attempted the vision quest by going to a remote area and fasting until he had a vision. He would be given a war song or dance by a guardian spirit and be told of the magical amulets (such as feathers, birds' beaks, or stones) that should be worn to give him power. Most failed and did not have a vision, in which case they would buy a bundle and its ritual. Individual bundles acquired much respect and gave its owner prestige, especially those associated with war such as headdresses and shields. (*Blackfoot*, Martin 1996)

Cherokee - Cherokee Indians can trace their history back more than one thousand years. Their society was based on hunting, trading, and agriculture, living in towns until they encountered the first Europeans in 1540, when Spanish explorer Hernando de Sota led an exploration through Cherokee territory. By the time European explorers and traders arrived, Cherokee lands covered a large part of what is now the southeastern United States. In the early 1800's, Cherokee Indians began a period of change. The Cherokee Nation was established with a democratic government composed of a Chief, Vice-Chief, and 32 Council Members who were elected by the members of the tribe. A constitution and code of law were implemented for the nation. (Smoky Mountain Mall, Cherokee)

Cheyenne Comanche - The Comanche Indians numbered as many as 20,000 in their heyday. Today, there are approximately 10,000 members of the Comanche Nation. Today, the majority of Comanche Indians live in Oklahoma. Those not located in Oklahoma can be found living in Texas, California, and New Mexico. Historically, the Comanche Indians lived in New Mexico,

Colorado, Oklahoma, Kansas, and Texas. The name Comanche is believed to come from the Komantcia, the Spanish, which is their way of saying the Ute word Kohmahts, which means "people." (Comanche Indians, Indians.org)

Chickasaw - One of the well-known Five Civilized Tribes, the Chickasaws were relocated to Indian Territory (which was to become the state of Oklahoma) from the central Appalachian Mountain region of Kentucky and Tennessee and formed their nation in 1855 from the western half of the Choctaw Nation. Long before white settlers came, the Chickasaws enjoyed a constitutional form of government (their constitution was written in 1856), an advanced public school system, a powerful judicial system and a strong economy. They even had their own newspaper, The Chickasaw Times, which survives today. Much of their culture was eradicated, however, when the U.S. Government phased out all tribal governments and combined them under the designation of Indian Territory in 1890. The boundaries of their nation today coincide almost exactly with those of their nation before statehood. Today they are strong once again, with a multifaceted economy and a modern approach to caring for their people. The Chickasaw Nation is credited with being largely responsible for the concentrated cooperative effort that resulted in construction of the sophisticated 53-bed Carl Albert Indian Hospital in Ada, Oklahoma. (The Chickasaw Nation, Indian Health Services)

Chippewa - Today's proud Saginaw Chippewa Indian Tribe works with the greater Central Michigan area to promote education and programs not only for the Indians of the area, but for all community members. The Tribe works to further the progress of other Indian Nations as well by working through state and federal legislation. Being located in the middle of Michigan, where they have lived for over 100 years, and close to their historic land base, the members of the Saginaw Chippewa Indian Tribe remain uniquely focused on the present and future, while still remembering the past. While current tribal land is concentrated near the cities of Mt. Pleasant and Pinconning, the Saginaw Chippewa Indian Tribe originally lived, hunted, fished and traded in southern and Midwestern areas of what is today's State of Michigan. The Tribe also occasionally lived in some parts of what is now Canada. (sagchip.org)

Choctaw - Traditionally, the Choctaws lived around Nanih Waiya in Central Mississippi, and spread to Southern Mississippi, as well as, Western portions of Alabama. Today, the Choctaw Nation of Oklahoma comprises over 175,256 Choctaws, worldwide, and they have moved their tribal complex to Durant, Oklahoma. (Choctaw Nation, rootsweb.com)

Creek - Today, the Creek Nation is the third largest federally recognized tribe in the United States. Like the United States government, the Creek government is composed of executive legislative and judicial branches. The Executive Branch administers a variety of service programs for the Creek people. The Division of Human Development provides education and vocational training. The Division of Community Services provides hospitals and clinics, and the Division of Tribal Affairs oversees Tribal Lands, Agri-Business and Natural Resources. Law Enforcement is under the Lighthorse Commission. The Executive Branch also includes the Chief and National Council. Despite the conveniences, technology and influences of the twentieth century, the Creek people maintain many traditional values. Family ties are strong and Creek values and beliefs continue to be passed down from generation to generation. Tribal Towns and ceremonial grounds, along with the mikko (Town Chief), still exist. Each ceremonial ground is the site for sacred ceremonies like the "Green Corn," a ritual that dates to pre-removal times. (The Muscogee (Creek) Nation Today, nps.gov)

Iroquois - The Iroquois people of today live in seventeen scattered communities in New York State, Oklahoma, Wisconsin, Ontario, and Quebec. Some also live in eastern urban centers such as

Rochester and Brooklyn. The Iroquois are six nations who joined together to form a confederacy of the Mohawk, Oneida, Onondaga, Cayuga, Seneca, and Tuscarora Nations. Today, each community has its own separate government. Some communities are run by chiefs elected by vote, and others are administered by hereditary chiefs appointed by the traditional clan matrons. The hereditary chiefs meet periodically as the continuing Iroquois Confederacy that conceives of itself as being independent of U.S. or Canadian control. Despite the fact the Iroquois are separated by miles of land now in the possession of the United States, they continue to maintain strong links to each other whether it be through family, political or religious beliefs, or art. Iroquois identity continues to remain strong and aims to unify the people. (The Iroquois Today, iroquoismuseum.org)

Lumbee - The Lumbee Indian Nation is fighting for Federal recognition. "Federal recognition" does not "make" an Indian tribe. No bona fide Native tribe needs any alien government's approval to be its own Tangible Reality. Recognition comes from the Creator and the People of the Tribe. But Federal recognition is extremely important. The large Lumbee Nation is based in southern North Carolina, with many of its members scattered into the urban areas of Maryland and Pennsylvania, but always maintains close connections with the home Nation, and for decades has been fighting hard for full Federal recognition. The Lumbees are certainly bona fide Native Americans. They emerged as a distinctive nation when a number of tribal remnant groups in the Southern Atlantic coastal region came together in the 1600's and early1700's in the wake of the genocidal European onslaught. (Lumbee Indian Nation, hunterbear.org)

Navajo - The Navajo Nation extends into the states of Utah, Arizona and New Mexico, covering over 27,000 square miles of unparalleled beauty. Today, the Navajo Nation is striving to sustain a viable economy for an ever-increasing population that now surpasses 250,000.

In years past, Navajo land often appeared to be little more than a desolate section of the Southwest, but it was only a matter of time before the Navajo Nation became known as a wealthy nation in a world of its own. The discovery of oil on Navajo land in the early 1920's promoted the need for a more systematic form of government. (Welcome To The Navajo Nation, navajo.org)

Osage - Today, the Osage Nation claims more than 10,000 members. The Osage Museum in Pawhuska, Oklahoma, the oldest existing tribal museum in the country, documents their history. The Osage began treaty-making with the United States in 1808 with the first cessation of lands in Missouri (Osage Treaty). Subsequent treaties and laws through the 1860's reduced the lands of the Osage and finally provided for a reservation in the Cherokee Outlet in 1870. The Osage moved from their homelands on the Osage River in 1808 and moved to western Missouri. The major part of the tribe had moved to the Three-forks region of what would become Oklahoma soon after the arrival of Lewis and Clark. Since this part of the tribe did not participate in the negotiations for the treaty of 1808, their assent was obtained in 1809. (Osage Nation)

Paiute - The early Native Americans who lived in what is now Zion National Park were the Southern Paiutes. The Paiutes were nomadic, that is, they moved around as the seasons changed. In summer, they grew corn and squash, which they irrigated (watered) during dry periods. The Paiutes also gathered the seeds, roots and leaves of native plants. Pinyon pine nuts were a favorite. They also hunted for mammals, birds, insects and reptiles. Skilled weavers, the Paiutes made hunting nets and baskets from plant fibers, and wove warm robes from straps of rabbit pelt. Today, the Paiutes still live in southern Utah and northern Arizona. (Zion National Park Profile, infowest.com)

Pima - Today, the Pima Indians of the Gila River Indian Community are still an agricultural people, nurturing orchards of orange trees, pistachios and olives. Eleven thousand strong, the members of the Gila River Indian Reservation have participated in 30 years of research that will help people avoid diabetes, have healthier eyes, hearts, and kidneys, and understand how and why people gain weight and what can be done to prevent it. (The Pima Indians, Pathfinders for Health)

Potawatomi - The Potawatomi are among the wave of Algonquian-speaking people who occupied the Great Lakes region from prehistoric times through the early 1800's. Oral traditions explain the ancient Potawatomi people were once part of an immense group that had traveled down the eastern shores of North America along the Atlantic Ocean. This large group, the Chippewa (Ojibwa), Ottawa (Odawa), and the Potawatomi all constituted a single tribe where they later split at Georgian Bay, Ontario, Canada and went their separate ways. Through early historic records, it has been confirmed the Potawatomi were living in Michigan and had established an autonomous tribal identity at least 500 years ago. The last quarter of the twentieth century was a period of great success for the Citizen Potawatomi Nation. In fact, the Citizen Potawatomi Nation is the largest of the eight federally recognized Potawatomi tribes and the ninth largest tribe in the United States. Under sound leadership and a tribal membership of over 26,000, the Citizen Potawatomi Nation has experienced growth in administration, tribal enterprises, and its community outreach programs. (Citizen Potawatomi Nation, potawatomi.org)

Pueblo 2 - The Pueblo Indians are a group of native tribes who inhabit regions of northeastern Arizona and northwestern New Mexico. Today, the Pueblo are divided in eastern and western divisions. In the eastern division are the New Mexico Pueblo while the western Pueblo comprise the Hopi, the Zuni, Acoma and Laguna, who live in western New Mexico with about two dozen other bands. The Pueblo are the descendants of the ancient Anasazi people. For hundreds of years these people lived in relative peace in small, scattered villages in Colorado and Utah. By the early 1100's, however, they had left these small villages in favor of larger, more compact Pueblos. In the 1200's a long period of drought affected the people, and the failing crops and lack of water forced the Pueblo south. Around 1300 they drifted south to the Rio Grande. (Pueblo Indians, esortment.com)

Salish - The Salish nation is just one of many Salish speaking tribes discovered by the white man when he came to the northwest. Quite a few others, such as the Quinault and Upper Skagit resided to the west of the Salish. What differentiated this group of Salish-speaking Native Americans was that they did not practice the custom of head flattening. Coastal Salish frequently tied padded boards to their foreheads and over a gradual process tapered their heads by the time they reached adulthood. To whites, it was the Montana Salish who possessed the "flat heads" and the coastal Salish seemed to have tapered or pointed heads. Although the reservation retains the name Flathead Reservation, the people have reverted to the name they have bestowed upon themselves, the Salish. Other Salish people, especially members of the Kalispell and Spokane tribes, joined them there. (The Flathead Nation of the Salish & Kootenai Tribes)

Seminole - In the early 1700's a group of Creek Indians left their homes in Georgia and moved to north and central Florida. They were joined by other groups of Indians from Georgia, Alabama, and South Carolina. In the mid and late 1700's, still other Indians arrived who spoke a different language, Muskogee. These groups were to become known as Seminoles. The word "Seminole" is derived from the Muskogee word "simano-li," taken originally from the Spanish "cimmarron." meaning wild or runaway. Together with the Choctaws, Chickasaws, Creeks and Cherokees, the Seminoles were called "The Five Civilized Tribes." The name was coined because these tribes in particular adopted many ways of the white civilization. They lived in cabins or houses, wore clothes similar to the white man and often became Christians. (Seminole, Native Americans.com)

Sioux - The early Sioux Nation consisted of about 20,000 people in 7 different tribes throughout the Great Plains. Free nomads of the Plains, they took great advantage of available horses which were originally brought to the Americas by Cortez and the Spanish in 1519. The horse allowed them the mobility to pull their tepees as they traveled and were an invaluable aid in hunting buffalo, their main staple. The Sioux today are a deeply spiritual people, who commune with the spirit world through music and dance. The Sun Dance is considered one of the most religious ceremonies of the Sioux. This twelve-day summer ritual of self-sacrifice is a testimony to individual courage and endurance in serving the Great Spirit. As a shared experience among men, the Sun Dance also instills a sense of tribal unity. By dancing and enduring the pain of self-inflicted wounds, each participant reasserted his identity as an Indian warrior. (The Great Sioux Nation, Native American People Tribes)

Tlingit - There is no book of Tlingit History. From time immemorial, the land and the peoples, reflect history. Legends speak of events in ancient times. In the last great iceage, North America was a silent, frozen landscape. As the ice began to melt, it uncovered a beautiful expanse of land, surrounded by water. Today, this land is known as Southeast Alaska. (Bob Sam-Tlingit Storykeeper) The Tlingit nation is built upon the values of respect and balance. Respect extends to all things living and dead, and balance is maintained by following the rules of protocol. Protocol is like the construction of a house, the foundation of which is respect. Balance is illustrated in that one wall cannot stand alone without another wall for support. Balance must be maintained throughout. The support for the structure of the Tlingit Nation comes from the clan. (Bob Sam-Tlingit Storykeeper, sitcatribal.com)

Tohono O'Odham - The Tohono O'odham of today is a nation with a population of more than 24,000 people. They live on four separate land bases totaling more the 2.7 million acres. The land bases are comprised of the main reservation, San Xavier District, San Lucy District and Florence Village. The main reservation is located in south central Arizona with the Sells community which serves as the Nation's Capital. The San Xavier District is located just south of Tucson. The San Lucy District is located near the city of Gila Bend. Florence Village is near the city of Florence southeast of Phoenix. For years, many have known the people as Papago, but during the 1980s, Papago was officially changed to the Tohono O'odham, meaning Desert People in the O'odham language. The Tohono O'odham are closely related to the Pima Tribe and are most likely descendants of the prehistoric Hohokam Culture. Many O'odham who reside on the four land bases are Catholics but are very aware of their "himdage" which means "way of life." Many traditions and beliefs of the O'odham elders continue to be handed down from one generation to another. The O'odham language is thriving. There are several different dialects, and these dialects come from different parts of the reservation. (San Xavier del Bac Mission)

Yaqui - The Yaquis are a tribe of 30,000 people living in Sonora (northern Mexico) and Arizona (USA). At the turn of the century, thousands of them migrated to Arizona for political reasons. Their language belongs to the 'Cahitan' branch of the Uto-Aztecan group. Although we know relatively little about the archaeology of the area, the Yaquis and their ancestors must have practiced irrigation farming for centuries. Their staple crops were corn, beans, and squash; they also hunted and fished. Traditionally they lived on the banks of the Rio Yaqui in small and dispersed settlements, the so-called rancherías. Their country was part of 'la gran Chichimeca', the fringe of Meso-America. Because of their geographical isolation, the Yaquis were never conquered by the Toltecs or Aztecs.

They probably had a fixed territory with well-defined borders when the Conquistadores arrived. (Yaqui: A Short History, lasculturas.com)

New Thought

This Faith represents less than 2.0% of the world population. (Religious Tolerance.org)

Christian Science – Christian Science was started in 1879 as a healing ministry by Mary Baker Eddy. Christian Science is a universal, practical system of spiritual, prayer-based Christian healing, available and accessible to everyone. Adherents believe God is Divine Love, Father-Mother, Supreme. The true nature of each individual as a child of God is spiritual, and God's infinite goodness, realized in prayer, heals. Most Christian Scientists believe God can heal all illness and afflictions, and there is no need to go to doctors or outside sources for help. (Christian Science, Encyclopedia.com)

Unity – Unity and The Association of Unity Churches International are the largest of the several metaphysical organizations and are part of the New Thought Faith. Charles and Myrtle Filmore started Unity in 1889 after they both had miraculous healings through prayer the year before and after Charles began to publish the magazine, "Modern Thought." Unity churches offer a liberal degree of freedom of belief among their members. Unity teaches what it terms as "practical Christianity." This term is defined as "what is believed to be the primitive Christianity of Jesus and the Apostles" (Melton: 1015). Unity School of Christianity encourages persons to explore and apply Unity teachings based on one's own spiritual understanding. They believe this spiritual understanding is enhanced through reflective prayer and meditation. The five basic ideas that make up the Unity belief system are: 1) God is the source and creator of all. There is no other enduring power. God is good and present everywhere. 2) We are spiritual beings, created in God's image. The spirit of God lives within each person; therefore, all people are inherently good. 3) We create our life experiences through our way of thinking. 4) There is power in affirmative prayer, which we believe increases our vibrational connection to God. 5) Knowledge of these spiritual principles is not enough; we must live them. Unity believes in one God and in Christ, the Son of God, who is made manifest in Jesus of Nazareth. Unity teaches Jesus is divine, and divinity, in itself, is not confined to Jesus alone. All people have God within them as an inborn quality of being as children of God. (Unity School of Christianity).

Religious Science – Today, Religious Science, also known as Science of Mind, is taught by two different organizations, Religious Science International and United Church of Religious Science. There is no difference between the religious beliefs of the two organizations, only in their corporate structure and church administration. Begun in 1923 by Dr. Ernest Holmes as a philosophy of science and reason and similar to Unity, Dr. Holmes wrote, "What We Believe" which is the cornerstone of Religious Science. It states: "We believe in God, the living Spirit Almighty; one, indestructible, absolute, and self-existent Cause. This One manifests Itself in and through all creation but is not absorbed by Its creation." The manifest universe is the body of God; it is the logical and necessary outcome of the infinite self-knowingness of God. Followers believe in the incarnation of the Spirit in everyone and that all people are incarnations of the One Spirit. They believe in the eternality, the immortality and the continuity of the individual soul, forever and ever expanding and that Heaven is within each person, and persons experience it to the degree that they become conscious of it. They believe the ultimate goal of life is to be a complete emancipation from all discord of every nature and that this goal is sure to be attained by all. They believe in the unity of all life and that the highest God, and the innermost God is one God. They believe God is personal to all who feel this Indwelling Presence, and they believe in the direct revelation of Truth through the intuitive and spiritual nature of the individual and any person may become a revealer of Truth who lives in close contact with the indwelling God. They believe the Universal Spirit, which is God, operates through a Universal Mind which is the Law of God, and we are surrounded by this Creative Mind which receives the direct impress of our thoughts and acts upon it. They believe in the healing of the sick through the power of the Mind and in the control of life's conditions through the power of this Mind. They believe in the eternal Goodness, the eternal Loving-kindness and the eternal Givingness of Life to all. They also believe in our own soul, our own spirit and our own destiny; for we understand the life of all is God." (Science of Mind Magazine)

The Science of Mind also states seven main attributes of Infinite Intelligence, or God: love, light, life, power, peace, beauty, and joy. It describes God as a "triune unity" (Holmes' phrase) of Spirit, Soul, Body. God is viewed as Omnipotent, Omniscient, and Omnipresent. (Rev. Abigail Albert)

Independent – "The 'Affiliated New Thought Network' (ANTN) was founded by independent Religious Science ministers who envisioned a spiritual community that would provide heart-centered connection, support and networking for independent Religious Science ministries. They also envisioned a community in which Consciousness was the sole authority. Based on those visions, ANTN was formed in 1992. Since its inception, ANTN has evolved to include not only independent Religious Science ministries, but all New Thought ministries who desire to be a part of such a spiritual community. Its mission is to foster the growth of unique New Thought communities that encourage the consciousness of service, spiritual growth and integrity. The Vision of ANTN is to create global transformation and healing through empowering New Thought ministries that encourage creativity, caring community, education, and spiritual support." (antn.org)

Other much smaller New Thought denominations include: Divine Science, Divine Unity, Home of Truth, Universal Foundation for Better living, One Spirit Ministries, Church of Truth and Seicho-No-Ie.

Sikhism
This Faith represents less than 1.0% of the world population. This faith has no recorded divisions. (Religious Tolerance.org)

Taoism
This Faith represents less than 1.0% of the world population. This faith has no recorded divisions. (Religious Tolerance.org)

Rev. Dr. Stephen L. Albert

*"We could call order by the name of God,
but it would be an impersonal God.
There's not much personal about the laws of physics."*
Stephen Hawking

THE LAWS OF SCIENCE

Evolution versus Creationism

Since the late 1800's, a battle has been raging over the origin of the Universe and mankind. It is a battle which has unnecessarily separated one man from another for a very simple reason, that of ego. Men of Science and of Faith have drawn the battle lines with each side using various scientific and non-scientific theories as their weapons. Before science developed instruments which could date objects as existing for thousands or even millions of years, mankind had only "what we believe" as the basis for discussing life and the origin of this planet. On one side we have the Evolutionists and on the other side the Creationists. Evolutionists believe the scientific evidence that all life on Earth shares a common ancestor, just as you and your cousins share a common grandmother. They believe there is a single "tree of life" which over billions of years has changed into the various species of life which exists on earth today. Creationists on the other hand, believe life was created by an intelligent supernatural being (God) as is depicted in the Judeo-Christian Bible and that all the various species on our planet were created during the first six days of God's creation. Although many people believe that each person has to be solely on one side or another, IT REALLY DOES NOT MATTER. In fact through the combination of the two sides, we accomplish a much more complete and stronger theory of OUR creation which does not reduce the intensity of either side.

Rev. Dr. Stephen L. Albert

The "Big Bang" theory, which most scientists believe happened as our universe was formed so many billions of years ago, had to be under the control of intelligence when it happened because of the way everything in our universe, and every other universe, has developed. IT IS ORDERLY! The evolution of all life had to start somewhere, and whether or not that somewhere was non-human at some point, it became human when "the intelligence" ("God") called it so. No matter which side of the argument you are on, you are right! Knowing the minute details of how we orderly progressed to where we are today will not change the way we treat our neighbor tomorrow. Nor will it change the shape of a plant or an animal or the way mankind reasons out complex issues. In fact, most people would prefer to shy away from arguing about complex issues rather than get into an intense dialog of "Where did we come from?"

As much as we hope people will use correct ethical reasoning to discuss and solve problems, many people seem to shy away from what is ethical when they are solving complex problems. For example, take the area of killing. Each one of the major faiths' holy books covered in this manual believes it is wrong to "commit murder" which is the correct translation from the Hebrew Torah rather than "Thou shall not kill." Not committing murder is different from not killing because murder has intent behind it. The Torah makes a clear distinction between killing, which is sometimes necessary to protect oneself or society and that which is premeditated and self-serving. "Thou shall not kill" would not be the correct usage of God's commandment if the death was accidental or if an animal was killed to feed a family. Yet over the centuries, more wars have been fought and more people killed in the name of "religion" than for any other reason. Killing, by some, is rationalized as a way to gain the power to promote "their" god, even though premeditated killing is a violation of "their" sacred laws. The choices we have are to obey our own laws or not consider ourselves part of the faith which believes them. (Marilyn Clements)

The only faiths which believe in creationism based on the biblical interpretation are the Biblical Christian sects, Orthodox Judaism and Orthodox Islam. All the rest of the faiths hold to a position somewhere between contemporary notions of evolution and creationism or evolution itself.

The Names We Use for "God"

Since around 1730 B. C. when Abraham, who is considered by many to be the father of Monotheistic Faith, was directed by God, to form Judaism, there has always been the question of what to name the "Supreme Being." Monotheistic faiths believe there is and can be only one unique Supreme Being, while Polytheism means the faith believes in several coexisting deities. The conceptions of the various beings vary widely; however, the word "God" in English and its counterparts in other languages are normally used for all of them. As you will see, most of the faiths have a deep emotional reaction to the name "God" and to those adjectives which further define Him/Her/It. In fact, the name "GOD" becomes much more than just a name and is further associated with feelings and connections to past and present generations and their beliefs.

Bahá'í - The Bahá'í belief in one God means the universe and all creatures and forces within it have been created by "an unknowable Essence," which they know as God. This Essence has absolute control over His creation (omnipotence) as well as perfect and complete knowledge of itself (omniscience). Bahá'ís believe although we may have different concepts of God's nature, and although we may pray to Him in different languages and call Him by different names—Allah or Yahweh, God or Brahma—nevertheless, we are speaking about the same unique Being. (Bahá'íNet)

Buddhism – Buddhism is unique among the religions of the world because it does not have any place for God in its soteriology (the

Doctrine of Salvation). Indeed, most Asian religions (with the possible exception of some extremely devotional forms of Hinduism) are essentially non-theistic, in that God does not occupy the central place that is accorded to him in monotheistic religious traditions. But Buddhism goes beyond most of these other religions in that it is positively anti-theistic because the very notion of God conflicts with some principles which are fundamental to the Buddhist view of the world and the role of humans in it. Buddhism is not concerned primarily with refuting the notion of God. It is principally concerned with developing a method of escape from the world's ills. This involves undertaking a method of mental discipline and a code of conduct, which is sufficient to satisfy the most demanding of spiritual requirements. Indeed, only very few of the Buddha's voluminous discourses deal directly with the question of God. He was more interested in expounding a way to achieve personal salvation, and to improve the role of mankind both in this world and in the worlds to come. It is this task which makes up most of the discourses of the Buddha, which later came to be compiled into the various Canons of Buddhism. (*The Buddhist Attitude to God,* buddhist information.com)

Christianity – Christians use the name God, Lord and "Our Father" to refer to God. Jesus said, "The Father is greater than I." They also refer to Jesus as God and believe him to be God-filled. Mormons believe there are many Gods. Brigham Young-Journal of Discourses 7:333 states, "How many Gods there are, I do not know. But there never was a time when there were not Gods. God the Father is an exalted man (a man who has progressed to godhood) with a body of flesh and bones. God the Father became a God after learning truth, aggressively pursuing godhood, and being obedient to the laws of the gospel. (contenderministries.org) The Hebrew name Jehovah is used for God by Jehovah's Witnesses. In The Lord's Prayer, as spoken by Jesus in the Aramaic language and documented in Matthew 6:9-13 and Luke 11:1-4, Jesus uses the term "ABBA" for Lord meaning "my dear Father." This word creates a very different and intimate relationship between God and 'his children.' "It is almost as if God was asking his child to come sit on his lap while he told him about life and protected him from evil." Christians also refer to God as "Light" "Love" and many other endearing adjectives. (Rev. Glen Larsen)

Confucianism – The term "Heaven," as understood by Mencius is a Conscious Being and it is interchangeable with their term for God. Heaven may be seen to symbolize the active and conscious creative principles of God. (Confucianism, alislam.org)

Hinduism – The Hindu faith has unlimited names for God which they refer to as "The Nameless." The following is taken from (geocities.com). Every name that occurs in these *sahasr-nAmas* reverberate with the concept of Divinity, or a glory of His, or an Action of His in the mythological yore, or a facet of His greatness. The fourteen names below are examples from the VISHNU SAHASRANAMA. He is:

1. anAdiH, beginningless, because he is the Cause of everything, and He owes Himself no Cause. Compare His own statement in the gItA: Whoever knows me as unborn and beginningless and as the Lord of the Universe, he is the one among men without delusion and he is absolved of all sins: (10 - 13):
   Compare also '*brahmaNyo brahmakRt brahmA brahma brahma-vivardhanaH*' in the *vishNu sahsra-nAma* itself. The two names *brahmA* and *brahma* denote that He is the creator-cause of everything but He himself has no cause, because He is *brahman* itself.
2. **hariH**, because the word *har* means to destroy. He destroys *samsAra* as well as sins of man. He carries away the sins of even evil-minded people.
3. **mArgaH**, the path, because there is no other path towards Him. Compare, *purusha sUkta*:

4. **sadgatiH**, the one obtained by those who understand the truth that *brahman* exists as the only reality: (- *taittirIyopanishad, II - 6 - 1*):
5. **kathithaH**, that is, the One who is spoken of. 'He is the One who has been declared as the One by all the vedas'; 'He is the One to be known by all the Vedas'.
6. **sambhavaH**, the One who, according to his promise in the *gItA*, manifests Himself by His own free will and for the good of the world and in the manner He chooses:
7. **svayambhUH**, the One who appears, manifests, 'is born', totally independent of anything else, all by Himself. Even when He was 'born' as an infant in the *avatAras* of Rama and Krishna, he was 'born' independent of any genetics or biology! He just appeared; that was all.
8. **kRtajnaH**. He knows what was done. Whatever man does, He knows. But even a little devotion, a little good deed, is remembered by Him and man is rewarded accordingly. In the *mahAbhArata*, in Udyoga parva, he laments with regret the delay He made in going to the help of Draupadi when she was most in distress. It is to be noted here that He did not go to her help until she cried 'O Govinda, help me'. *'Even the vilest sinner, if He remembers me with sincerity, I will consider Him to be noble because He has taken the forward step'* says He in Ch.9 of the *gItA* 9 - 30:
Even the offering of leaves, fruits or flowers is acceptable to Him provided it is done with an intensity of feeling of devotion: gItA 9 - 26:
In the *avatAra* of Rama there is a classical example of this in the description of Rama's characterisitics: (Valmiki Ramayana 2 - 1 - 11): *He (Rama) felt gratified (even) with a single good turn casually rendered and did not take to heart (even) a hunbred wrongs because of his mastery over his self.*
9. **kRtAkRtaH**. *kRtam* means that which is artificially made to happen. *akRtam* means that which happens without any action, that is, that which is natural. He is both the (*kArya*) Effect (which has an antecedent cause) and the (*kAraNa*) Cause (which has no antecedent cause). Again, He is both the effect in the form

of works done and the cause in the form of works which are only latent. He has a *kRta* form, which comes and goes, and He has an *akRta* form which is subtle, which has no perceptible qualities. In other words He is both the concrete and the subtle. Also, He has two facets of *dharma* both inherent in Him, namely, that which gives a temporal spatial benefit (this is kRta) and that which has a permanent immutable benefit (this is *akRta*).

10. Each name of God is interpreted as indicative of a certain quality of His, perhaps the name itself has arisen because of that quality or attribute in Him. He is eternal, **SASvataH**. He is auspicious, *SivaH*; never-changing, *acyuta*. All beings are drawn to Him as the originator; hence He is *Adi-devaH*. He revels in the great knowledge of the Atman, ignoring all trifles - hence He is *mahA-devaH*. Great are His activities of creation, etc.; therefore, He is *mahA-karmA*. By His brilliance, the Sun derives its brilliance, so He is *mahA-tejaH*. He deserves praise by all, but none has to be praised by Him; so He is *stavyaH*. He is one who delights in praise, so He is *stava-priyaH*. Praise is uttering the divine qualities, that is God Himself, so He is also that by which He is praised - *stotram*. And He who praises is also Himself, so He is *stotA*.

11. Not only is the Lord living in each one of us as its innermost resident, but, He is, at once, the all-pervading essence in which the entire universe exists and, as such, He alone is the abode in which we live, breathe and act. He is the abode, therefore, *vatsaraH*. He is also **vatsalaH**, the supremely affectionate, who loves His devotees deeply. His love for all of us is greater by far than all the maternal and paternal love we have ever enjoyed. He is Supreme Love, vatsala. All living things are His children and He is the father of them all, therefore He is *vatsI*.

12. He is **kAlaH**, one who measures the merits and demerits of each individual and apportions the appropriate results. *I am the time of reckoning*, says the Lord in the *gItA*: *kAlo'smi*. He is kAlaH also because He is the death or annihilator of all His enemies, the misdirected sense organs.

13. He is ***ugraH***, the terrible, that is, the one who instills fear in those who are diabolically evil. The Upanishad declares *'For fear of Him the Wind blows, the Sun shines, the fire burns and Indra rules':*
14. He is also ***manoharaH***, the one who plunders the mind; the charming one; He is beauty incarnate; He compels the attention of the devotee, drawing it away from all other sense objects to dwell upon His enchanting form. Recall the story of Dhanurdasa being charmed away from his ladylove, on seeing the infinitely winning personality of the reclining VishNu of Srirangam. (geocities.com)

Islam - Muslim people follow the faith of Islam and have 99 Names of God, also known as The 99 Attributes of God (**Arabic transliteration**: Asma' Allah al-Ḥusná), are the **names of God** revealed in the **Qur'an** and **Sunnah**. It is not possible to perfectly translate the names and attributes of Allah from their original Arabic into English. However, here are some fairly close explanations.

1. **Allah** - Allah, He who has the Godhood which is the power to create the entities.
2. **Ar-Rahmaan** - The Compassionate, The Beneficent, The One who has plenty of mercy for the believers and the blasphemers in this world and especially for the believers in the hereafter.
3. **Ar-Raheem** - The Merciful, The One who has plenty of mercy for the believers.
4. **Al-Malik** - The King, The Sovereign Lord, The One with the complete Dominion, the One Who's Dominion is clear from imperfection.
5. **Al-Quddoos** - The Holy, The One who is pure from any imperfection and clear from children and adversaries.
6. **As-Salaam** – The Source of Peace, The One who is free from every imperfection.
7. **Al-Mu'min** - Guardian of Faith, The One who witnessed for Himself that no one is God but Him. And He witnessed for His

believers that they are truthful in their belief that no one is God but Him.
8. **Al-Muhaimin** - The Protector, The One who witnesses the saying and deeds of His creatures.
9. **Al-^Azeez** - The Mighty, The Strong, The Defeater who is not defeated.
10. **Al-Jabbaar** - The Compeller, The One that nothing happens in His Dominion except that which He willed.
11. **Al-Mutakabbir** - The Majestic, The One who is clear from the attributes of the creatures and from resembling them.
12. **Al-Khaaliq** - The Creator, The One who brings everything from non-existence to existence.
13. **Al-Bari'** - The Evolver, The Maker, The Creator who has the Power to turn the entities.
14. **Al-Musawwir** - The Fashioner, The One who forms His creatures in different forms.
15. **Al-Ghaffaar** - The Great Forgiver, The Forgiver, The One who forgives the sins of His slaves (His creations) time and time again.
16. **Al-Qahhaar** - The Subduer, The Dominant, The One who has the perfect Power and is able to overcome anything.
17. **Al-Wahhaab** - The Bestower, The One who is Generous in giving plenty without any return.
18. **Al-Razzaaq** - The Sustainer, The Provider.
19. **Al-Fattaah** - The Opener, The Reliever, The Judge, The One who opens for His *"ABD"* (slaves who He loves) the closed world and religious matters.
20. **Al-^Aleem** - The All-knowing, The Knowledgeable; The One nothing is absent from His knowledge.
21. **Al-Qaabid** - The Constrictor, The Retainer, The Withholder, The One who constricts the sustenance by His wisdom and expands and widens it with His Generosity and Mercy.
22. **Al-Baasit** - The Expander, The Enlarger, The One who constricts the sustenance by His wisdom and expands and widens it with His Generosity and Mercy.

23. **Al-Khaafid** - The Abaser, The One who lowers whoever He willed by His Wisdom to teach them to be humble and raises whoever He willed by His Endowment (to test them) to be grateful.
24. **Ar-Raafi^** - The Exalter, The Elevator, The one who can raise people up.
25. **Al-Mu^iz** - The Honorer, He gives esteem to whoever He willed, hence there is no one to degrade Him; And He degrades whoever He willed, hence there is no one to give Him esteem.
26. **Al-Muthil** - The Dishonorer, The Humiliator,
27. **As-Samee^** - The All-Hearing, The Hearer, The One who Hears all things that are heard by His Eternal Hearing without an ear, instrument or organ.
28. **Al-Baseer** - The All-Seeing, The One who Sees all things that are seen by His Eternal Seeing without a pupil or any other instrument.
29. **Al-Hakam** - The Judge, He is the Ruler and His judgment is His Word.
30. **Al-^Adl** - The Just, The One who is entitled to do what He does.
31. **Al-Lateef** - The Subtle One, The Gracious, The One who is kind to His slaves and endows upon them.
32. **Al-Khabeer** - The Aware, The One who knows the truth of things.
33. **Al-Haleem** - The Forbearing, The Clement, The One who delays the punishment for those who deserve it and then He might forgive them.
34. **Al-^Azeem** - The Great One, The Mighty, The One deserving the attributes of Exaltment, Glory, Extolment, and Purity from all imperfection.
35. **Al-Ghafoor** - The All-Forgiving, The Forgiving, The One who forgives a lot.
36. **Ash-Shakoor** - The Grateful, The Appreciative, The One who gives a lot of reward for a little obedience.
37. **Al-^Aliyy** - The Most High, The Sublime, The One who is clear from the attributes of the creatures.

38. **Al-Kabeer** - The Most Great, The Great, The One who is greater than everything in status.
39. **Al-Hafeez** - The Preserver, The Protector, The One who protects whatever and whoever He willed to protect.
40. **Al-Muqeet** - The Maintainer, The Guardian, The Feeder, The Sustainer, The One who has the Power.
41. **Al-Haseeb** - The Reckoner, The One who gives the satisfaction.
42. **Aj-Jaleel** - The Sublime One, The Beneficent, The One who is attributed with greatness of Power and Glory of status.
43. **Al-Kareem** - The Generous One, The Bountiful, The Gracious, The One who is attributed with greatness of Power and Glory of status.
44. **Ar-Raqeeb** - The Watcher, The Watchful, The One that nothing is absent from Him. Hence it's meaning is related to the attribute of Knowledge.
45. **Al-Mujeeb** - The Responsive, The Hearkener, The One who answers the one in need if he asks Him and rescues the yearner if he calls upon Him.
46. **Al-Wasi^** - The Vast, The All-Embracing, The Knowledgeable.
47. **Al-Hakeem** - The Wise, The Judge of Judges, The One who is correct in His doings.
48. **Al-Wadood** - The Loving, The One who loves His creation. His love to His creation is His Will to be merciful to them and praise them.
49. **Al-Majeed** - The Most Glorious One, The Glorious, The One who is with perfect Power, High Status, Compassion, Generosity and Kindness.
50. **Al-Ba^ith** - The Resurrector, The Raiser (from death), The One who resurrects His creations after death for reward and/or punishment.
51. **Ash-Shaheed** - The Witness, The One who nothing is absent from Him.
52. **Al-Haqq** - The Truth, The True, The One who truly exists.

53. **Al-Wakeel** - The Trustee, The One who gives the satisfaction and is relied upon.
54. **Al-Qawiyy** - The Most Strong, The Strong, The One with the complete Power.
55. **Al-Mateen** - The Firm One, The One with extreme Power which is un-interrupted and He does not get tired.
56. **Al-Waliyy** - The Protecting Friend, The Supporter.
57. **Al-Hameed** - The Praiseworthy, The praised One who deserves to be praised.
58. **Al-Muhsee** - The Counter, The Reckoner, The One who can and will take account from all on the day of judgment.
59. **Al-Mubdi'** - The Originator, The One who created the human being. That is, He created him.
60. **Al-Mu^eed** - The Reproducer, The One who brings back the creatures after death.
61. **Al-Muhyi** - The Restorer, The Giver of Life, The One who took out a living human from semen that does not have a soul. He gives life by giving the souls back to the worn out bodies on the resurrection day and He makes the hearts alive by the light of knowledge.
62. **Al-Mumeet** - The Creator of Death, The Destroyer, The One who renders the living dead.
63. **Al-Hayy** - The Alive, The One attributed with a life that is unlike our life and is not that of a combination of soul, flesh or blood.
64. **Al-Qayyoom** - The Self-Subsisting, The One who remains and does not end.
65. **Al-Waajid** - The Perceiver, The Finder, The Rich who is never poor. Al-Wajd is Richness.
66. **Al-Waahid** - The Unique, The One, The One without a partner.
67. **Al-Ahad** - The One.
68. **As-Samad** - The Eternal, The Independent, The Master who is relied upon in matters and reverted to in ones needs.
69. **Al-Qaadir** - The Able, The Capable, The One attributed with Power.

70. **Al-Muqtadir** - The Powerful, The Dominant, The One with the perfect Power that nothing is withheld from Him.
71. **Al-Muqaddim** - The Expediter, The Promoter, The One who puts things in their right places. He makes ahead what He wills and delays what He wills.
72. **Al-Mu'akh-khir** - The Delayer, the Retarder, The One who puts things in their right places. He allows what He wills and delays what He wills.
73. **Al-'Awwal** - The First, The One whose Existence is without a beginning.
74. **Al-'Akhir** - The Last, The One whose Existence is without an end.
75. **Az-Zaahir** - The Manifest, The One that nothing is above Him and nothing is underneath Him, hence He exists without a place. He, The Exalted, His Existence is obvious by proofs and He is clear from the delusions of attributes of bodies.
76. **Al-Baatin** - The Hidden, The One that nothing is above Him and nothing is underneath Him, hence He exists without a place. He, The Exalted, His Existence is obvious by proofs and He is clear from the delusions of attributes of bodies.
77. **Al-Walee** - The Governor, The One who owns things and manages them.
78. **Al-Muta^ali** - The Most Exalted, The High Exalted, The One who is clear from the attributes of the creation.
79. **Al-Barr** - The Source of All Goodness, The Righteous, The One who is kind to His creatures, who covered them with His sustenance and specified whoever He willed among them by His support, protection, and special mercy.
80. **At-Tawwaab** - The Acceptor of Repentance, The Relenting, The One who grants repentance to whoever He willed among His creatures and accepts his repentance.
81. **Al-Muntaqim** - The Avenger, The One who victoriously prevails over His enemies and punishes them for their sins. It may mean the One who destroys them.

82. **Al-^Afuww** - The Pardoner, The Forgiver, The One with wide forgiveness.
83. **Ar-Ra'uf** - The Compassionate, The One with extreme Mercy. The Mercy of Allah is His will to endow upon whoever He willed among His creatures.
84. **Malik Al-Mulk** - The Eternal Owner of Sovereignty, The One who controls the Dominion and gives dominion to whomever He willed.
85. **Thul-Jalali wal-Ikram** - The Lord of Majesty and Bounty, The One who deserves to be Exalted and not denied.
86. **Al-Muqsit** - The Equitable, The One who is Just in His judgment.
87. **Aj-Jaami^** - The Gatherer, The One who gathers the creatures on a day that there is no doubt about, that is the Day of Judgment.
88. **Al-Ghaniyy** - The Self-Sufficient, The One who does not need the creation.
89. **Al-Mughni** - The Enricher, The One who satisfies the necessities of the creatures.
90. **Al-Maani^** - The Preventer, The Withholder.
91. **Ad-Daarr** - The Distresser, The One who makes harm reach to whoever He willed and benefit to whoever He willed.
92. **An-Nafi^** - The Propitious
93. **An-Noor** - The Light, The One who guides.
94. **Al-Haadi** - The Guide, The One whom with His Guidance His believers are guided, and with His Guidance the living beings have been guided to what is beneficial for them and protected from what is harmful to them.
95. **Al-Badi^** - The Incomparable, The One who created the creation and formed it without any preceding example.
96. **Al-Baaqi** - The Everlasting, The One that the state of non-existence is impossible for Him.
97. **Al-Waarith** - The Supreme Inheritor, The Heir, The One whose Existence remains.
98. **Ar-Rasheed** - The Guide to the Right Path, The One who guides.
99. **As-Saboor** - The Patient, The One who does not quickly punish the sinners. (jannah.org/articles/names)

Jainism - Jains have a different concept of God. It is not God, but godhood which can be attained by every soul. He/she who attains it, is omnipotent. He knows everything about all the past, present, and future at the same time. He is free from the four major Karmas. They call these great souls *Arihantas*. There have been many Arihantas. In the present time cycle, there were twenty-four of them who set up the religious order afresh to help them cross the cycles of birth and death. They also re-established the order of the *Jain-Tirth* formed of *sadhus, sadhvis*, male and female house holders and that is why they are also called Tirthankaras. The Jains worship them. They are also called Jinas, Vitrag, or Arihants. They lead them to the spiritual path and ultimately to liberation. Before renouncing their worldly life, some of them were kings, or princes, while others were ordinary people. (jainworld.com)

Judaism – In Judaism, the name of God is more than a distinguishing title. It represents the Jewish conception of the divine nature, and of the relationship of God to the Hebrew people. To show the sacredness of the names of God, and as a means of showing respect and reverence for them, the scribes of sacred texts took pause before copying them, and used terms of reverence so as to keep the true name of God concealed. The various names of God in Judaism represent God as he is known, as well as the divine aspects which are attributed to Him. An example of this usage occurs in Ex. 3:13-22: Moses asks God what His "name" is. Moses is not asking "what should I call you;" rather, he is asking "who are you; what are you like; what have you done." That is clear from God's response. God replies that He is eternal, that He is the God of our ancestors, that He has seen our affliction and will redeem us from bondage. In many orthodox writings you will see a hyphen used in place of the "o" in the word G-d. This is because many Jewish teachers believe God's name is so holy it should not even be written. (*The Name of God*, jewishencyclopedia.com)

Native American –Native American tribes have many Gods and Godesses and some Gods have several names. According to Native American Mythology, there are 329 names in total. (godchecker.com) In 1994, Dan Moonhawk Alford wrote a paper entitled, "God is Not A Noun" and made the point that in the Native American tradition, "God" is more a verb than a noun which carries a past and future time element with it. (enformy.com)

New Thought - The name "God" and "Spirit" is used interchangeably throughout the New Thought faith to refer to the Holy Spirit and the Ultimate Consciousness which exists in all, as all and is all. Other names are: Love, Creative Intelligence, First Cause, Creative Power, The One Mind and Divine Love, Mother-Father God, Divine Intelligence, Universal Energy. In prayer, God is referred to as Omnipotent, Omniscient, Omni-loving and Omni-active in and through all. For those who spiritually grow through 12-Step programs, the term "Higher Power" is also used to refer to God.

Sikhism - In Sikhism - The Lord God revealed himself to Guru Nanak and enlightened him. In praise of the Lord, Guru Nanak uttered; "There is but One God, God's name is Truth, God is the Creator, God fears none, God is without hate, God never dies, God is beyond the cycle of births and death, God is self-illuminated, God is realized by the kindness of the True Guru. God was True in the beginning, God was True when the ages commenced and has ever been True, God is also True now." (Japji)

Taoism – In Taoism, there is a single supreme ONE who sustains the cosmos. This ONE is neither male nor female, yet this ONE encompasses both male and female. This ONE is unknowable and incomprehensible. It is fathomless, without beginning or ending, before all things. There are as many names for this ONE as there are tongues to speak them; there are as many faces to this ONE as there are eyes to behold them; there are as many paths to this ONE as there are feet to walk them. No name is the complete name; no face is the complete face; no path is the complete path. This ONE does not seek or need worship, love, praise, or obedience. It transcends all human emotions.

Like Lao Tzu, we call this ONE the TAO because we do not know what else to call it. You may call it God, Buddha, Christ, Krishna, Aphrodite, or Gaia, or anything else if you wish but when either of us calls it anything at all, we have "defined" the ONE, put it in a semantically contrived" box" of human constructs, and, therefore, we can no longer truly be talking about the indefinable ONE. We have given rise to dividing the indivisible and in doing so we have caused division among ourselves. (exploretaoism.com)

"If you were all alone in the universe with no one to talk to, no one with which to share the beauty of the stars, to laugh with, to touch, what would be your purpose in life? It is other life, it is love, which gives your life meaning. This is harmony. We must discover the joy of each other, the joy of challenge, the joy of growth."
Mitugi Saotome

Part 4
What we Strive to Achieve in Life
Our Search for Meaning

The opening quote by Mitugi Saotome has such meaning for me because without the people who shared my past, the activities of those times, good or bad, would have been meaningless. Mindless facts and experiences really cannot exist in a world where having 'feelings' makes up so much of our lives. I truly believe the numbers of significant experiences we have in our life, and our conscious understanding of those experiences, direct us to being able to appreciate the intricacies of life at a deeper level and afford us the ability to enjoy each moment beyond just noticing that something is happening. The feelings I had when I was in the process of learning to drive a car, graduating from college, getting married, watching my godson being born, listening to beautiful music, giving a sermon after which, a congregant said, "Your words helped me" and the billions of other experiences I have had, all helped me develop my faith and who I am today. To me, each of these experiences is the meaning of life and perhaps even previous soul incarnations are also helping me strive to achieve who I am becoming.

Bahá'í - In the Bahá'í faith Baha'u'llah taught the purpose of religion is the evolution of human consciousness and civilization and the achievement of unity, peace and justice.

Buddhism - In the Buddhist faith the goal of Buddhism is to escape the wheel of birth and death. Since suicide leads only to reincarnation, the only effective way to escape this world is by attaining *nirvana*, a transcendental state of consciousness which serves as an exit pass from the wheel of birth and death.

Christianity - In the Christian faith, Christianity gives one answer to this question of what is the meaning of life. The reason that we are here, according to Christianity, is that God created us to have a relationship with him. This is why God created a universe fit for human life, and why he laid down guidelines for how we are to live our lives. According to Christianity, each one of us is created for communion with God; God wants to know us, to love us, and to rejoice with us. Mormons believe in the Plan of Salvation as to why we are here which takes followers through a specific chain of events forcing them to live by faith as they progress back to Salvation.

Confucianism - In the Confucian tradition, a divine being does not have a significant role; his philosophy is man-centered and relies on self-effort. A human being is sufficient to attain the ideal character through education, self-effort, and self-reflection. The goal of life is to live a good moral life. After his death, Confucianism evolved, combining with Chinese traditional religions and Buddhism to add a spiritual component. (*Confucius*, Probe Ministries, leaderu.com)

Hinduism - The Hindu faith recognizes the need for being disciplined, and it also recognizes the need for the individual to pursue abundance and joy in life. This is the core concept of the *purushArtha* which means "meaning of life" or essence of life. There are four purushArthas or the things to seek in one's life. They are *dharma, artha, kAma, moksha*. That is virtue, wealth, joy and liberation. You do not need to keep worrying all your lifetime about the discipline and keep fearing life after death. There is more to life and Hinduism fully supports you to pursue them along with virtue and God. You do not lose out either way. (*Hindu Perspective of Life*, shaivam.org) Hindus believe every individual is forever a living soul and as his or her acts of *Puja* (offerings to God) extend to daily living, those acts of devotion are tied to the growth of his or her *Atman* which is the spirit of God within. As you awaken the power of God within you, you also awaken the power of good.

Islamic - In the Islamic Faith, Muslims believe the purpose of life is Ibadah. Ibadah is to worship Allah out of deep love and a correct knowledge and gratefulness of who Allah is in a way which was taught to Prophet Muhammad the last messenger to mankind. Ibadah is submitting to Allah. The five pillars of Islam are the basis of their worship. They are Shahadah, Salat, Zakah, Sawm and Hajj. The Shahadah is the declaration of faith to Allah and proclaiming that Prophet Muhammad is the servant and messenger of Allah. "There is no god worthy of worship except God, and Muhammad is His messenger." Salat is the establishment of the daily prayers for the individual and the Muslim community established for the remembrance and purification of the individual and society. Zakah is concern for and almsgiving to the needy and to one's relatives; Sawm is self-purification through fasting and Hajj is the pilgrimage to Makkah (Mecca) for those who are able to follow the way of Ibraheem and his wife, Hagar. (*Purpose of Life*, islamtommorrow. com) The five pillars, however, become "lip service" by themselves. To build your faith of Islam, there needs to be a learned foundation and training giving the Muslim "knowledge of God." Together with five daily prayers, which are held in all Mosques or can be said wherever you are, the Friday prayers and use of the five pillars, the Muslim brings balance into his or her life and becomes available to help and give to other people. From there the Muslim will hopefully grow to share the teachings and eventually stand up with courage for what Islamic Truth believes. (Imam Bassem Syed)

Jainism - For Jains, the purpose of life is to attain *moksa,* or release, from the cycle of rebirth. The only way to do this is through non-violent actions and getting rid of negative karma. There are five levels on the path of human development: 1). *Sadhus* (monks) and *sadhivas* (nuns) 2). *Upadhvayas* (teachers of the Jain scriptures) 3). *Acharyas* (spiritual leaders) 4). *Siddhas* (liberated souls) and 5). *Arihantas* (liberated souls who have obtained salvation; both Ordinary and Tirthankar). (religionfacts.com/Jainism) Each morning and evening the Jains pay penance, meditate and ask for forgiveness for anything they may have done which might have caused hurt to any person or life form. They understand that although actions by others might be harmful or hurtful, their reactions to those actions are under their control. (Rohak Vora)

Judaism - In the Jewish faith, there is nothing a human being can do for God. God has no needs. Yet at the same time He gives us everything - air, water, food, sun. And He gave us the Torah as instructions for deriving maximum pleasure from this world. Mystic Judaism says that God needs us to relieve suffering in the world. In the Shema, the Jewish pledge of allegiance, we are commanded to love God B'chol Nafshecha - "with all your soul." You have to be willing to sacrifice your life rather than deny God. This is the pleasure of clarity and commitment. If you can perceive something as so important that you will sacrifice your own life for it, then your life has weight and purpose and direction. Until you know what you are willing to die for, you have not yet begun to live. According to Kabbalah, every physical object possesses sparks of holiness. By using an object in the way ordained by the Torah, the sparks are released and can ascend. Jews believe they are here in this world to elevate the entire creation. (Rabbi Noah Weinberg, *The Meaning of Life,* simple to remember.com)

Native American - In the Native American faith, most follow the principle of "All you have to do is equate the word 'meaning' with the word 'purpose.' The purpose of this life is simply this: We are here to help as many other people as we can while we live on this earth. Many years ago, when the Native Americans had extra skins, food, moccasins, or whatever, they put them in a storehouse. Anyone who needed to use a particular item went to that storehouse and took the item or items they needed. This act was not considered stealing; this act was merely tradition. Native American legends reflect the view that human beings are no more important than any other thing, whether alive or inanimate. In the eye of the Creator, they believe, man and woman, plant and animal, water and stone, are all equal, and they share the earth as partners, even as family. (*The Meaning of Life*, members.tripod.com)

New Thought - In the New Thought Faith, the mission of life is to raise our consciousness to know our Oneness with and in God and embody the attributes of God. They believe we are spiritual beings in a human existence and blend their spirituality in practical, everyday living to create a life of love, joy, success, health and prosperity. "The whole purpose of The Science of Mind is to reconcile the apparent separation of the spiritual world, which must be perfect, with the material world which appears imperfect." (Ernest Holmes) Always striving for a higher consciousness is the purpose those in New Thought seek. Congregational members learn to respect all living things and to nurture their relationship with all people, all faiths, all cultures, all creeds. Understanding that our life is created by what we think and how we feel, cause and effect, New Thought followers realize their constant responsibility to themselves and everyone they meet.

Sikhism - According to the Sikh faith, which accepts the idea of reincarnation, life as a human being is considered the last step before realizing God. Whether or not one attains union with God depends on a person's actions in this life. According to Sikh philosophy, human beings should free themselves from the cycle of reincarnation (births and deaths) by abandoning self-centeredness and embracing God-centeredness. In Sikhism, God is metaphorically known as Truth. With this in mind, a human being who embraces God-centeredness is living a life devoted to the fulfillment of Truth. (Gangadeep Kapur)

Taoism - To be a Taoist means many things to different people in the faith. To be a practitioner of Contemporary Taoism simply means to have realized we are all minute parts of an indescribable large Whole (the Tao), and to choose therefore to 'Flow Like Water' and live in harmony in a spontaneous, natural manner. (The Contemporary Taoist) Lao Tzu believed that human life, like everything else in the universe, is constantly influenced by outside forces. He believed "simplicity" to be the key to truth and freedom. Lao Tzu encouraged his followers to observe and seek to understand the laws of nature; to develop intuition and build up personal power; and to use that power to lead life with love, and without force. (lucidcafe.com)

"Two reactions are expected from the believers once they are exposed to any suffering, in order to deserve the price of either erasing their sins or elevating their rank in Paradise. The first one is to show patience, and the second is to show gratitude to God for sending them this test. God says in Qur'an what means: *{ ... those who patiently persevere will truly receive a reward without measure... }*
(Az-Zumar 39:10)

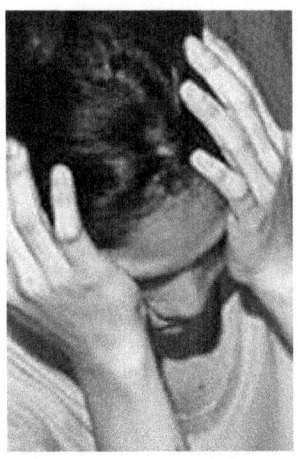

SUFFERING

Suffering seems to be one of those fundamental human experiences we all have in common and is perhaps the one we would all gladly give up. We often feel oppressed and frustrated by suffering because we do not understand it nor the reason we have to experience it. It can pierce the heart of our being and our identity and shakes every assumption we hold about ourselves and the world. It often seems to destroy our will-power and, to our dismay, can overthrow our commitments. My stroke experience in 2003 scared me and had me asking, "Why me, God?" Only in the aftermath have I learned why and I am eternally grateful I am able to use my stroke and other not-so-pleasant life experiences for the benefit of others as well as myself.

Bahá'í - Pain is an inescapable fact of life in the Bahá'í way of thinking. Physical pain arises from injury and illness. Psychological pain accompanies many experiences from loss to betrayal. Although we know we can't escape it, we often wish we could live without pain. Yet we need to realize that pain is an integral part of God's design. It is not in itself an evil thing, unpleasant though it may be. It plays a significant role in protecting us, educating us, and motivating us to progress. The presence of pain in the world is not a sign that there is no loving God, nor is it a sign of a "fallen creation." Paradoxical as it may seem, it is a sign of God's infinite love for us. (*The Goodness of Pain*, planetbahai.org)

Buddhism - Regarding suffering in Buddhism, Tonglen, which means giving and receiving, teaches how one must learn to embrace and work through one's suffering and bear with others in their pain. The Four Noble Truths, which comprise the foundation of Buddhism, are: 1). In this world one sees suffering, 2). The cause of suffering is ignorance (not understanding the nature of reality), hatred (aversion to that which we do not like) and unhealthy desire (attachment to that which is not healthy for us), 3). The cessation of suffering is the cessation of ignorance and elimination of attachment to desire and aversion, 4). The cessation is achieved through practicing the Noble Eight-fold Path, which includes right speech, right action, right livelihood, etc. Taoists and Buddhists believe it is completely possible to find happiness by eliminating our own suffering and the suffering of others in the world (Tonglen). This is done by practicing four steps. **The first step** – or truth – is to recognize the suffering within our own life and define the exact things which cause us to suffer. **The second step** is to take the sufferings we identified and to understand they come from inside ourselves. **The third step** is training our mind to perceive the world in a different way. We realize we can eliminate suffering because we created it within our minds to begin with. **The fourth step** is staying mindful throughout the day and practicing the eightfold path which will bring us lasting happiness and keep suffering away forever as we learn to deal with discomfort.

Christianity - In Christianity suffering in life is very much a part of each Christian's experience. *"Suffering is the evidence against God, the reason not to trust him. Jesus is the evidence for God, the reason to trust him.* It is significant that Jesus rose from the dead with a body that still bore the marks of his sufferings in his hands, his feet and his side." Christians believe that throughout all eternity Jesus will bear those scars. It is because of them that you and I may, if we choose, share that eternity with him as "co-heirs" of his glory (Romans 8:17). *(Making Sense out of Suffering,* Peter Kreeft) Christians look to how Jesus dealt with suffering and how He is a model to each person as to how we should deal with suffering in our life. Suffering will happen, and the process has the ability to transform us to see the hidden purpose and good of each incident and each situation we go through. (Rev. Glen Larsen)

Confucianism – In his teachings, Confucius avoided spiritual issues. He can be categorized as an agnostic who believed in spirits and the supernatural, but he was not interested in them without connection of human flourishing. Because of his very difficult childhood, Confucius sought to transcend suffering by cultivating good character and ethics. He was humanistic and rationalistic in his outlook. "His position on matters of faith was this: whatever seemed contrary to common sense in popular tradition and whatever did not serve any discoverable social purpose, he regarded coldly." (John Noss, *Man's Religion*, p. 392.) Confucius taught a very pragmatic and utilitarian system. However, people are not able to survive for an extended period in this kind of system. Soon they will need a metaphysics that supports the ethical system, that gives them ultimate meaning for their existence, and offers them hope when facing unjust suffering and evil. (Rev. Dr. John Berthrong)

Hinduism - Many Hindus believe suffering is a result of past-life greed, hatred, and spiritual ignorance, which returns as suffering (karma). Coping with suffering is viewed as valuable in furthering spiritual growth. Suffering is also seen as illusory, in that it results from attachment to bodily pleasure and pain, and only the Absolute, or God, truly exists. (beliefnet.com) Suffering is a result of *Avidya (ignorance)* which is forgetting who we really are, which happens when we focus on the outer realm of our life which is heightened by our senses. *Maya* is the illusion of the senses and our ability to control what we experience. Hindus speak of the seven levels within each person and how the first four, the physical body, the etheric (vital) body, the emotional feeling body and the mental body are all experienced by our senses. The last three, the soul, will and God-spirit are all invisible. If these levels are not in balance in our life, we experience suffering and a lack of connectedness with God.

Islamic - According to the Holy Qur'an for Muslims, our present life, with all its joys and sufferings, is merely transitory and illusionary. The passage of human life continues after crossing the valley of death. Our present life is but temporary and fleeting, and the life after life is permanent and perpetual. Death may be the ultimate human suffering in this world, but it is certainly not the end of life. Death is just like a door through which we have to pass to enter into a new dimension of life. In Islam, the next life is a reality beyond any doubt. Both the dimensions of human life — the life in this world and life yet to come — are welded together, one merging into the other like a splendid waterfall turning into a mighty river. The only difference is the second phase of human life is reflective of how we conduct ourselves in the first phase of life. The joys for those who did good in this life shall continue in the life Hereafter. (*God and Human Suffering*, irfi.org) "The suffering will be for those who did bad in this life and died without getting God's forgiveness. Suffering makes you strong and has a hidden mercy, that of no pain, no gain."(Imam Baseem Syed)

Jainism – Jains believe suffering comes from lack of Ahimsa (desire) and that we must give up unhealthy desire to experience Nirvana (paradise). As with the law of Karma (deeds) in which every action sets up a vibration which attracts a particular type of response (favorable or unfavorable), negative Karma clogs the soul and obstructs its natural wisdom or omniscience. This causes suffering such as soul stains and clogs which Jain teachings can remove and move us forward in life.

Judaism - In Judaism, the best answer regarding suffering is provided by Rabbi Harold Kushner in his work <u>When Bad Things Happen To Good People</u>. He concludes that while we will never know "why," what we need to do is learn how to respond in the face of suffering. If one is forced to make any "choice" about God's nature, he must conclude that God is all-knowing, all-present, all-good, etc. but not all-powerful because He has given us free-will. Too often we hold

God responsible for tragedy and suffering that we as human beings, individually and collectively, should have and could have prevented! Our higher self knows what we should do to reduce our sufferings.

Native American – Despite centuries of suffering, Native American tribes have worked hard to become self-sufficient. They believe they must suffer the ordeal of the heat in order to purify themselves. Black Kettle of the Cheyenne tribe said, "Although wrongs have been done to me, I live in hopes. I have not got two hearts….Now we are together again to make peace."

New Thought - New Thought believes "man should be free from sickness, lack, unhappiness' because God does not want man to suffer. God is a loving, giving God. It is not up to man, who has the inherent qualities of God, to use the Law of Mind (It is done unto you as you believe) to endure any life suffering. Suffering comes from a State of Consciousness. As long as the man feels poor, he will remain in poverty. As long as a man feels ill, he will remain ill. As long as man talks about being unhappy, he will be unhappy" (*Science of Mind*, Holmes, p110). Minor suffering occurs to the ego and the physical body when our poor choices reduce the chances of our achieving our goals. Major suffering happens to redirect us back towards the important goals for which our soul chose to come into the physical dimension in the first place. How we react to the conditions we are given, affects the amount of suffering we experience. New Thought followers believe we create our heaven or hell on Earth by the conscious choices we make and the thoughts we think. Ernest Holmes said; "Change Your Thinking, Change Your Life." Our thoughts are our responsibility, and we do create the life we live by our thoughts, words, and deeds. Any suffering is brought on by us and our thinking negatively. There is no one "out there" to blame. We bear the sole responsibility for our lives. (Rev. Abigail Albert)

Sikhism - Sikhism is not a philosophy of suffering. Even so, human suffering and death are the two running themes in the Sikh poetic tradition. The poet-philosophers of Guru Granth Sahib the holy scripture, and practically all the commentators and interpreters of the Sikh faith, repeatedly stress these twin facts of human life, not for highlighting them, but to encourage men and women to face them and to conquer them. According to Sikhism, suffering is created by the consequences of our own actions (Karma), and is the mechanism by which we get back to God-consciousness. The Guru Granth Sahib Ji, the Sikh Holy Scripture says, "Suffering is the medicine, and pleasure the disease, because where there is pleasure, there is no desire for God."

Taoism – Similar to Buddhists, those who follow Taoism believe human suffering comes from not accepting the inability to get what you wish for. Realizing we all suffer and that life is not simple, are the first steps to removing the ignorance about being able to live without suffering. It is a conscious understanding, which then creates the life we would choose for ourselves. Suffering then is, quite simply, that the human intellect experiences limits. One of our primary weaknesses as humans is that we do not want to accept this fact. As a result we overestimate our own intellectual abilities and we try to define what cannot be defined, Tao. Acutely aware of this tendency, students of Tao embrace their innate human weakness, thus freeing themselves to better understand their own limitations while working to enhance their natural abilities and reduce their suffering. (*On The Absolute Tao*, tao.org)

In terms of suffering, some Taoists believe we are born with a certain destiny/*ming*, which is like a curriculum of things we are to learn in this life. Ming would be different for everyone. That destiny arises from the Tao and resides in the expression of the "true will." But because of social conditioning, that true-will can become obscured, and that is the social will, which is the motivations of a worldly life based on separation from the One, mistrust of the universe and the desire for self- gratification. To practice Daoism, we must uncover our "true-will" and see what our destiny/ming is in this life and then live it out. The way the true will can be uncovered is by meditation and by communing with nature. (Michael Arnold, Taoist)

West Virginia Interfaith
P.O. Box 226
Talcott, WV 24981

REV. DR. STEPHEN L. ALBERT

*"Original sin is that thing about man
which makes him capable of conceiving
of his own perfection and incapable of achieving it."*
Reinhold Niebuhr

Original Sin & Salvation

The faiths are very much divided with regard to whether a man or woman is born from original sin and whether he or she can ever reach salvation in this life. Christianity (not all of its divisions) believes in the concept of original sin and the other faiths do not.

Bahá'í - Bahá'ís do not think of salvation in terms of salvation from the stain of "original sin," nor does it protect us from some external evil force or devil. Rather, salvation delivers people from the captivity of their own lower nature, a captivity that breeds private despair and threatens social destruction. Salvation means drawing nearer to God and progressing on the path to a deep and satisfying happiness. This deep and satisfying happiness is due to the spiritual condition of feeling nearness to God. Bahá'u'lláh repeatedly stressed that only revealed religion can save us from our imperfections. It is because God has sent his Messengers to show us the path to spiritual development and to touch our hearts with the spirit of God's love that we are able to realize our true potential and make the effort to be united with God. This is the "salvation" that religion brings. (*On Good and Evil*, bahai.org)

Buddhism - In Buddhism there is no original sin and therefore no need for salvation. Buddhists believe the root of human suffering is not sin, but our confusion about ego. We suffer because we believe in the existence of an individual self. This belief splits the world into "I" and "other." Also, they believe, sin should not be equated to suffering. There is no almighty God in Buddhism. There is no one to hand out salvation on a supposed Judgment Day. (Stephen Butterfield, *Tricycle*: The Buddhist Review, Vol. I, #4) However, it is even more than this... (although not all Buddhists believe this), the highest teachings (third turning of the wheel of Dharma) is that all living beings have the Buddha-Nature and have the inherent capacity for good and awakening good, not evil, and will become Buddhas. (Sondra Buschmann & Rinpoche Zhai Xhuoma)

Christianity - In Christianity, "original sin" refers to the idea that the sin of Adam and Eve's disobedience (sin "at the origin") has passed on a spiritual heritage, so to speak. Some Christians teach that human beings inherit a corrupted or damaged human nature in which the tendency to do bad is greater than it would have been otherwise, so much so that human nature would not be capable now of participating in the afterlife with God. Believing in "original-blessing" which comes from the teachings of Genesis 1 versus "free-will" which comes from Genesis 2, divides many who follow Christianity. Original sin is not a matter of being "guilty" of anything; each person is only personally guilty of their own actual sins of "missing the mark" of what they are striving for. However, this understanding of original sin is what lies behind the Christian emphasis of the need for spiritual salvation from a spiritual Saviour, who can forgive and set aside sin even though humans are not inherently pure and worthy of such salvation. (helium.com) Jesus the Christ's choice of dying on the cross (the atonement) canceled the penalty of death imposed on ALL men through Adam's sin, thereby ensuring that all men would be redeemed, resurrected and given immortality (the reuniting of spirit with body) as a gift. "If there had been no atonement, temporal death would have remained forever, and there never would have remained forever, and there never would have been a resurrection. The body would have remained forever in the grave" (Mormon Doctrine, 1977 ed., p.63) The other element about sin is that its actions are deeper than disobedience to God. It is seen as creating a separation from God; it is a transgression against God. Confession (witnessing) in Christianity is designed to create a bridge so that man may repent and he and God may be reunited. (Rev. Glen Larsen)

Confucianism - The basic goal of Confucianism is to become more fully human. *Jen* (pronounced Ren) is "human heartedness," living up to true humanness - our innate potential for goodness, empathy and love. There is no "original sin" in Confucianism. The goal of the kind of person to be is to live by moral values rather than for selfish, personal gain. Such a person who emulates Jen is called a *"chun tzu"* - a "great man", a man of virtue in the Confucian sense. (Confucianism, nvcc.edu) Salvation is viewed as realizing one's natural goodness, which is endowed by heaven through education. The superior man always knows the right and follows his knowledge. (*Eastern Beliefs*, ksuweb.kennsew.edu)

Hinduism – There is no original sin or fall of man in the Hindu teachings. Hinduism does not view sin as a crime against God, but as an act against dharma, moral order, and one's own self. It is thought natural, if unfortunate, that young souls act wrongly, for they are living in nescience, *avidya*, the darkness of ignorance. Sin is a course of action which automatically brings negative consequences. The term sin carries a double meaning, as do its Sanskrit equivalents: 1) a wrongful act, 2) the negative consequences resulting from a wrongful act. (Sabdavali, himalayanacademy.com)

Islam - There are many elements to Human nature and each one has the potential to bring benefits. So there is no "Original Sin" in Islam. It is that when Man contradicts God's commandments or His will, he commits sins. The Islamic view of sin, is similar to the Jewish view. In fact, the religion of Islam is the natural culmination of the progressive revelation of God from the very first prophet to the last one, Prophet Muhammad (pbuh). Consequently, Islam believes in all prophets of God, from Adam to Muhammad, including Abraham, Moses and Jesus (peace be upon them all). According to the Islamic creed, the original religion taught by all these prophets is and was always Islam, which is the peaceful submission to the One and Only God. Thus, the concept of sin as taught by all prophets of God ought to be the same. (*Adam & His Sin*, readingislam.com)

Jainism – Jains believe spiritual salvation is possible through a rigorous practice of Ahimsa which is complete non-violence, non-injury and harmlessness in deed word and thought and absolute respect for all forms of life. How you live your life is the most important thing and how you choose to burn off your negative karma is up to the individual. You can burn negative karma each day and each moment throughout your life or in one shot during a major feat of caring or forgiveness. Jains believe the misery or happiness all comes with you when you die. (Rohak Vora)

Judaism does not accept the doctrine of original sin. Jews believe we each have an inclination within us to do good and to do evil. Life is about channeling our energy and mastering our passions so we will truly live a moral and just life. For the Jews, the Torah is a blueprint for living however, we each have our own free will. (Marilyn Clement). While there were some Jewish teachers in Talmudic times who believed that death was a punishment brought upon mankind on account of Adam's sin, the dominant view by far was that man sins because he is not a perfect being, and not because he is inherently sinful. (*Original Sin*, sullivancounty.com)

Native American - Although many differences can be seen between the creation myths of different Native American tribes, two similarities stand out in sharp contrast with Judeo-Christian creation mythology: 1) there is no concept of original sin, no initial wrong-doing by humans which has resulted in our being cast out of the place we truly belong, and 2) the Earth home, there is no 'Kingdom of Heaven' awaiting us which is our 'true' spiritual home, with time on Earth to be used as a 'testing ground.' (Donna Ladkin, *Native American Spirituality*, greenspirit.org)

New Thought - In New Thought, the belief of original sin is not accepted, and the term "Original Blessing" is used in place of it in discussion and rituals. They believe each person is pure spirit, pure love, pure God Essence and therefore capable of going and sinning no more. Baptisms for children are preformed without water in Christian traditions (typically used to "wash away" a child's sins) but instead, the rite uses rose pedals sprinkled on the child to denote the original beauty which God has bestowed on the child. Sin is seen as the archery term it came from meaning "missing the mark" and therefore gives the person who once or more failed in something, the chance to try again.

Sikhism - Forgetfulness of God is the greatest sin in Sikhism. They do not believe in the concept of original sin or Satan. Sikhs believe humans are inherently prone to succumb to temptations and that God created all and gave people free will. Salvation is enlightenment, granted by God's grace only, resulting in liberation from cycles of rebirth and the soul's merger with God (the Supreme Soul or Guru) after death. (Sikh.net)

Taoism - Taoists don't use the word sin, and they believe "people are compassionate by nature." They do not believe Humans have any need to be saved from anything although they agree there is much change needed in society as far as curing social ills. (*Lessons in Sarva Dharma*, books4saikids.com) Human beings are always trapped into own self definition of "sin." If we agree to define sin as an act which causes others to suffer a loss or a disadvantage, Taoism teaches Its people to act according to "Hek Ching, Hek Li, Hek Fa." It means our act must follow etiquette and all existing rules in society. On top of that, it must also follow constitutions. In daily life, we sometimes need to lie, don't we? (not for a bad purpose). Like "cheating during a test", it is not causing others to suffer, but it causes our own self to suffer. It makes us lazy and dependent to others, etc. And in the end, it would lower our "character," also creating difficulties to our life. It is true that in Taoism as if there is no "prohibition," however It requires Its people to think deeply and logically. So they could see things clearly and could also decide which are the things that can be done, must be done, or must be avoided, etc. Such thinking is more precious to own by human. (tao-tsm-en.siutao.com)

> *"I have so much to do*
> *that I spend several hours in prayer*
> *before I am able to do it."*
> **John Wesley**

World Prayer Symbol
Galesburg First Church of the Nazarene
1501 Webster Street
Galesburg, IL 61401

Prayer

I know prayer is different for everyone; however, I cannot believe that once anyone has made it a daily habit, how anyone can live without it. I have watched myself when I am rushed and forced to wake up and be almost instantaneously in a decision-making mode; I make somewhat poorer decisions than when I get the chance to pause, go within, and connect to that God presence in my Soul. The power of daily prayer for me has changed my attitude, increased my health, my prosperity level and my ability to multi-task in ways I had never considered before. For something which is free to obtain, prayer for me is a wonder drug for all which ails me.

Bahá'í - The Bahá'í teachings prescribe daily prayer and intimate communion with God as the foundation for a life devoted to spiritual advancement and service to humanity. In addition to practicing private prayer and meditation, Bahá'ís gather in their homes and communities for collective worship. Devotional gatherings are scheduled regularly to share a devotional spirit of joy, love and fellowship. Readings are taken from the Bahá'í writings and may include the scriptures of Christianity, Islam, Judaism, Hinduism, Zoroastrianism and Buddhism. Participants are encouraged to bring their prayer books or favorite passages from the scriptures to share. These gatherings often offer prayers for healing or assistance to those in need. Musical selections are diverse, coming from a variety of cultures and styles. There is no established ritual and no solicitation of funds. (*Prayer and Devotion*, Bahai.us)

Buddhism - In Buddhism, prayer is considered part of our spiritual journey, transforming confusion into clarity and suffering into joy. They believe in order for prayer to be effective it must be devoid of any self-centeredness and calculation, relying strictly on great compassion. It should be done to strengthen and open our hearts, and to benefit all beings. Buddhist prayer has nothing to do with begging for personal worldly or heavenly gains. Buddhist prayer is a practice to awaken our inherent inner capacities of strength, compassion and wisdom rather than to petition external forces based on fear, idolizing, and worldly and/or heavenly gain. Buddhist prayer is a form of meditation; it is a practice of inner reconditioning. Buddhist prayer replaces the negative with the virtuous and points us to the blessings of Life. (*Buddhist Prayer Explained*, buddhistfaith.tripod.com)

Christianity - Prayer in the Christian faith is thought of as communion with God. The key to prayer is hearing God and also being heard by God. Christians believe God won't listen if we are not sincere and he rewards those who seek Him. They also believe God always hears them and knows their heart. When we give our self fully to God we receive answers. (*Prayer*, christianfaith.com) Mormon doctrine requires followers to "make prayer meaningful" so as to feel the deeper meaning of life. Baptists also see prayer as the road to better know God.

Confucianism – Confucianism comes closest to achieving the karmic ideal of what the Christians and New Thought believers call "praying without ceasing" in that their lives are their prayers. The Confucian philosophy can best be described as "principles and precepts, not prayers!" The essence of Confucianism can be summed up by this simple phrase: "the cultivation of the person is the root of everything!" Confucius himself believed prayers detracted from life in that too much focus on them interfered with the all important "cultivation of the person." (*Confucianism Precepts*, healpastlives.com)

Hinduism - In Hinduism prayers are used to invoke gods or various supernatural powers for the welfare of particular individuals or the entire community. The Vedic hymns are some of the most powerful prayers ever known to mankind. In Hindu prayers the content of the prayer and the sounds involved in the utterance of prayers are equally important. A great emphasis is directed to the manner and method in which the prayers are recited. If a prayer is not correctly chanted, if the syllables are not properly pronounced, it is believed the prayers may not yield desired results and may even harm the individuals. (*Hinduism and Prayer,* experiencefestival.com)

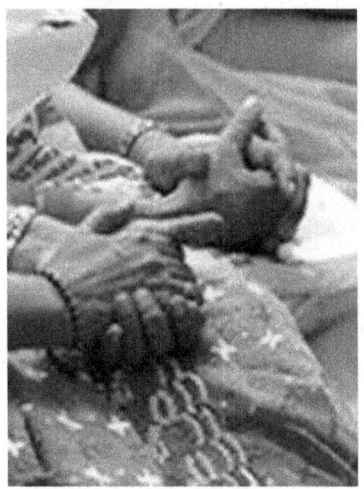

Islam - Muslims are called to prayer from the minaret in a *Masjid* (Mosque) if it has one. In the days before sound amplification, this was the way the call to prayer was announced. Today a microphone and loud speaker will suffice. The man who calls them to prayer is called a muezzin. There are no pictures or statues in a mosque. They are decorated with patterns and words from the Qur'an. They have very little furniture in them because Muslims use prayer mats for prayer. All Muslims go to the mosque on Friday which is a special day of sermon and prayer and every day, five times a day, if a Masjid is close by. When people go into the mosque they take off their shoes as was Moses commanded to take off his shoes in the sacred Valley of Tuwa. This is to keep it clean for prayer. There is a bathroom called *"Inuzu"*, or at least an area with water where people can purify their hands, face, feet and arms, head and neck and ears with water. Women pray in the same place as men unless, as in more orthodox mosques, there is a screened off area for them. When Muslims pray they are required to face towards Mecca. This direction is called *"Quibla."* All mosques have an Imam, a prayer leader. If He is not around, any adult male who is righteous may lead the prayers. (*An Introduction to Islam*, bbc.co.uk/Birmingham/faith/islam) (Imam Baseem Syed)

Jainism - Jain prayers are not like God-focused prayers found in other religions. Instead, Jain prayers tend to recall the great acts of the tirthankaras and remind the individual of the various teachings of Mahavira. Jain prayer is part of a being's spiritual development; it is a means to an end and not an end in itself. Jains do not pray to ask the tirthankaras for grace or material favours, but to inspire them in their practice. Prayers are spoken in the ancient dialect of Ardha Magadhi (which is as old as Aramaic, the language spoken by Christ). One of the most important Jain prayers is the Namaskara Sutra which praises the five great beings of Jainism. This prayer does not worship any particular individual. It worships the virtues of the arihantas, the siddhas, the acharyas, the upadhyayas and sadhus. This prayer is learned by all Jain children. It is often the first prayer a Jain will say when rising in the morning and the last prayer said before going to sleep for the night. (Religion and Ethics, *Worship, Jain Prayers*, bbc.co.uk/religion)

Judaism - Recitation of prayers is the central characteristic of Jewish worship. These prayers, often with instructions and commentary, are found in the Siddur, the traditional Jewish prayer book. Orthodox Jews are expected to recite three prayers daily and more on the Sabbath and Jewish holidays. While solitary prayer is valid, attending synagogue to pray with a *minyon* (quorum of 10 adults) is considered ideal. This lends support to each other as each person recites their intention whether it is a prayer to feed the hungry, clothe the poor or for something more personal. Proper concentration (*kavvanah*) is considered essential for prayer, and there are certain prayers such as the *Shema* that are invalid if recited without the required awareness and intention. The Shema reads, "Hear o' Israel, the Lord our God, the Lord is One." (Marilyn Clement)

Native American – Native Americans believe the purpose of prayer is to "give back" to the creator your thanks for the gift of creation. It's not about taking." They believe the prayers and thoughts contained in the smoke of the pipe are carried to the Creator. To pray in this way requires clarity, choice, cleaning out any obstructive forces in the mind, such as feelings/beliefs of unworthiness, guilt, fear or limitation, to the intent of the prayer, being able to clear all the channels to the higher self, and having enough power (manna) to set it all in motion. A breakdown in any of these factors and the system doesn't work. And, of course, before asking, make sure you are in balance by having given thanks for all the other gifts in your life. Prayer in this way is about opening your heart to what you are seeking, then opening to Creator's heart and loving presence and to the field of infinite potential, which is this universe, and becoming an open channel for its expression and creative manifestation. The final step requires surrendering to the Mystery. "If what I have prayed for is not for my greatest good, I release it all to you and open to that which is truly for my greatest good, greatest healing and greatest outcome for all involved." (*Power of Prayer*, nierica.com)

New Thought - Those in New Thought believe prayer works and most of the different divisions of the New Thought faith actually began as prayer movements. They believe "prayer is a recognition of Spirit's Omnipresence, Omnipotence and Omniscience and a realization of man's unity with Spirit. The unity and oneness one feels while praying, open the doors to health, abundance and love individually and globally." (*Science of Mind*, Holmes, p149) Prayer is a way of life, a way to move through life with peace in our hearts. Prayer is a tool, which New Thought congregants use to know their oneness with/in God and to be closer to God. It is this awareness of God's presence that keeps them poised and centered in times of challenge. The New Thought approach to prayer is affirmative, based on positive prayers and affirmations that have universal, interfaith appeal. An affirmation is a simple statement of spiritual truth that calls forth a conscious recognition of our oneness with God. Focusing on these spiritual truths reinforces our awareness of God and all that God is. For more than 100 years, a division of Unity called "Silent Unity" has been serving people of all faiths from all parts of the world through prayer. What began as a small group of praying friends has grown into a worldwide prayer ministry with devoted staff prayerfully responding to thousands of requests that pour in each day by telephone, letter, e-mail, or through the Internet ministry. They believe true prayer goes beyond words. True prayer is an attitude of heart and mind, of receptivity and thanksgiving.

Religious Scientists believe people can achieve more fulfilling lives through a process called spiritual mind treatment, or affirmative prayer. Spiritual mind treatment is a step-by-step process, in which one states the desired outcome as if it is already known that it has happened. Each step flows logically from the last one. Treatment is to be stated as personal, positive, powerful, and present. The goal is to gain clarity in thinking that guides action to be consistent with the desired outcome. The treatment sets off a new chain of causation in Mind that leads one to act according to the good for which one is treating. (Rev. Abigail Albert)

Religious Scientists use a very powerful five-step 'Scientific Prayer Treatment' approach to prayer and those who follow this division of the New Thought faith, structure their prayers this way: 1). **Recognition** – (GOD IS): Omnipresent, Omnipotent, Omniscience, Omniactive and Omniloving in and through all people, places, things and experiences. 2). **Unification** – (I AM) Spirit and I are One. I live move and have my being in God. 3). **Realization** – (I ASK and ACCEPT). These are a series of statements affirming and declaring the desired outcome. **Thanksgiving** –(I AM GRATEFUL) Thanking God for the divine outcome, this or something better. 5). **Release** – (LET GO LET GOD)I release this prayer into the Law of Mind knowing it returns to me fulfilled for my highest good.

Sikhism - The Sikhs recite their set prayers in the morning, evening and at bedtime. They bow to the Holy Book and recite it with reverence. They believe that the Hymns composed by the Gurus and given in Guru Granth Sahib were revealed to them by God. Besides, the individual i.e. personal meditation on God, they perform "Kirtan" - sing God's praise, and meditate on God in the congregation. They hold their gatherings in the presence of the Holy Book in their place of worship called "Gurdwara"- Doorway to the Guru. Every ceremony is performed in the presence of their Holy Book. Their gatherings always end in "Langar" - common (community) food - sitting together and eating. It may be prepared singly, jointly, at home or at the Gurdwara. (Essays on Sikh Values, gurmat.info)

Taoism - In Taoism, there are many powerful and famous prayers quoted in history. It is not necessary to repeat any specific prayer or 'manthra' to benefit from prayer. However, many people find great comfort in meditating over some prayers. When praying, Taoists realize prayer is not the idle repetition of words or empty formula. They study the prayer, think about it, visualize it and repeat it. Taoism states that words are just signs to point to the non-conceptual ultimate reality. It is of value to not obsess over the conceptual pointer but to see the ultimate reality clearly. (beliefnet.com)

Rev. Dr. Stephen L. Albert

*"The only work that will ultimately bring
any good to any of us
is the work of contributing to the healing of the world."*
Marianne Williamson

HEALING

After my stroke in April of 2003, I spent a year healing in so many ways. As well as the physical healing which was so obviously needed, I drew upon my spiritual beliefs to help me heal emotionally and mentally as well. Without the help of the various doctors, nurses and therapists I could never have achieved the abilities I now have today. That said, without my belief that I COULD GET WELL, and that God had my Soul going through the stroke experience to prepare me for helping others to heal, I know I would not have been able to accept myself as HEALED.

Bahá'í - Bahá'ís believe that religion and science must be harmonized; therefore, one consults competent physicians and also beseeches God for healing. The view is wholistic rather than dualistic. According to Bahá'í teachings, all work performed in spirit of service is considered as worship. Thus, Bahá'ís applaud medicine. However, there is room for belief in "divine" healing through formalized healing prayers. They believe there is a direct correlation between emotional and spiritual condition and physical health. The Bahá'í promote following a good diet and eating in moderation. (Beliefs about the Bahá'í faith, allaboutreligion.org)

Buddhism - Buddhist healing uses the laws of cause and effect to find the root of disease and treat it. Without faith Buddhists believe most mental healing practices won't work.

Christianity - Healing in Christianity is a matter of faith. People can be healed if they believe in the healing power of God. Prior to performing a healing on anyone, the Bible records Jesus always asking the person, "Do you believe you can be healed?" If the answer was positive, Jesus' healings would happen. "Yet the news about him spread all the more, so that crowds of people came to hear him and to be healed of their sicknesses." (Luke 5:14-16)

Confucianism – Confucianism, with its belief in social equality and respectful relationships, places within the individual the innate ability to deal with the many issues we all face in life. By using self-restraint and moderation, they feel the need for healing is reduced.

Hinduism – Ayurveda is the traditional Hindu science of medicine of long life practiced in one form or another by 80% of people of Indian descent. Around the Pacific rim, peoples from Fiji, Indonesia, Malasia and Singapore use Ayurveda practitioners when seeking help for physical and mental disorders. Ayurveda, like other forms of medicine, is not just the reliance on past practices, but continues to be up-dated as more knowledge is known. Consider the term Ayurveda, which is a combination of dyus, meaning "life, vitality, health, longgevity," (Crawford, 1989, p. 3), and veda, meaning "science or knowledge (Crawford, 1989, p. 3). Since 1947 the Indian government has regulated Ayurveda practices and Ayurveda medical colleges continue to train healers, publish papers and encourage research. (*Ayurveda*, educ.uvic.ca)

Islam – Islam is a religion of healing for humans on all levels of their being: mind, body, and soul. Seeking medical help is recommended in many prophetic traditions asserting that "there is a remedy for every malady and it's excellent to get treatment." (Narrated by Muslim.) In addition to seeking medical assistance from a professional to cure the body on emergencies or chronic cases, Islam offers the sick and the ailing, cure for their souls and minds through an array of Qur'anic verses and supplications called *ruqyah*. They believe words create chemical reactions of which the outcome is controlled by God. Healing is from God and comes through the remembrance of God at a divine time. "Healing" words heal; Divine words have Divine healing. A Muslim believes that Allah is the Creator of everything in the universe, including germs, illness, accidents, natural disasters, etc. So, after seeking medical assistance, Muslims are instructed to turn to Allah to seek complete and comprehensive healing for the marvelous miracle that is the human body. (*First Aid and Healing*, reading islam.com) As the human body needs food to stay strong, the *Rooh* (Soul) needs spiritual food to replenish itself. The complete person is a balance of Body and Spirit in which God is the light. (Imam Baseem Syed)

Jainism – Medicine as a social science evolves with the influence of various cultures. Western medicine has its roots in Greek culture. Ayurveda in olden days was called Hindu medicine. In the same way the origin and development of Pushpayurveda is associated with Jainism. Founded upon the philosophy of non-violence, Jainism has contributed many good things to humanity. Pushpayurveda, a science that explores the healing power of flowers (pushpa) is considered an offshoot of Jainism. (*Pushpayurveda; The science of healing and way to happiness*, Dr. Job Thomas, Kerala Caling, Sept. 2004) Jainism also uses the many Homeopathic and Ayurvedic healing techniques of the Hindu faith.

Judaism – The Jewish healing movement falls into the category of *z'aka*. Everything we do, from healing services, the use of psalms, the assistance we give to caregivers, the training we offer clergy and others help people fulfill this unstructured *mitzvah* (commandment) of crying out to *Hashem* (the name for God) in times of pain and trouble. We do this because the Torah guides us in this manner and because it helps. The rabbis of old intuitively knew this. Their understanding is reflected in *Torah* sources and wisdom which guide us in seeing how visits and prayer can make a difference in the life of someone living with illness. The unstructured crying out to God in times of trouble is the central theme of the Jewish healing movement. It can be seen as fully sanctioned by our tradition and has been clinically shown to truly help those in need. With sensitivity to *Halakhic* issues, our work can be shared with an ever-widening circle of Jews in need of the Torah's healing power. (Is Jewish Healing Kosher? Rabbi Joseph S. Ozarowski author of To Walk in God's Ways: Jewish Pastoral Perspectives on Illness and Bereavement)

Native American - Shamanism is a Native American healing tradition that has existed since the beginning of time. A shaman can be defined as a man or woman who can travel between alternative states of consciousness at will, traveling in spirit or mind between this world and other worlds in order to find healing, knowledge, wisdom, guidance and help. Shamans have traditionally filled the role of priest, magician, metaphysician and healer. Healing and guidance are the shaman's major purposes, whether for themselves or someone else in the community. Shamans use various methods to heal the body such as herbalism used by the Yaqui Indians, chants used by Hopi Indians, sand mandalas used by Navajo Indians and trance-inducing dance used by Yoruban Africans. Healing of the spirit usually involves more esoteric healing, such as guided meditation and imagery. Knowledge sought through shamanism can be gained through vision quests as performed by Lakota Indians and Aranda Aborigines[2], and initiation ceremonies as performed by Australian Aborigines. Some shamans also use psychotropic herbs, plants and cacti, including the Mescalero Apache and Huichol Indians. Wisdom-seeking is an integral aspect of shamanism, whereby the individual may look to spirit or totem animals for guidance through journeying. With such powerful inspiration, shamans perform services such as divination, elemental manipulation, soul retrieval and guiding souls after death. Spirit guidance is also represented in the form of wise women/men, ancestors, spirit teachers, spirit healers, power animals, nature spirits, patron gods/goddesses and angels. (*Shamanism*, wellbeing.com)

New Thought – New Thought believes Spirit is perfect, whole and complete in each person. To the degree we realize it, the healthier we are. Since those in the New Thought faith believe everything is consciousness, they believe by healing the mind and emotions, the body will be healed also. "What you believe manifests" is an often-heard quote. Regarding how to heal, New Thought believers recite something like the following when a body is in pain. "God in me, as me, is me. Divine perfection is who I am." "I know this Spirit is complete and perfect. Therefore, it must be complete and perfect in me." "I know this Spirit is now operating in my affairs. It is manifesting its beauty and harmony in everything I do. I know my body is a spiritual idea, manifesting in form. I know every organ of my body, being a manifestation of pure Spirit, contains within itself a pattern of joy, of peace, of divine order, of harmony, and complete perfection. And so it is." (Rev. Abigail Albert)

Sikhism – Sikhs believe Divine name is the medicine for all ailments. (Sarab Rog Ka Aukhad Naam (asthpadi 9/4 Sukhmani Sahib) The Sikh religion founded by Guru Nanak (1469-1539) believes in one transcendent, inexpressible and formless divinity, who is manifest everywhere in the world God has created. They believe by meditating on the name of the God, the true nature and essence of the God could be revealed. Sikhs believe religion is useless if the worshipper's heart remained immersed in the material world. The Gurus have stated any ailment which cannot be cured by innumerable remedies, vanishes with the application of Naam (the recitation and remembrance of God in prayer). It is fully effective for removing all mental, physical or spiritual pain and suffering. (*Prayer of Abundance*, 1stwholistic.com)

Taoism - (Taoism) has been called China's indigenous high religion and stands alongside Confucianism and Buddhism as one of the Three Teachings (sanjiao) of that civilization. Pranic healing encompasses a broad array of therapeutic approaches, both ancient and modern, based on the notion that illnesses of body or mind involve an imbalance and/or blockage in the flow of vital life energy. In ancient India, this energy was known as *prana*, as it still is in the contemporary practice of yoga and Ayurvedic medicine. (*Eye on Religion*, ccat.sas.upenn.edu)

For the Taoist, the laws of yin and yang and the Five Elements connect the macrocosm of nature and the microcosm of man. At the macrocosmic level, the laws manifest at the elements and seasons, while at the microcosmic level they manifest as the organs and energies of the human body. Each element corresponds not only to a quality of energy, but also to a particular season, pair of organs (yin and yang), and color. Fire corresponds to summer, the heart and small intestine, and red; water to winter, the kidneys and bladder, and blue; wood to spring, the liver and gallbladder, and green; metal to fall, the lungs and colon, and white; and earth to Indian summer, the spleen and stomach, and yellow. What's more, each pair of organs—especially their meridians, their energetic pathways—is associated with a particular set of virtues and negative emotions. For example, the heart/small intestine pair represents love and hate/ the kidneys/bladder, gentleness and fear; the liver/gallbladder, kindness and anger; the lungs/colon, courage and grief; and the spleen/stomach, openness and worry. This emotional energy map indicates that for the Taoist there is nothing wrong with negative emotions as long as they are in balance with virtue—in short, as long as they are not excessive. In fact the Taoists point out that any excessive emotion, positive or negative, can upset the overall quantity and flow of energy in the organism and thus cause imbalance and illness. (Taoist Healings, authentic breathing.com)

THE INTERFAITH MANUAL

Institute for Interreligious, Intercultural Dialogue
Temple University
1114 W. Berks Street, Ste. 511
Philadelphia, PA 19122

*"Prosperity is a way of living and thinking,
and not just for money or things.
Poverty is a way of living and thinking,
and not just a lack of money or things."*
Eric Butterworth

Material Wealth

I do not believe material wealth makes us happy; it may give us the means to obtain physical stuff which may alter the way we live in a positive way, yet by itself it has no power. Understanding "material wealth" is at its highest when we come close to losing everything. In the 2007 San Diego wildfires, my wife and I came close to losing our home and all our possessions. Yet when the flames came close enough for the reverse 911 call to come telling us we had to evacuate, we knew we had friends to stay with and that together we could overcome any challenge. To us, prosperity is the non-tangible assets we possess in our minds and hearts which allows us to see beauty when the appearance says otherwise. That is what we call "the Good Life."

Bahá'í – A statement prepared by the Bahá'í International Community Office of Public Information, Haifa, was first distributed at the United Nations World Summit on Social Development, Copenhagen, Denmark. It was entitled "The Prosperity of Humankind." In it the Bahá'í Faith stated, "Social Development must be galvanized by a vision of human prosperity in the fullest sense of the term — an awakening to the possibilities of the spiritual and material well-being now brought within grasp. Its beneficiaries must be all of the planet's inhabitants, without distinction, without the imposition of conditions unrelated to the fundamental goals of such a reorganization of human affairs." (*The Prosperity of Humankind*, statements.baha'i.org)

Buddhism – Buddhists seek prosperity by creating inner peace within themselves. According to Woody Hochswender, "You may be a Buddhist and not even know it: "We all believe in the oneness of the world. We all believe there's spiritual truth inside us, an indwelling kernel. We all seek the happiness of others as a gateway to our own prosperity. (*Seeking Prosperity*, asp.usatoday.com)

Christianity – Christian beliefs about material wealth vary from church to church and from such extremes as believing, "Do not love the world or the things in the world. If anyone loves the world, the love of the Father is not in him" from 1 John 2:15. to Revelation 3:17 — "I am rich, have become wealthy, and have need of nothing." Certain churches preach Jesus' words, "If the world hates you, you know that it hated Me before it hated you. If you were of the world, the world would love its own. Yet because you are not of the world, but I chose you out of the world, therefore the world hates you." (John 15:18-19). Christian minister Joel Olsteen preaches, "We can get what we want from God by our faith-filled words, and as a child of God we should be receiving "preferential treatment" by everyone." Bringing heaven to Earth is a goal for most Christians.

Confucianism – From the Book of History, Confucian followers believe a religious and moral work, which traces the hand of Providence in a series of great events in past history and inculcates the lesson that the Heaven-god gives prosperity and length of days only to the virtuous ruler/person who has the true welfare of the people at heart.

Hinduism – Hindus believe "Prosperity is not for the envious, nor is greatness for men of impure conduct. - *Tirukkural 14:135* Artha is prosperity or success in worldly pursuits. Although the ultimate goal of Hinduism is enlightenment, the pursuit of wealth and prosperity is regarded as an appropriate pursuit for the householder (the second of four life stages). It also ensures social order, for there would be no society if everyone renunciated worldly life to meditate. But while Hindus are encouraged to make money, it must be within the bounds of dharma. (*The Purpose of Life in Hinduism*, religionfacts.com)

Islam – In the Qur'an, God promises prosperity in return for generosity to the poor. The Qur'an insists, therefore, that individuals transcend their pettiness and enlarge themselves and by doing so, they will develop the inner moral quality that the Qur'an calls *taqwa*. (history.com/minisite) *Taqwa* is: awareness of God, love of God, obedience to God, motivation to do good, fear of God's punishment, desire to serve God, understanding of God, the intention with which you do good to please God and not humanity, the behavior one should have, the attitude in life towards self, others and God, and state of mind, body and soul as God's presenter. (Imam Baseem Syed) By this quality of taqwa, humans can discern right from wrong and, above all, can evaluate their own actions properly, escaping self-deception, a danger to which they are always exposed. Often people think they have done something consequential, but the deed has no importance in the long run. The real worth of a person's deeds can be judged only through his intention behind the good deed. Muslims believe God will judge us according to our intentions behind good deeds and not the appearance of good deeds.

Jainism – Jain scriptures guide them on the path of inner growth. They show how to move on from the creation of material wealth to the next state - the creation of spiritual wealth. Jain philosophy says, a true guru is, the supreme embodiment of patience who removes doubts and gently leads people to clarity and enlightenment. He not only tells his people how to live their life, but sets out an ideal. He leads by suggestion and example. He does not bind his pupils in a miasma of theory and ritual. He does not blind them by the brilliance of his own personality, but opens their eyes to truth, beauty, love and wisdom. The Jain philosophy of Anekantavada (multitude beliefs) tells us there are no absolute theories or formulae that can describe reality in absolute terms. Rather, our belief of Anekantavada tells us that we do not know the complete truth. We can learn from others as well. Let truth prevail, say Jains. Truth in its final analysis is wholesome and one, which leads us to love and understanding. And that is the very necessary essence of all religions. (Jainism: Let Truth Prevail, experiencefestival.com) Jains believe their wealth comes from the good karma they earn in life and their success comes at the end of life by how much they have made other people happy. They also say, "You cannot take it with you" and "We come and go with nothing." (Rohak Vora)

Judaism – Much of Jewish prayer is expressing appreciation for all of the goodness which comes their way. (Marilyn Clement) The Abrahamic covenant with God provided physical healing, material prosperity and family well-being for Old Testament Judaism. Many of the Jews of the Old Testament believed prosperity and spirituality were inseparable as Jews believe today. In the Book of Job in the Old Testament, Job's prosperity including his family, land, cattle, etc. were taken away. After a discussion with God, Job came to realize everything he values was God's anyway and even without those material things, he still had his relationship with God which was the most important thing. (*Healing, Prosperity and Family Well-Being*, jaysnell.org)

Native American – Most Native Americans do not believe that material wealth comes to an individual, but rather to the whole tribe. That is why they do not draw any attention to 'self' but can show how they contribute to the Tribe. Believing in the 'good of the Tribe' naturally encompasses 'Family Values', thus prospering brings Families closer together, as well as wealth to the whole Tribe. (Evans Craig, Navajo) They believe by living by a core set of values and beliefs for the tribe, true prosperity can be found. Unfortunately, many who have kept to the basic principles of the faith feel the majority of people live far beyond their means and have lost the connection with the true prosperity which is found in relationships with family and friends. (*How American Values Have Overshadowed our Values and Beliefs*, helium.com)

New Thought – New Thought authors such as Catherine Ponder, use prosperity concepts which came from the Old and New Testaments to teach that everything comes from God and God indwells each and every person. Therefore, all the material wealth which IS God is in and around each person. New Thought followers believe in being 'One-in-God' without separation. All the good God is, is inherent in each person only to be realized. Therefore, prosperity in the form of good health, wealth, loving relationships and successful work is already within. New Thought followers believe in having a close relationship with God and they accept their material wealth in the form of good health, wealth, in their relationships and in their work. The "Law of Attraction" which is described in the 2006 movie "The Secret," explains we attract prosperity to us by the intentional words and actions we use. New Thought teaches when we speak positive words and believe we are prosperous, despite any appearance; the prosperity we seek will begin to seek us.

Sikhism – Sikhism believes every Sikh is a member of the universal brotherhood and every member should live in prosperity. A Sikh is required to care for others, and it is known for a very special concept of *Wand Chhakna*. It is a concept of giving something out of the bounties bestowed by God for the welfare of needy, less fortunate and deserving people. It is a concept of co-operative and corporate living. It is a concept of serving each other without selfish motives and sharing wealth and the knowledge of God with each other. It is a concept to eliminate poverty of mind and body. It is a concept for social and economic equality through social responsibility. It is tantamount to sharing of earnings, physical labor, wealth, God given wisdom and knowledge for welfare of human beings as a whole without discrimination of caste, color, creed and gender. (Sikh Missionary Society U.K.)

Taoism – Taoists who look for universal unity, believe by meditating on the concept of prosperity, through a symbol or picture, material wealth and all aspects of their lives will come into order and balance. Taoists seek happiness, prosperity and good health by worshipping and appeasing the spirits and treating all people and things with respect. The principles of Dynamic Balance and Complementary Cycles are embodied in the symbol of the Yin-Yang, which depicts the two opposite energies from whose interaction the universe is believed to have emerged. When these opposites are equally present, everything is calm, which is where the Taoist emphasis on balance comes from. This is also seen in the elements of fire, water, wood, metal, and earth, which should be balanced wherever possible to create fortune, as well as in the practice of feng shui, which aims to balance the way the home is set out, in order to generate greater prosperity. (Taoists, The Chaplaincy and Pastoral Care Department, West Suffolk Hospital, wsh.nhs.uk)

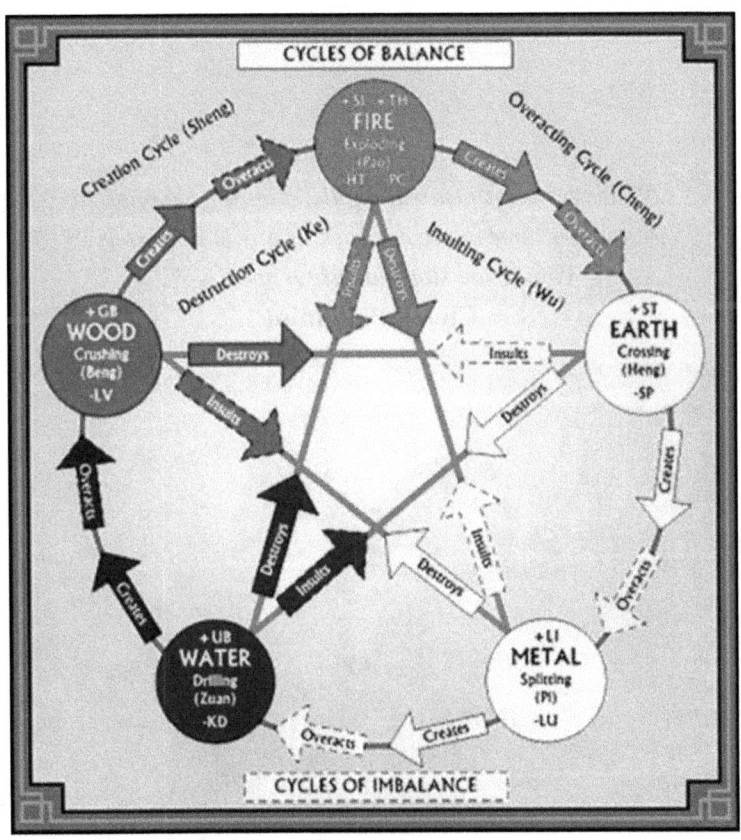

Interactions of Five Chinese Elements
Cycles of Balance and Cycles of Imbalance

Rev. Dr. Stephen L. Albert

"If death meant just leaving the stage long enough to change costume and come back as a new character… Would you slow down? Or speed up?"
Chuck Palahniuk

Part 5
Where we are Going From Here
Death and Dying

Possibly the most emotional time a man or woman can have is when they are going through the loss of a loved one. Whether it is a revered family member or a close friend who is dying, the sense of loss, and the acknowledgement that someday this will also be me, can be very scary and lonely. When asked to speak at my father's graveside funeral, I was faced with the choice of saying what I believed about death or telling the family and friends who had gathered what they expected to hear. I was amazed to find my choice of words, which echoed my spiritual beliefs of the Soul's continuation throughout time, was received with open arms and love. If we are truly here for a divine purpose, never block saying what you know to be true deep down.

Bahá'í - "Bahá'ís believe the experience we call death leads to a life immeasurably richer and more beautiful than we can ever imagine in this world. We should prepare for it and look forward to it with expectation and hope, remembering that God's love is not limited to this life on earth but will surround us throughout eternity. After death, a person's soul permanently departs from the material plane and enters the world of the spirit in which it can indefinitely progress and advance. The nature of that spiritual world is essentially different and superior to our earthly life here. Bahá'ís consider

Heaven as nearness to God and Hell as distance from God or lack of awareness of spiritual realities. Our spiritual development while we are alive can be considered as preparation for our life after death. (Bridging our Faith) (Bahá'í Prayers, Bahá'í Publishing Trust) There are many beautiful Prayers for the departed in Bahá'í belief and the following is a fine example, attributed to 'Abdul'l-Baha', of what the faith believes.

> O my God! O my God! Verily, Thy servant, humble before the majesty of Thy divine supremacy, lowly at the door of Thy oneness, hath testified to Thy word, hath been enkindled with the fire of Thy love, hath been immersed in the depths of the ocean of Thy knowledge, hath been attracted by Thy breezes, hath relied upon Thee, hath turned his face to Thee, hath offered his supplications to Thee, and hath been assured of Thy pardon and forgiveness. He hath abandoned this mortal life and hath flown to the kingdom of immortality, yearning for the favor of meeting Thee.
>
> O Lord, glorify his station, shelter him under the pavilion of Thy supreme mercy, cause him to enter Thy glorious paradise, and perpetuate his existence in Thine exalted rose garden, that he may plunge into the sea of the light in the world of mysteries. Verily, Thou art the Generous, the Powerful, the Forgiver and the Bestower.

Buddhism - According to Buddhist teaching, all things are impermanent, in a constant state of flux, all is transient, and no abiding state exists. This applies to humanity as much as to anything else in the cosmos; thus, there is no unchanging and abiding self. Our sense of "I" or "me" is simply a sense belonging to the ever-changing entity which (conventionally speaking) is us, our body, and mind. This idea expresses in essence the Buddhist principle of anatta (Pāli; Sanskrit: anātman).

Buddhists hold the belief of a permanent, abiding self as one of the main root causes for human conflict on the emotional, social and political levels. They add that understanding of *anatta* (or "not-self") provides an accurate description of the human condition, and this understanding allows "us" to go beyond "our" mundane desires. Nirvana (the perfect condition) is solely recognized as being distinct. Buddhists can speak in conventional terms of the soul or of self as a matter of convenience, but only under the conviction that ultimately "we" are changing entities. At death, the body and mind disintegrate; if the disintegrating mind contains any remaining traces of karma (the existence of all things which came before that moment), it will cause the continuity of the consciousness to bounce back as an arising mind to an awaiting being, that is, a fetus developing the ability to harbor consciousness. Thus, in Buddhist teaching, a being who is born is neither entirely different nor exactly the same as it was prior to rebirth.

Many modern Buddhists, particularly in Western countries, reject the concept of rebirth or reincarnation as incompatible with the concept of *anatta*. They take the view that if there is no abiding self and no soul then nothing remains to be reborn. Stephen Batchelor, notably, discusses this issue in his book *Buddhism Without Beliefs*. However, the question arises: if a self does not exist, who thinks/lives now? Buddhists hold the view that thought itself thinks: if you remove the thought, there is no thinker (self) to be found. A detailed introduction to this and to other basic Buddhist teachings appears in *What the Buddha Taught* by the Buddhist monk Walpola Rahula. The Greek mystic Gurdjieff taught, "Man has no soul." Rather, man must create a soul while incarnate whose substance could withstand the shock of death. Without a soul, Gurdjieff taught, man will "die like a dog."

If we are requested to perform a funeral rite for someone who has recently died, we can use this Sadhana Heartfelt Prayer. This is a funeral service in which spiritual practitioners gather together to make heartfelt prayers and dedications for the deceased person to take a fortunate rebirth. Because it is a Buddhist service, the prayers are addressed to the assembly of Buddhas and other holy beings. The prayers presented in this ritual are only the basis for a funeral service and may be adapted as appropriate. The power of our prayers depends upon the strength and purity of our intention. In this service it is very important for everyone to have a mind of compassion for all living beings in general, and for the deceased in particular. If we have a genuinely compassionate motivation, our prayers will definitely be effective.

The service begins with Heartfelt Prayers followed by Preliminary prayers, Prayer of the Stages of the Path and then a Remembrance of the deceased followed by Dedication prayers. The Remembrance of the Deceased portion is below.

> Buddha taught all life is impermanent and all those who are born must eventually pass from this life. However, everyone has within them the seeds of their past virtues, which have the power to bring a fortunate rebirth in the future.
>
> We pray through the power of this virtue, through the blessings of the holy beings, and through the force of our heartfelt prayers, our dear friend, _____, will experience great good fortune and everlasting peace and happiness.
>
> We also pray for the bereaved relatives and friends, that they may be comforted in their loss and find peace of mind and strength of heart.
>
> May all beings without exception be released from suffering and find true happiness and everlasting peace.

Christianity - Most Christians regard the soul as the immortal continuous essence of a human, and after death, God either rewards or punishes the soul. Different Christian groups dispute whether this reward/punishment depends upon doing good deeds, or merely upon believing in God and in Jesus. Many Christian scholars hold, as Aristotle did, that "to attain any assured knowledge of the soul is one of the most difficult things in the world." Augustine, one of the most influential early Christian thinkers, described the soul as "a special substance, endowed with reason, adapted to rule the body."

Philosopher Anthony Quinton said the soul is a "series of mental states connected by continuity of character and memory, [and] is the essential constituent of personality. The soul, therefore, is not only logically distinct from any particular human body with which it is associated; it is also what a person is." Richard Swinburne, a Christian philosopher of religion at Oxford University wrote, "it is a frequent criticism of substance dualism that dualists cannot say what souls are.... Souls are immaterial subjects of mental properties. They have sensations and thoughts, desires and beliefs and perform intentional actions. Souls are essential parts of human beings..." The origin of the soul has provided a sometimes vexing question in Christianity; the major theories put forward include creationism, traducianism (soul inherited from the parents) and pre-existence. From The Book of Common Prayer (1979), Christian prayers would include the following:

For all who have died in the hope of the resurrection, and for all the departed, let us pray to the Lord.

Lord, have mercy. Depart, O Christian soul, out of this world; In the Name of God the Father Almighty who created you;
In the Name of Jesus Christ who redeemed you; In the Name of the Holy Spirit who sanctifies you. May your rest be this day in peace, and your dwelling place in the Paradise of God.
I am the resurrection and the life, saith the Lord;
he who believeth in me, though he were dead, yet shall he live; and whosoever liveth and believeth in me shall never die. I know my Redeemer liveth, and he shall stand at the latter day upon the earth; and though this body be destroyed, yet shall I see God; whom I shall see for myself and mine eyes shall behold, and not as a stranger. For none of us liveth to himself, and no man dieth to himself. For if we live, we live unto the Lord and if we die, we die unto the Lord. Whether we live, therefore, or die, we are the Lord's.

Blessed are the dead who die in the Lord; even so saith the Spirit, for they rest from their labors.

Confucianism - The Master said, ""All the living must die, and dying, return to the ground; this is what is called *kuei*. The bones and flesh smolder below, and, hidden away, become the earth of the fields. But the spirit issues forth, and is displayed on high in a condition of glorious brightness. The vapors and odors which produce a feeling of sadness, (and arise from the decay of their substance), are the subtle essences of all things, and also a manifestation of the shen nature." (*Book of Ritual* 21.2.1 from *Readings from World Scriptures* - by Prof Andrew Wilson) (kheper.net/topics/bardo) (china-sd.net/eng/qiluculture/confucius)

Confucius seldom speaks of prayer. Suppliant prayer, not to mention magic prayer, is far from him, for he implies his whole life is prayer. The words of a Japanese Confucian in the ninth century are quite in the spirit of Confucius: "If only the heart follows the path of truth, you need not pray, the gods will protect you."

"Death and life are the will of heaven;" "From the beginning all men have had to die." Such maxims express Confucius' candid acceptance of death. Death offers no ground for emotion; it is not situated in any field of essential meaning. He can indeed lament premature death: "That some things germinate but do not flower; that some things flower that do not mature-alas, that happens." But: "To die at nightfall, that is not bad." Death has no terrors: "When a bird is dying, his song is mournful; when a man is dying, his speech is good." It is meaningless to inquire about death: "If you do not know life, how should you know death?" But when asked whether the dead know of the offerings sacrificed to them, he replies: "Knowledge of this is no concern of ours." He judges the answers pragmatically, by their results, and concludes no answer is the best: "If I say yes, I must fear that pious sons may spend their substance for the departed - if

I say no, I must fear impious sons may neglect their duty toward the departed."

Hinduism - In Hinduism, the Sanskrit word most closely corresponding to soul is "Atman," which can mean soul or even God. It is seen as the portion of Brahman (the life force) within us. Hinduism contains many variant beliefs on the origin, purpose, and fate of the soul. For example, advaita or non-dualistic conception of the soul accords its union with Brahman, the absolute uncreated (roughly, the Godhead), in eventuality or in pre-existing fact. Advaita or dualistic concepts reject this, idea instead identifying the soul as a different and incompatible substance. (hindugateway.com/library/prayer) This simple four line prayer followed by the beautiful words of this poem, reflects much of what Hindu belief is all about.

> Lead us from the unreal to the real, Lead us from darkness to light, Lead us from death to immortality. OM, peace, peace, peace.
>
> Ah, my God, I see all gods within your body; Each in his degree, the multitude of creatures; See Lord Brahma enthroned upon his lotus;
>
> See all the sages, and the holy serpents. Universal Form, I see you without limit, Infinite of arms, eyes, mouths, and bellies — See, and find no end, midst, or beginning. Crowned with diadems, you wield the mace and discus, Shining every way — the eyes shrink from your splendor; Brilliant like the sun; like fire, blazing, boundless.

Islam - According to the Qur'an of Islam (15:29), the creation of man involves Allah "breathing" *Rooh* (Spirit/Soul) into *Nafse* (self). This Nafse is raw and untamed, uncultured and has the potential of growing and achieving nearness to God if the person leads a righteous life. At death the person's body is buried and Rooh is taken to Allah. Upon dying, the Angel of Death is sent by Allah to take away the human life and the Rooh resides in an interim place called "*barzakh*" between this world and the hereafter. This permanent place for the Nafse can be pleasant (Heaven) or unpleasant (Hell) depending on the degree to which a person has developed or destroyed his or her Nafse during life. Islam believes both Rooh and Nafse have rights and needs. (Qur'an 91:7-10). (alkhidmat.no/artikler/ghusl) The two minute death prayer rite starts with the takbir (saying Allahu Akbar - Allah is the Greatest) at the pronouncement of which hands are raised to the ears and placed in the same position as in prayer. There are four takbirs in all, the final takbir being followed by a salaam as in the ordinary prayer.

First Takbir:

After the first takbir the following prayer called Thana (praise to Allah), followed by the opening chapter of the Qur'an, called AI-Fatihah, are recited.

Glory to You, O Allah, and to You is the praise, and blessed is Your name, and exalted is Your majesty, and there is none to be served besides You.

"Praise be to Allah, the Lord of the worlds, the Beneficent, the Merciful, Master of the day of Requital. You do we serve and You do we beseech for help. Guide us on the right path, the path of those upon whom You have bestowed favors, not those upon whom wrath is brought down, nor those who go astray."

Second Takbir:

Then follows a second takbir without raising the hands to the ears, and the following prayer known as as-salaah 'alan Nabiyy, i.e., salutations to the Holy Prophet Muhammad, is recited:

O Allah! Exalt Muhammad and the true followers of Muhammad, as You did exalt Abraham and the true followers of Abraham, for surely, You art Praised, Magnified. O Allah! bless Muhammad and the true followers of

Muhammad as You did bless Abraham and the true followers of Abraham, for surely You are Praised, Magnified.

Third Takbir:

The third takbir is then pronounced in a manner similar to the second takbir, and a prayer for the forgiveness of the deceased is addressed to Allah. Different forms of this prayer are reported as having been offered by the Holy Prophet (pbuh), thus prayer in any form is permissible. O Allah! Grant protection to our living and to our dead and to those of us who are present and those who are absent, and to our young and to our old folk and to our males and to our females. O Allah! Whomsoever Thou grantest to live among us, cause him to live in Islam (submission) and whosoever of us You cause to die, make him die in faith. O Allah! Do not deprive us of this reward and do not make us fall into a trial after him.

Jainism – Jainists believe in a *jiva*, an immortal essence of a living being analogous to a soul, subject to the illusion of *maya* and evolving through many incarnations from mineral to vegetable to animal, its accumulated karma determining the form of its next birth. Jainists believe the prayers, good thoughts or good wishes and *Kirtan* (call and response chanting) become helpful to the departed souls. They can be of invaluable assistance to the dead. Prayer or Kirtan is a mighty force which helps the departed souls in their progress towards heaven and their quiet passage through the intermediate state. The departed souls remain in a state of swoon or unconsciousness immediately after death. They cannot feel they are detached from their previous gross material bodies. Prayers, Kirtan and good thoughts from the relatives and friends can give real solace to the departed souls. They create a potent vibration and an awakening in their stupefied condition of mind and bring back their veiled consciousness. The souls begin to realize they are not really in their gross material bodies. Then they endeavor to cross the borderland, a narrow river of ether, which is known as Vaitarani by the Hindus, Chinavat bridge by the Parsis and Sirat by the Muslims. (*What Becomes Of The Soul After Death*, Sri Swami Sivananda.)

According to the theory of transmigration, even if the individual is to take another birth immediately after his death, the performance of Sraaddha adds to his happiness in his new birth. So, it is the imperative duty of everybody to perform the Sraaddha ceremony for his parents and forefathers. Sraaddha ceremony should be performed with great Sraddha (faith) as long as you live. Faith is the main support for religion. In olden days the question whether to perform Sraaddha ceremony or not, did not arise. Then people were full of faith and had reverence for the scriptures. In these days when faith is almost-dwindling into an airy nothing and when the list of non-performers of Sraaddha has increased, others of wavering faith begin to doubt whether it is necessary to perform Sraaddha and whether any good will accrue out of it. This lack of faith in the Sastras has degraded them to the present deplorable condition. *Sraddhavan labhate jnanam*... the man of faith attains knowledge and thereby immortality and eternal peace is the declaration of the Gita. (*What Becomes Of The Soul After Death*, Sri Swami Sivananda*)*

Judaism – In general, Jewish views about why we are here and where we are going falls into the statement, "We don't know. What we do know is that it is more important to lead a good life in which people remember you for the good you do and are grateful to know you for your positive influence." "They feel, "A good name is its own reward." (Marilyn Clement) Other Jewish views of the soul begin with the book of Genesis, in which verse 2:7 states, "the LORD God formed man from the dust of the earth. He blew into his nostrils the breath of life, and man became a living being." (New JPS) Jewish life is more focused on the issues of the day and living rightly versus where they may end up in an afterlife. The Hebrew Bible offers no systematic definition of a soul although various descriptions of the soul exist in classical rabbinic literature. In Judaism, death is not a tragedy, even when it occurs early in life or through unfortunate circumstances. Death is a natural process. Our death, like our life, has meaning and each life is part of God's plan. In addition, Orthodox Jews have a firm belief in an afterlife, a world to come, where those who have lived a worthy life will be rewarded. Orthodox Judaism thought argues that after death, the soul has to be purified before it can go on the rest of its journey. The amount of time needed for purification depends on how the soul has dealt with life. One Jewish tradition states a soul needs a maximum of 11 months for purification, which is why, when a parent dies, the Kaddish (memorial prayer) is recited for 11 months. The Pharisees believed the souls of evil men are punished after death. The souls of good men are "removed into other bodies" and they will "have power to revive and live again." The Sadducees, who believed everything ended with death, did not accept the idea of reincarnation. Jewish ideas included the concept that people could live again without knowing exactly the manners by which this could happen. (near-death.com/experiences/judaism06)(simpletoremember.com/vitals/Kaddish)

If you have read the Kaddish Prayer, one should realize although Jewish Law requires the Kaddish be recited during the first eleven months following the death of a loved one by prescribed mourners, and on each anniversary of the death (the "Yahrtzeit"), and by custom in the State of Israel by all Jews on the Tenth of Tevet ("Yom HaKaddish HaKlali'), there is no reference, no word even, about death in the prayer! The theme of Kaddish is, rather, the Greatness of G-d, Who conducts the entire universe, and especially his most favored creature, each individual human being, with careful supervision. In this prayer, they also pray for peace, from apparently the only One Who can guarantee it, peace between nations, peace between individuals, and peace of mind. Paradoxically, this is, in fact, the only true comfort in the case of the loss of a loved one. That is, to be able to view the passing of the beloved individual from the perspective that the person's soul was gathered in, so to speak, by the One Who had provided it in the first place. The

Kaddish prayer is said in appreciation for a life in which we were permitted to share with _____ (a family member, a great teacher, a friend, etc.). (Marilyn Clement)

Glorified and sanctified be God's great name throughout the world which He has created according to His will. May He establish His kingdom in your lifetime and during your days, and within the life of the entire House of Israel, speedily and soon; and say, Amen. May His great name be blessed forever and to all eternity. Blessed and praised, glorified and exalted, extolled and honored, adored and lauded be the name of the Holy One, blessed be He, beyond all the blessings and hymns, praises and consolations that are ever spoken in the world; and say, Amen. May there be abundant peace from heaven, and life, for us and for all Israel; and say, Amen. He who creates peace in His celestial heights, may He create peace for us and for all Israel; and say, Amen.

Native American - Navajo people believe that when someone dies, they go to the underworld. Certain precautions must be taken during the burial process to ensure that they don't return to the world of the living. These visits are to be avoided at all costs, and for this reason, Navajos are very reluctant to look at a dead body. According to traditional Navajo beliefs, birth, life and death are all part of an ongoing cycle. It is the natural course of things. Crying and outward demonstrations of grief are not usually seen when someone dies. This is not to be interpreted as a lack of caring; according to Navajo burial customs, the spirit's journey to the next world can be interrupted if too much emotion is shown. It is believed the spirit can attach itself to a place, an object or a person if this important part of the process is interrupted. (*Navajo Burial Customs*, dying. lovetoknow.com)

According to Erna Johnson, RN, director of nursing at Parker Indian Hospital in Parker, Ariz., and a member of the Quechan tribe, one Navajo belief is that when people die at home, their spirits remain in the home; therefore, many patients choose to die in the hospital. Tom-Orme adds that Diné (Navajo) women who view the hospital as a place to die may choose not to give birth there. Johnson notes one Pima belief shared by several other tribes is any body part removed during life, such as by amputation, must be put back with the body when a person dies. Otherwise, the person will go on to the afterlife incomplete. In Papago (Tohono O'odham) culture, when a person dies, the family bathes the body and combs his or her hair. All hair that comes out in the brush or on the floor must be bound and placed with the dead body so the spirits will take the entire deceased person with them. (minoritynurse.com/features/nurse_emp/02-14-01b)

In general, Native religions have no precise belief about the soul after death. Some believe in reincarnation, with a person being reborn either as a human or animal after death. Others believe humans return as ghosts, or people go to another world. Others believe nothing definitely can be known about one's fate after this life. Combinations of belief are common. (religioustolerance.org/nataspir) (aaanativearts.com/article1143) There are many different Native American Tribes which have different prayers for the dead. This prayer is taken from the Lakota Sioux Tribe:

GrandMother East:
From you comes the sun which brings life to us all; I ask that you have the sun shine on my friends here, and bring a new life to them — a life without the pain and sadness of the world; and to their families, bring your sun for they also need your light for their lives. Here, do so without the nightmares that we have had for so long. Let your stars and moon shine on my friends in a gentle manner; and as they look at the stars, they remember those stars are the spirits of my friends shining on them and those friends are at peace.

GrandFather North:
You are the Warrior, you have ridden alongside my friends here into battle, you have also felt their love and caring when you were wounded or lonely; ride alongside of them,

for now they are in this the hardest battle for their life, the battle for inner peace. Now is the time for you to care for them.

GrandFather Sky:
May your songs of the winds and clouds sweep the pain and sadness out of my friends' hearts; as they hear those songs, let them know the spirits who are with those songs are at peace.

GrandMother Earth:
I have asked all the other GrandFathers and GrandMothers to help my friends rid themselves of the troubles that weigh so heavy on their hearts. This way, the weight they carry will be less; and they will walk more softly on you.

GrandMother Earth:
From your womb all spirits have come when they return to you; cradle them gently in your arms and allow them to join their friends in the skies. If they want to hurry themselves to you, tell them you are not ready; and they must wait, for now they can pass on peace to others. May the Great Spirit watch over you, and may you be at peace.

GrandFather South:
You bring the storms from the south which brings the rains to nourish us and our crops. Be gentle when you fall on my friends; and as the rain touches them, let it wash away the pain and sadness they carry with them.

GrandMother West:
You take the sun from us and cradle it in your arms, then you bring darkness onto us so we may sleep. When you bring the darkness to my friends in a gentle manner; and as they look at the stars, they remember that those stars are

the spirits of my friends shining on them and those friends are at peace.

New Thought – Those who follow New Thought believe God is a loving Infinite Intelligence, operating through and in all of life, never separate from anyone or anything. Spirit is eternal and therefore the Spirit within each person is eternal. The body dies and the spirit lives on. Religious Science and Unity teach the eternality of life. They accept the idea that our physical bodies operate within a natural cycle of birth and death. However, even though we may have a body, we are not just our body. What we really are is the Life that animates our body, and that Life is infinite and immortal. As we become increasingly identified with our divine and eternal nature, our underlying fear of death begins to dissolve, and our experience of life becomes more joyous.

Religious Science and New Thought in general, neither endorses nor rejects any particular theory or concept of reincarnation. Since life is eternal, there are an unlimited number of possibilities for its evolvement after the experience of physical death. In Religious Science, a follower accepts the on-goingness of life and deals with what is before one in the present moment. (ccrs.org/FAQs)

Unity defines heaven and hell as conditions in the here and now. They are not places where people go to spend eternity. Some members believe in a reincarnation. They cite references from the Christian Scriptures which show that the concept of reincarnation was common during Jesus' time. In the Gospels of Matthew and Mark, John the Baptist is referred to as the reincarnation of Elijah. In Matthew, some of the populace guessed Jesus was a reincarnation of Elijah; still others guessed Jeremiah or one of the other prophets. Jesus neither criticized the people for their beliefs, nor declared reincarnation to be heresy. Among believers in reincarnation, each lifetime is viewed as a time of preparation for the next life, leading towards eventual perfection. (religioustolerance.org/unity) Unity's Poet Laureate James Dillet Freeman, wrote the following about death.

Rev. Dr. Stephen L. Albert

There Is No Death

I am standing on the seashore.
A ship at my side spreads her white sails
to the morning breeze and starts for the blue ocean.
She is an object of beauty and strength,
and I stand and watch her until at length
until she is a speck of white cloud just where the sea and sky
come to mingle with each other.
Then someone at my side says, "There! She's gone!"
Gone where? Gone from my sight, that is all.
She is just as large in mast and hull and spar
as she was when she left my side,
and she is just as able to bear her load of
living weight to her destined harbor.
Her diminished size is in me, not in her.
And just at the moment
when someone at my side says, "There, She's gone!"
there are other eyes watching her coming, and other voices
ready to take up the glad shout, "There she comes!"
And that is dying.

Sikhism - The word "soul" to a Sikh is the same as God, and they believe there is no separation between God and human. Sikhs believe in Karma; how well you lived your life on earth will determine how your next lives will be formed. During the funeral ceremony (Antim Sanskar) the body is usually cremated and The Kirtan Sohila and Ardas prayers are performed. The bedtime prayer, Kirtan Sohila is usually recited just before sleeping at night. Its name means 'Song of Peace'. Kirtan Sohila is composed of five hymns, the first three by Guru Nanak Dev, the fourth by Guru Ram Das and the fifth by Guru Arjan Dev. This hymn is usually recited at the conclusion of evening ceremonies at the Gurdwara and also recited as part of Sikh funeral services. (sikhs.org/transl)

Gauri Purbi Measure, Guru Arjan Dev
My friend, I request that this is the
opportune time to serve the saints.
Earn divine profits in this world and live in peace
and comfort in the next one.
Life is shortening day and night.
O' mind, meet the Guru and set right your affairs.
This world is engrossed in sins and evils;
but Gods Divines will swim across it.
He/She, who is awakened by God, drinks
the Nectar of (person's Name)
and comes to realize the Ineffable God.
Purchase the commodity, for which you have come in this world,
and then God will come to reside in your
heart with the Gurus Grace.
You will easily obtain your Real Home and
will not suffer transmigration.
O Searcher of hearts and Fulfiller of desires!
Kindly fulfill my heart's desires.
Nanak says: I, your servant,
pray that I may become
the dust of the Saints feet
join the society of saints.

Taoism - In terms of hun and po, the two souls, they are not necessarily seen as being in conflict. Po is very physical and primal, the drive to survive and exist, while hun is like the group mind or the universal mind - that fragment of consciousness which has undertaken to dream that specific dream of a person's life. That is one aspect of Daoist divination - the shaman goes into a trance and the hun travels into the universal hun and the shaman accesses that part of the universal hun which is the person's life and so can know something of their past and future. The purpose is to help the person prepare to meet the challenges of their *ming*/destiny. The view is that if we try to avoid our ming, we are simply reborn in a more intense version of the original situation so we have a chance at getting the lesson again. (Michael Arnold, Taoist)

The Chinese Taoists like the ancient Egyptians were greatly concerned with ensuring the survival of the individual after physical death. Their metaphysics was based on the ancient Chinese conception of the polarity of Dark and Light, Negative and Positive, Yin and Yang; the two fundamental principles in the Cosmos. According to the Chinese, just as the Cosmos consists of and comes about through the interaction and interchange of Yin and Yang (as superbly illustrated in that magnificent Chinese Oracle, the *I Ching* - pronounced "Yee Jing"), so, in a similar way, the human personality consists of and comes about through two principles or "souls," a Yin soul and a Yang soul, which are welded together during life, but separate at death. Their separation means the end of the personality as such, even though the Yin and Yang principles survive. One Jungian writer, Cary Baynes, summarizes the matter as follows:

"In the ... bodily existence of the individual ... are ... two ... polarities, a *p'o* soul (or anima) and a *hun* soul (animus). All during the life of the individual these two are in conflict, each striving for mastery. At death they separate and go different ways. The anima sinks to earth as *kuei*, a ghost-being. The animus rises and becomes *shen*, a spirit or god." [*The Secret of the Golden Flower*, Cary Baynes, ed.; Richard Wilhelm and C. G. Jung, (Harcourte Brace Jovanovich, 1962), p.64) (yesmagazine.org/article.asp?ID=1040)

Be still and know I am with you, says the Lord.
Be still and know I am you, says the Tao.
We are part of nature and nature is part of us.
We are held by the Hand of God
and we are the Hands of God.
Do not try to live as if you are separate.
You are not.
You are of God, part of the Tao.
You are within the landscape.
You are elements of the seasons.
You are of both heaven and earth.
Be known for what you are,
and make your actions
harbingers of a better future.
Flow like water around obstacles.
Do not batter your head against a brick wall.
Flow under it and when it collapses,
You will be long gone.
Hold true to God, rest in the Tao,
and you will be carried to where
the future needs you.

Spirals 2

Rev. Dr. Stephen L. Albert

"Begin to see yourself as a soul with a body rather than a body with a soul."
Wayne Dyer

THE SOUL

As you can see, almost every faith believes the Soul of a person exists in one form or another. No matter which faith you investigate, a person's body is believed to have an energy within it which cannot be defined and that energy is believed to transcend the human condition. Many of the faiths believe the soul prepares itself to move into another physical plane after it has reconciled the karmic (see next topic) debt it owes to other souls, with what it still needs to learn for its own growth. Therefore, as souls we choose to spiral forward, similar to a DNA spiral, for the benefit of ourselves and for others. The benefit to others or ourselves may not seem to be a positive one when we look at a particular situation; however, since we can never know the entire picture, we cannot judge one way or the other. The Soul is an eternal energy form and has been here since the beginning of time. It exists in, through and around all living entities and changes form as it moves from one life experience to the next. The soul's purpose is to awaken in consciousness and become fully expressive no matter what form it is in. (In experiments with people dying in beds set on sensitive scales, the soul has been weighed at 21.3 grams (0.75 ounce) when it leaves the dying body).

Rev. Dr. Stephen L. Albert

*"The person whose mind is always free from attachment,
who has subdued the mind and senses,
and who is free from desires,
attains the supreme perfection of freedom
from Karma through renunciation."*
Bhagavad Gita

Karmic Law

Karmic Law is fundamental, with small variations, to most religions. The good and righteous actions yield pleasant and happy fruits or awards and those who perform mistaken actions bring forth painful and unhappy fruits or results here in this world or hereafter. The New Testament expresses the thought: "whatsoever a man soweth, that shall he also reap." That is just what karma means — it is a Sanskrit term used in Hindu and Buddhist philosophy to signify deed-'action' followed by reaction. Every religion has stressed the doctrine of moral responsibility. The Moslems speak of Kismet as representing one's individual portion or lot in life. The ancient Greeks had their Nemesis or goddess of retributive justice; they also personified past, present and future as the three Moirai or Spinners of Destiny. So too those born in the Jewish faith are familiar with the Mosaic injunction: "an eye for an eye, and a tooth for a tooth." All of these are different ways of describing the universal law of harmony and balance, which insures that every cause set in motion will, some time in the future, bring about its corresponding effect. (*Karmic Law*, geocities.com) Marilyn Clements believes this is mostly misunderstood and that current rabbinic thinking says it is talking about just compensation for loss inflicted by another. She feels it is not karmic at all but early Tort Law. Mahatma Gandhi said, "An eye for an eye just makes the whole world blind." If someone blinds you and then he or she is blinded also, that person can never make amends to you and your family's loss.

Along the same lines in the New Thought faith, adherents believe in the Law of Cause and Effect. Our thoughts and feelings, consciousness, (cause) our life experiences (effect). Our life becomes a 'mirror' of our consciousness. What we think, say and do to others returns to us in some way and in some form. There are no actions in life which do not stem from what we think, say and do prior to the act we chose to take. If we choose to be hateful and violent, we will suffer the results of those acts. Laws, whether they are karmic or man-made, impose consequences on those who ignore them.

Members of each faith understand that the early years of life exist not just for physical growth but also for mental, emotional and spiritual growth as well. The more we balance out these four areas of life, the easier we will be able to "fit in" with our family and faith communities. Karmic law teaches if you ignore what is right to do with intent, you will receive a negative impact sometime in the future. That impact will coincide with the lessons your soul is here to learn.

**All actions stem
from what we think, say and do.**

THE INTERFAITH MANUAL

*"There were never in the world two opinions alike,
any more than two hairs or two grains.
Their most universal quality is diversity."*
Michel de Montaigne

The California Forum for Diversity
The University of California

Part 6
How we Consider Other Faiths

*A*lbert Einstein said, *"A person who is religiously enlightened appears to me to be one who has, to the best of his ability, liberated himself from the fetters of his selfish desires and is preoccupied with thoughts, feelings and aspirations to which he clings because of their super-personal value... regardless of whether any attempt is made to unite this content with a Divine Being, for otherwise it would not be possible to count Buddha and Spinoza as religious personalities. Accordingly, a religious person is devout in the sense that he has no doubt of the significance of those super-personal objects and goals which neither require nor are capable of rational foundation... In this sense religion is the age-old endeavour of mankind to become clearly and completely conscious of these values and goals, and constantly to strengthen their effects."* Einstein argues that conflicts between science and religion *"have all sprung from fatal errors."* However *"even though the realms of religion and science in themselves are clearly marked off from each other"* there are *"strong reciprocal relationships and dependencies"*... *"science without religion is lame, religion without science is blind... a legitimate conflict between science and religion cannot exist."* However Einstein makes it clear he does not believe in a personal God, and suggests that *"neither the rule of human nor Divine Will exists as an independent cause of natural events. To be sure, the doctrine of a personal God interfering with natural events could never be refuted... by science, for [it] can always take refuge in those domains in which scientific knowledge has not yet been able to set foot."* (Albert Einstein, Einstein 1940, pp. 605–607)

Predestination vs. Free Will

Are human beings free agents, or do we only suffer from the illusion of such? If God has foreknowledge of all things, in what sense do we have free will? Each Faith gives its followers different degrees of freedom when it comes to believing what its own faith teaches and also the amount of credibility its followers should have about what other faiths believe.

Bahá'í – The Bahá'í Holy Writings offer a startling perspective on the question of free will and destiny and believe they are not mutually exclusive. Rather, they are closely related realities of human existence. In *Some Answered Questions* 'Abdu'l-Bahá talks about the nature of free will (p. 248-250). His discourse is too lengthy to quote here, but His main points are: Good and evil actions (e.g., justice or injustice) are subject to free will. We are responsible for these acts. Other aspects of life are forced upon us (e.g., sleep, death, sickness, and misfortunes beyond our control). We are not responsible for these things. At the same time, "might and power belong especially to God" and we are therefore absolutely dependent upon God's help. In this manner, our "motion" comes from God, but our direction we set ourselves."

Buddhism – The basic problem according to Buddhism is that emotions like anger and hatred are based on projections and exaggeration, not on objectivity or *wisdom*, and thus basically incorrect. There is little need to explain what anger and hatred do to ourselves by means of the laws of *karma*; the misery we cause others will come back at ourselves. Nobody wants suffering, so next is a summary of methods which can not only reduce but even eliminate anger and hatred from our minds. It must be emphasized that to completely eliminate these negative emotions from our mind is a lengthy psychological process, requiring study, mindfulness, reflection and honest observation of one's own mind. To begin with, meditation is an ideal method to review a situation in which one became angry. This has the advantage that one is not exposed to the actual situation, but one can review it much more objectively. When regular meditation gives some insight into what anger is and what happens to oneself when feeling angry, then one can gradually try to apply it in real-life situations, preferably of course before one is already under complete control of anger. It is a slow process, but the change in your life and the ones around you can profoundly change for the better. (buddhism.kalachakranet.org/anger)

Christianity – Catholicism affirms Predetermination in which God invites man to be in relationship with Him. They believe if there is a God, then that God has no free will and no-one else has free will either. The Christian Bible frequently states that God creates our future and decides our fates, no matter what our own will is. Some of the foremost Christians in history have taught there is no free will, including St. Augustine (one of the four great founders of Western Christianity [Russell 1946, p335]), Martin Luther (founder of Protestantism) and John Calvin. (Bane of Monotheism, vexen.co.uk) Most of the other Protestant denominations do not agree with predetermination and instead believe in the Free Will of its congregants. In this manner the person becomes directly responsible for his or her behavior and actions; confession by itself does not preclude being judged. (Rev. Glen Larsen)

Confucianism – Confucianism prescribes family relationships and indicates the degree of intimacy and obligations. Anyone who is within this network is considered part of the family. Otherwise, he or she is an outsider. As a member of the family, one enjoys membership privileges such as trust, intimacy, and sharing. Confucians promote universal brotherhood and sisterhood by respecting others and observing propriety (Confucian Analects, Confucius 1971 [500 B.C.E.]). So while knowledge of the sages is important, Confucius affirms human free-will.

Hinduism – Hindus believe God is omnipresent and omnipotent and in the existence of God everywhere, as an all pervasive, self-efferent energy and consciousness. Hindu Dharma teaches that all forms of life are manifestations of the supreme self (Brahman). This basic belief creates the attitude of sublime tolerance and acceptance towards others. We each have the free will to act accordingly. (*Gratitude as Viewed in Hinduism*, Una Mysorekar, yale.edu)

Islam – According to Muslims, living Islam means living, modeling, guiding, teaching, and counseling with loving care and concern. It is a life of trust, struggle, and noble effort. "The obedience demanded by Islam is obedience as a result of *taqwa* that is, obedience to Allah. This obedience comes after one acknowledges that God created me and God gave me everything. God has given me this life as a trust, that I must love, thank and obey God to keep myself on the right path according to the teachings of Prophet Muhammad. (Imam Baseem Syed)

Jainism – Jains believe each faith's perspective on life is true in its own way, and they respect all persons for their beliefs. They say our next life is decided approximately two-thirds of the way through the one we are in and it is based on how well we conquered our personal desires, anger and greed. (Rohak Vora) One of the most fundamental doctrines of the Jains is their division of souls (*jives*) into two unalterable categories called Bahavya and Abhavya: those who are capable and those who are incapable of the release from the bondage of transmigration (*sansara*). (*Bahavyatva and Abhavyatva: A Jaina Docterine of Predestination*, Padmanabh S. Jaini, Chapter 5) In Jain thinking there are five factors called: (1) *Kaal* (time) (2)

Swabhav (nature or disposition) (3) *Purakrit* (past karma) (4) *Niyati* (destiny) and (5) *Pursharth* (human exertion) which are known as the five Samvay. Jain thinkers have considered that all the five Samvay jointly are responsible for the world phenomena. All these together contribute to the success and failure, or pain or pleasure. None of these five viz. time, disposition fate, past karmas, and exertion is individually effective. It is only when all the five come into play that crop shall grow in the field. (jainworld.com)

Judaism – Judaism's basic teachings concern tolerance and acceptance of others. Orthodox Rabbi Naftali Brawer says, "the Jewish ethical outlook has been that "the world endures by three things: truth, justice, and peace... if there is no justice there can be no peace." Marilyn Clement believes the world stands on three things: 1). Torah Law, 2). work and service and 3). acts of loving kindness. In Judaism there is an "on-going-ness" about life and how each person brings their own stuff to help them interpret God's law (the Torah). This "wrestling" with God's law versus our own free will, makes life meaningful and in constant conversation. Leviticus 19 tells the Jew, "Don't mistreat other people for you know what it feels like to be the stranger." When you voluntarily join and live by the laws of the Torah, you are never a second class citizen.

Native American – Although not accepted in the "white" world in America for so many generations, the basic spiritual life of the American Indian teaches love and brotherhood among all people. Many Indian tribes continue to stay among their own people and interact with outside groups only after they are sure they have been accepted as equals. The most common factor about people amongst all Tribes is **"One Planet, One People."** When they pray to the Creator, they end their prayers with **"All My Relations."** That does not mean just their relatives but refers to *'all living things on Mother Earth,'* including earth, rocks, trees, plants, two-leggeds, four-leggeds, water & sky people. (Evans Craig, Navajo)

New Thought – The basic teachings of New Thought affirm the complete acceptance of all peoples no matter who they are, what they do, where they came from etc. They see each individual as a manifestation of God and therefore choose to honor that spirit in each person they meet. Each person has the free will to accept any spiritual belief or deny it, and each person has the free will to change their beliefs at any time. God has given us Free Will and there is a Divine Purpose in our lives. The followers believe the divine purpose will manifest when the person is ready to pursue it. All paths lead to God. Ernest Holmes says, "Be open at the top!"

Sikhism – Sikhs have a mission to stand up and defend the rights of all vulnerable adults and children regardless of caste, creed, or gender. Sikhs believe that Sikhism is only one of many paths to realizing God. It is the free will of the human to choose the correct path for him/herself and then to follow it to the best of their capabilities to attain God.

Taoism - Taoism's founder, Lao-tzu, (although he did not have the intention of starting a faith movement) was a Chinese philosopher who preceded Socrates and Plato by a century, composed the maxims found in the text known as the *Tao Te Ching* over 2,000 years ago. The Taoist idea of acceptance meshes nicely with what modern science tells us about happiness. The Taoist precept of accepting all life works because it allows them to dynamically redefine what makes them happy. True Taoist masters always find happiness in life because they define happiness by their current situation of acceptance of all things and all people. (*Taoism and The Job Market*, B. Ho, chronicle.com)

For the more literal followers, the concept of immortality means physical immortality of this body. Then other schools will so know a person's immortality without the need for this body. The most advanced understanding is not that we achieve immortality but we become aware of the immortality that we already are. (Michael Arnold, Taoist)

Rev. Dr. Stephen L. Albert

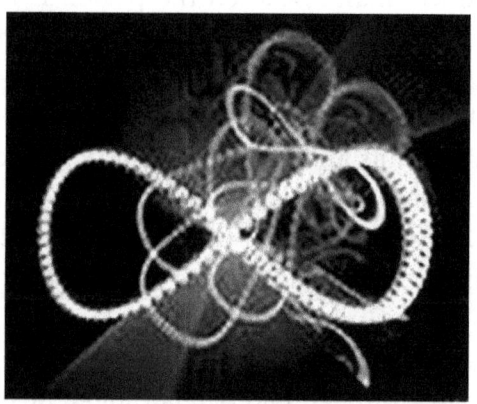

"Say: We believe In God, and in what Has been revealed to us And what was revealed To Abraham, Ishmael; Isaac, Jacob, and the tribes, And in the Books Given to Moses, Jesus, And the Prophets, From their Lord: We make no distinction between one and another among them, and to God do we submit in Islam."
The Qur'an

*"Love All, Serve All
Help Ever, Hurt Never."*
Sathya Sai Bába

*"Be well, my children, and think good thoughts
of peace and togetherness.
Peace for all life on earth and peace with one another in our
homes, families and countries. We are not so different
in the Creator's eyes.
The same great Father Sun shines his love on each of us daily
just as Mother Earth prepares the substance for our table,
do they not? We are one after all."*

Chief Dan Evehema

Prophets

In religion, a prophet (or prophetess) is a person who has directly encountered God, of whose intentions he or she can then speak as if a formal representative of God. In popular usage, especially among Christians, a prophet is believed to be someone who can foretell the future *and not do it for personal gain*. The biblical prophets in the Hebrew Bible claimed to speak for God and taught social or religious messages to the masses. They were Abraham, Sarah, Isaiah, Samuel, Ezekiel, Malachi and Job. "The Hebrew prophets were not fortune tellers but "forth" tellers because they told it like it is; "If you continue to behave badly, your life will be miserable." (Marilyn Clement) Moses brought the Ten Commandments from God to the Hebrew People which was later accepted by Muslims and Christians. The Ten Commandments are:

1: 'You shall have no other gods before Me.'
2: 'You shall not make for yourself a carved image—any likeness of anything that is in heaven above, or that is in the earth beneath, or that is in the water under the earth.'
3: 'You shall not take the name of the LORD your God in vain.'
4: 'Remember the Sabbath day, to keep it holy.'
5: 'Honor your father and your mother.'
6: 'You shall not murder.'
7: 'You shall not commit adultery.'
8: 'You shall not steal.'
9: 'You shall not bear false witness against your neighbor.'

10: 'You shall not covet your neighbor's house; you shall not covet your neighbor's wife, nor his male servant, nor his female servant, nor his ox, nor his donkey, nor anything that is your neighbor's.'

According to some views, prophecy is not a gift that is arbitrarily conferred upon people; rather, it is the culmination of a person's spiritual and ethical development. When a person reaches a sufficient level of spiritual and ethical achievement, the Shechinah (Divine Spirit) comes to rest upon him or her. Likewise, the gift of prophecy leaves the person if that person lapses from his or her spiritual and ethical perfection. There have been other prophets, mystics, seers, soothsayers, theorists, psychics, etc. throughout history who say something which either comes true and helps you understand yourself or something better, or offers you wisdom which you take and use as a gift from God. (Prophets and Prophecy, jewfaq.org)

Bahá'í - The Bahá'í Faith refers to prophets as *Manifestations of God*, or simply *Manifestations* (*mazhar*). In expressing God's intent, these Manifestations are seen to establish religion in the world. Thus they are seen as an intermediary between God and humanity. Bahá'u'lláh referred to several historical figures as Manifestations. They include the figures in the Abrahamic Faiths such as Noah, Abraham, Moses, Jesus, and Muhammad, but also include the founders of great non-Western religions such as Zoroaster, Krishna, and Buddha. (baha'i-library.org)

Buddhism - The Buddha was considered a prophet. He was an Indian Prince, Siddhartha Gautama, who lived in the 5th century BCE and who became known as the "Enlightened One" (the Buddha) when he understood the cause of suffering and the way to end suffering. Although he is not directly worshipped as a deity, there is very little difference between the veneration shown to the Buddha by the Buddhists and the manner of worship of God found in other religions. They revere him and pay homage to him, bow to his images and statues and prostrate themselves before them like the adherents of any other religion in the world which worships idols. (alislam.org)

Christianity – Christians share the Jewish belief that a prophet is a person who speaks for God, in the name of God, and who carries God's message to others. Some Christian denominations teach that a person who receives a personal message not intended for the body of believers (where such an event is credited at all) should not be termed a prophet. The reception of a message is termed revelation; the delivery of the message is termed prophecy. For Christians the authenticity of a prophet is judged by their fruits as Jesus said, "one should judge a prophet by his fruits." Christians regard Jesus as The Son of God and as the main prophetic figure in their faith. Christians also accept the prophets of the Hebrew Bible (Old Testament) as prophetic figures also.

Confucianism – In Confucianism, the Chinese sages can be considered to be the equivalent of prophets as mentioned in the Qur'an or the Bible, i.e. men who are representatives or messengers of God or Heaven. Confucius expressed his complete conviction that the eventual transcendence of truth was assured by an unchanging decree of God in whose safe hand he was a mere instrument. "God does not allow those He has directly guided to perish without having accomplished their task of establishing truth, even though they may stand alone against seemingly all-powerful odds." This is exactly the picture given of the prophets in the Bible and the Qur'an. Those who are worthy to be chosen for such tasks are men who have excelled in emulating God's attributes. (alislam.org)

Hinduism – Being the oldest faith on Earth, this faith path offers thousands of Hindu gurus, reflecting the huge variety of teachings. India is the sacred land which has given birth to countless sages, Rishis, Yogins, saints and prophets. India is the land that has produced many Acharyas or spiritual preceptors like Sri Sankara and Sri Ramanuja; many saints like Kabir, Ramdas, Tukaram and Gauranga Mahaprabhu; many Yogins like Jnana Dev, Dattatreya and Sadasiva Brahman; many prophets like Buddha and Nanak. The Hindus believe Buddha is their flesh and blood. A guru, or teacher, is someone who has gained enlightenment through knowledge and practice. A Hindu today wanting to follow a particular path of prayer, meditation and devotion usually has a guru such as Shirdi Sai Báb a or Sathya Sai Báb a. (*Hinduism: Hindu Religion*, All About Hinduism, Sri Swami Sivananda) One such following, which is well known around the world is Krishna Consciousness. The main differences between Krishna Consciousness and mainstream Hinduism are: 1). Krishna Consciousness comes from liberation from samsara through sankirtana (congregational singing), 2). The followers believe they can attain a personal relationship with Krishna, 3). Hell is a temporary experience after death for people who have sinned, 4). Devotees need a spiritual master who is in a line of succession from the Guru Caitanya and 5). The Krishna energy in food prepared for and offered to God purifies the body. (Religious Tolerance .com)

Islam – According to Muslims, none of the teachings of the prophets who preceded Muhammad (the last Prophet) are denied. From Adam (the first Prophet) and Abraham to Solomon and Jesus, the Biblical and even extra-Biblical prophets are affirmed, many of their actions and utterances being lauded in the pages of the Qur'an. For this reason Muslims do not subscribe to the Jewish view, which according to Jewish tradition asserts that prophecy ceased about 400 B.C. so that there could be no new scriptures after that time. Muslims regard Muhammad, Moses and Jesus as prophetic and as such were assigned a special mission by God. Muslims maintain and believe every subsequent prophet who served in the world, no matter where, was to affirm the correct teachings of previous prophets. God sent each prophet with refined guidance that, the revelations communicated through him supersede, even as they mark the culmination of all earlier scriptures and those inserted by man. (muslim-canada.org)

Jainism – The Jain religion is contemporary to Buddhism and bears much resemblance to it. It was founded around 500 B.C. by Mahavira, the 24th and last of the Jain prophets called as Tirthankars or "finders of the path." Mahavira cannot be called the founder of Jainism, rather its transmitter. The first Jain prophet was Rsabha who is mentioned in the Vedas and hence Jainism can be considered to be of great antiquity. (IndianMirror.com) The last of its great prophets was contemporary with Sākya Muni, the Lord Buddha, but He was the last of a great succession, and simply gave to Jainism its latest form. There were great cycles of time believed in by the Jains as by the Hindu; and we find that in each vast cycle, which resembles the day and night of Brahmā, twenty-four great prophets come to the world, somewhat, though not entirely, of the nature of Avatāras. They always climb up from manhood, while, in some cases, the Hindu is loath to admit an Avatāra is a perfected man. The Jain has no doubt at all on this point. His twenty-four great Teachers, the Tirthankaras, as they are called, are perfected men. (*Jainism*, Annie Besant, theosophical.ca)

Judaism - The Hebrew word for a prophet, navi comes from the term niv sefatayim meaning "fruit of the lips," which emphasizes the prophet's role as a speaker. The Talmud teaches there were hundreds of thousands of prophets: twice as many as the number of people who left Egypt, which was 600,000. But most of the prophets conveyed messages intended solely for their own generation and were not reported in scripture. Scripture identifies only 55 prophets of Israel. A prophet is not necessarily a man. Scripture records the stories of seven female prophets and the Talmud reports that Sarah's prophetic ability was superior to Abraham's. Orthodox Jewish tradition asserts that prophecy ceased about 400 B.C. (jew-faq.org) Reform Jews believe we meet prophets today who continue to tell the Truth to each other and not for his or her own gain.

Native American – Native American prophets resembled the great prophets of Israel in preaching a definite message; the ordinary medicinal healer (shaman) had no such role. The Native American prophet in the late 18th and the 19th century normally foretold the regeneration of all indigenous peoples and the recapture of lands from foreign settlers, provided that Native Americans accepted the idea of ethnic brotherhood and that they follow prescribed religious practices. Frequently, prophets were connected with their military leaders, such as the Delaware Prophet with Pontiac, and the Shawnee Prophet with his brother, Tecumseh. Two later prophets of renown were Smohalla and Wovoka (of the Ghost Dance). Deganawidah (Iroquois), and Chief Dan Evehema (Hopi), have also been called prophets. (*Among Native Americans*, infoplease.com)

New Thought – The Metaphysical Bible Dictionary defines "Prophet" as "A teacher, one who receives the inspiration of Spirit, an understanding of spiritual law, and imparts it to others." They believe all people have God's Spirit within them, and the followers of the New Thought faith look for wisdom coming from anyone, young or old who act on spiritual principles and allow Spirit to express through them. This list includes the prophets and enlightened beings from the Old and New Testaments such as Moses and Jesus the Christ and Eastern leaders such as Buddha and even more modern teachers such as Ernest Holmes, Charles and Myrtle Fillmore, Michael Beckwith and Ekhart Tolle. However, they believe everyone has the God potential to be a prophet. We are truly all teachers for each other.

They believe Jesus Christ, as the full expression of the Christ within, was "The Son begotten of the only Father, not the 'only begotten Son of God.' Christ means the universal idea of Sonship, of which each is a member." We are of One Body, One Mind, One Spirit. Each partakes of the Christ nature to the degree that the Christ is revealed through him..." (Ernest Holmes)

Sikhism - Sikhism was founded in India by Guru Nanak (1469-1539 A.D.) and nurtured by the nine prophets who followed him to cope with changing times by instilling martial spirit to the dying morale of an oppressed society. The Guruship, held by a human prophet ended when the Tenth Prophet, Guru Gobind Singh (1675-1708 A.D.) passed the Guruship to the holy scripture, the Guru Granth Sahib, which enshrines the inspired writings of the Sikh Gurus and also of some holy saints and bards of Hinduism, Sufism, and Islam without any distinction as to religion, caste, creed or even sex. The basis of the teachings of Sikh prophets is the belief in absolute oneness of God and universal good-will and compassion. (*Sikhism*, members.tripod.com) (Gangadeep, Kapur)

Taoism – In Taoism there have been various prophetic figures, ranging from mythical emperors to semi-historical figures, such as Lao Tzu (5th century BCE) and Chang Tao Ling (2nd century CE), who founded popular Taoism. Taoists believe in one true God as the Eternal Truth as do the Christians, Hindus, Muslims and Jews. Lao Tzu said, "He who knows other men is discerning; he who knows himself is intelligent. He who overcomes others is strong; he who overcomes himself is mighty. He who is satisfied with his lot is rich; he who goes on acting with energy has a firm will. He who does not fail in the requirements of his position, continues long; he who dies and yet does not perish, has longevity." (*Lao Tsu*, wsu.edu)

Rev. Dr. Stephen L. Albert

"Being a Christian is more than just an instantaneous conversion - it is a daily process whereby you grow to be more and more like Christ."
Billy Graham

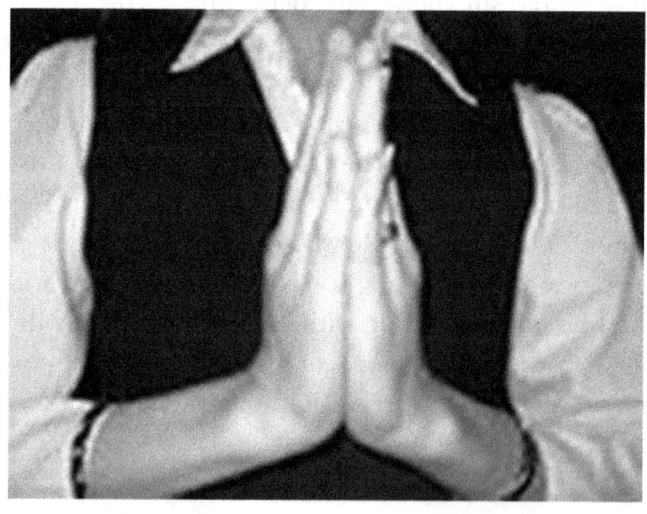

Conversion

In many faiths, the act of conversion can be a very touchy subject for people. Individually, it refers to a soul making a choice to change direction in how he or she will worship God. It is "to do and pay attention (harken)" to a different way. From the faith group which is being left, it can be seen as someone putting down their beliefs. Some families no longer talk to a family member who has chosen to seek another path. From the faith group who is accepting the converter, the converter may be viewed with skepticism and cautiousness. A faith must be lived and witnessed before it can be truly left for another. My experience with conversion is the beauty which develops by the blending of all the knowledge learned.

Bahá'í – People converting to the Baha'i faith will be asked to follow the Baha'i Faith laws, which were revealed by Bahá'u'lláh. They forbid gambling, alcohol, drug abuse, and gossip. The Bahá'ís strive to live a life of high moral standards, emphasizing honesty, trustworthiness, service to others, chastity, purity of motive, generosity, unity, and work as a form of worship. (Lynne Yancy, The Baha'i National Center)

Buddhism – People can convert to Buddhism by the correctness of their thoughts, words, and the small and large acts which they perform in a daily setting. It is the belief and knowledge of yourself in all you do which makes you a Buddhist. Follow the Buddhist advice: "Avoid the Evil, do good and above all cleanse the Spirit." It is in doing this practice where the real conversion lies; it is common in all real and authentic spiritual traditions in their essential verticality with Spirit and horizontality with mankind. (*Be Converted To The Buddhism*, bouddha.ch)

Christianity – Conversion to Christianity involves believing and having faith in God, repenting of (turning around) your sins, and accepting and confessing (witnessing) that Jesus Christ is the Son of God and that we will become Christ-like in our living. It involves a personal choice to focus on Christianity more than another religion. Most Christians understand it to mean the individual attains eternal salvation by a genuine conversion experience or act. Persons converting to Christianity through the Baptist church often choose to experience baptism (immersion in water or water on the forehead) as a sign of their conversion, although many Christian churches do not require baptism. A period of instruction in the faith is required by all denominations. Conversion follows a time of repentance when you come to realize you are going the wrong way and making the wrong decisions. Repentance actually means 'to turn about' from what you are doing or the actions you have been taking and to choose a different common denominator to help you find a way through life's struggles. (Rev. Glen Larsen)

Confucianism – There is no conversion process to the ethical system of Confucianism. Accepting the guides to loving and helping humanity and leading your life for the good of all is all that is required to be called a Confucian.

Hinduism – A convert to Hinduism must demonstrate formal severance from his previous religion or faith before formally entering the Hindu religion through the name-giving sacrament. Full religious conversion includes informing one's former religious or philosophical leader, preferably through a personal meeting, that the individual is entering a new religion. The six steps of conversion include: 1). Joining a Hindu community, 2). Studying Hinduism and presenting your understanding to a Hindu elder, 3). Severing ties with any former mentors of a previous religion, 4). Adopting a Hindu name which includes legally changing your name on all lawful documents (passports, driver's license, etc.), 5). Participating in Namakarana Samskara (the name giving ceremony) at a Hindu temple and 6). Publishing a three-day announcement in a local newspaper stating the name-change has been completed and he or she has entered the Hindu religion through the Namakarana Samskara. (himalayanacademy.com)

Islamic – A non-Muslim becomes a Muslim when he believes in his heart: *"There is no God but Allah, and I bear witness that Muhammad is His Messenger."* Hence, belief in the Unity and Oneness of God and that Muhammad is his Messenger makes one a Muslim at heart. The three steps to becoming a Muslim include officially converting by pronouncing the shahadah (pledge of conviction of faith) three times in Arabic thus: *"Ash HaduAllaa Ilaaha Il-lallaah Wa Ash Hadu Anna Muhammadar Rasullulah"* which means *"I bear Witness that there is no deity but Allah, and I bear witness that Muhammad is His Messenger"*. The pledge can be taken in front of at least two adult Muslim witnesses. (Imam Baseem Syed)

Jainism – There is no ritual to convert to Jainism. If you act like a Jain and truly believe you are a Jain, you are a Jain.

Judaism – A convert to Judaism is referred to as a **ger tzedek** (Hebrew: "righteous proselyte" or "proselyte [of] righteousness") or simply **ger** ("stranger" or "proselyte"). Orthodox, Conservative, Reform, and other branches of Judaism disagree somewhat as to conversion processes and requirements, and even within any particular movement there is bound to be disagreement. Many orthodox Rabbis hold it is necessary for a man to have a *brit milah* (circumcision) or *brit dam* (a drop of blood from the penis), that both men and women require immersion in a mikveh (ritual bath), and that the conversion must be allowed only at the end of a formal course of study, before a Bet Din (rabbinic court) which ensures the sincerity of a potential convert. (chabad.org)

Reform Judaism does not require ritual immersion in a mikveh, circumcision, or acceptance of mitzvot as normative. The converter is only to lead a Torah-based way of life, and then he or she is equal with someone born into a Jewish home. The saying in Judaism about someone who converts is, "The stranger shall be as the home born."

Native American – As much as you would like, studying or taking part in Native American rituals will not make you Native American. Only those born and raised as Native Americans can call themselves as such, and many choose to keep to themselves. Native American spirituality is appealing to many people, some of whom are presently forbidden by federal law from exploring their faith because of their ethnicity. Rather, for hundreds of years Native Americans have been enslaved and then converted to other religions by their conquerors, mostly those who called themselves Christians. (Evans Craig, Navajo)

New Thought – There is no conversion process when choosing to be a New Thought follower. Anyone who has followed or not followed any religion which is life-affirming is welcome in any New Thought faith center. The freedom of the faith, the belief God's Spirit is within each person and the absence of guilt, attracts many people who previously were followers of more orthodox faiths. All are responsible for their choices. (Rev. Abigail Albert)

Sikhism – Sikhs, as a rule, do not aim at the conversion of others. If someone wants to convert to Sikhism, they are inspired on their own. If someone is inspired and wants to become a Sikh, they are welcomed into the faith wholeheartedly. No person is shunned or turned away.

Taoism – There is no real conversion to Taoism; it is an awakening to the philosophy which many westerners have chosen to practice.

You can combine whatever faith you now follow with Taoism. Take what you like from your faith and combine it and harmonize it with Taoist teachings.

"*Everything that irritates us about others can lead us to an understanding of ourselves.*"
Carl Jung

Part 7

The Taboos to Know How Not to Insult

My greatest fear as I began to delve into New Thought was, I never wanted to insult someone of another faith by action or deed, and I certainly did not want to mispronounce their name. After years of trying to be perfect, I accept my actions that speak louder than my words. In general, when I meet new people from different faiths, I choose to be less expressive and spend more time listening to what they have to say. Yet at the same time, I make sure to ask questions on THEIR opinion about a situation or issue. I have learned with people who have a cultural background with the tendency not to be tactile with outsiders, my avoiding shaking hands and hugging, which I am prone to do, actually brings them closer to me because they are less worried I will overstep a physical boundary. It is just common sense to be less demonstrative when interacting with new people no matter which faith they come from.

Bahá'í - Bahá'ís believe in modesty in all things, including dress. Insulting Manifestations and denying God are irreverent, but if someone were to do these things in the presence of a Bahá'í, there would not be any "fall out." Bahá'í laws are enjoined upon only Bahá'ís. Bahá'ís don't expect people who are not Bahá'ís to observe the Bahá'í laws. Bahá'ís may not gamble. Discriminating against anyone of any sex, race, culture, religion, etc. is against all that Bahá'ís believe. Bahá'ís believe one God created one humanity; hence, all are equal in the sight of God. Therefore, any behavior contrary to unity, such as discrimination, is contrary to the will of God. (Lynne Yancy, Bahá'í National Center)

Guests are always invited to Bahá'í worship services and it is expected that each person will arrive on time when prayers are being recited. Clothing is your personal preference; appropriate reverent attire is normal, and no head covering is necessary. You can sit where you wish and may participate in all service activities. Non-Bahá'ís may NOT give an offering or tithe, although if they tried to, the Bahá'ís would not embarrass the giver by rejecting it. Only Bahá'ís who recognize Baha'u'llah may give. They feel it is a sacred duty and privilege to give and they do not want to feel "beholden" to anyone.

Buddhism – Buddhists are normally vegetarian in their diet. Buddhist priests in China wear a bao-tzo on their head similar to the Jewish yarmulka. It is proper to remove your shoes when entering a Buddhist temple. Other no-nos include using replicas of religious figures such as Buddha in any way. Guests, who arrive early, may be led to a meditation pillow and they do not enter or leave during the meditation. If you need to you may leave early. Participating is a personal choice, and there is no talking during the service. Contributions may be made in an offering box near the front door, and $1-$5 is a customary offering. At most temples men and women are expected to wear comfortable clothing, and no head covering is required. An important PRACTICE is putting one's hands/palms together, holding a nenju (prayer beads) and placing them in front of the chest, then head. This represents the individual and the Buddha coming together.

Christianity – Many Christians do not support abortion or gay rights. In general, men and women tend to dress up for a worship service, which is held on Sunday morning and led by the Priest or Minister Other worship services be scheduled on other days and times. Men typically wear a tie and jacket, and women wear dresses. Depending on the type of Christian church, a variety of ritual objects is used. A collection plate is passed during the service, and anyone may contribute any amount of money.

Confucian – Many Confucians are normally vegetarian in their diet, but most are not. Societal chaos and lack of civility are considered abhorrent for Confucianism. It is proper to remove one's shoes when entering a Confucian temple. (Rev. Dr. John Berthrong)

Hindu – To Hindus, beef is forbidden, as the cow is a holy animal for all Hindus. Normally, they consume a vegetarian diet. Hindus are also strict with certain habits. When cooking food, they never taste food from the dish. If food has to be tasted then, a small portion is placed in the right hand. When entering a Hindu temple it is proper to remove one's shoes. Orthodox Hindus are not permitted to shake hands with members of the opposite sex. Guests to their temples are asked to arrive on time and sit where they wish. You can come and go and participate at will. A contribution of $1 - $5 is recommended for the offering.

Islam – The Qur'an describes that clothing is meant to cover people's private areas, and be an adornment (Qur'an 7:26). Clothing worn by Muslims should be clean and decent, neither excessively fancy nor ragged. One should not dress in order to gain the admiration or sympathy of others. Women can wear head coverings, and many Muslim men can wear a *topi*, similar to the Jewish yarmulka. Islam has strict dietary laws with lawful food being called *halaal*. Lying, treachery, unlawful relations between men and women, oppression, cruelty to fellow beings, abusing and ridiculing others, lewdness, hot temper are the vices which Islam considers as the worst attributes, and Muslims should keep themselves away from these evil traits. It is proper to remove shoes when entering an Islamic place of worship. One of the basic rules of Islam is that men and women who are not intimately related are not allowed to have any form of physical contact. Muslims do not eat pork or drink alcohol.

One must remove shoes before entering the prayer room (musallah), which faces Mecca where all Muslims direct themselves. There are no pews or chairs. The room is uncluttered, in order to stand and bow in unison. There are facilities to wash hands, face and feet in order to purify oneself prior to prayers. Prayers are meant to be recited by memory and prayer books are used only by those who are learning the prayers. No ritual objects are used. Guests are asked to arrive early. There are two unit prayers being repeated by Muslims as they enter which is a way to greet the mosque. Guests will sit on the prayer rug and not leave during group prayer. Muslims donate whatever they can; however, non-Muslims are not expected to openly make a contribution. Regarding guest clothing, men wear casual shirt and slacks and no head coverings. Women are expected to wear a dress which covers their whole bodies. Women must also wear a scarf to cover their head. Wearing religious jewelry is discouraged.

Jainism – It is almost impossible to insult someone who lives the concept of "non-violence" to the degree the Jains do. If you said something offensive they would merely walk away from you. In the life of an ascetic, he may find himself in circumstances, likely to arouse his wrath. In spite of such provocation, he must avoid emotional disturbance and maintain peace of mind. This maintaining patience in the midst of provocation is called *Kashama* or forbearance. Jains are, for the most part, vegetarian. They should not become engrossed in pleasures of perfumes and scents that will increase their lust as well as others' lust. The foods they eat should be simple as should all things which come before their senses. (*Jainism Simplified*, Chapter 14, umich.edu)

Judaism – The greatest insult to a Jew is to deny the holocaust ever happened. Orthodox Jewish congregants do not eat pork products or shell fish, and they do not mix meat with dairy products at any meal. Judaism has strict dietary laws with lawful food being called *kosher*. Orthodox Jews always wear a head covering, *Yarmulka*, because they believe they are always in the presence of G-d. It is also a sign of humility for men, acknowledging what's "above" us (G-d). Conservative Jews always wear the Yarmulka in the sanctuary but not necessarily outside the synagogue. Orthodox Jews are not permitted to shake hands with members of the opposite sex.

In the sanctuary, whenever the Ark is opened exposing the Torah, everyone in the sanctuary stands in reverence for the belief that the Torah is the blueprint of their way of life, and as such they show it respect. It is respected not for the object but for the ideas it contains. In an Orthodox Synagogue, men and women will need a hat or head covering while in the sanctuary. Women's hemlines should be below the knees and extra jewelry, especially a symbol of another faith, is frowned upon. Guests are asked to arrive on time and sit where they wish and respect the separation of men and women in the Orthodox congregations. Do not enter when people are standing or during the Rabbi's sermon. No Collections (offering) are taken at the services; Jews are members of their congregations and pay dues. They also make donations throughout the year to commemorate a death, birth, anniversary, getting well after an illness, etc. (Marilyn Clement)

Native American – Native Americans value common sense, continuity and respect. They expect outsiders to obey all laws when visiting Indian lands as well as to 'respect the customs' of the Tribe they are visiting.. Native Americans use the word "regalia" for traditional clothing which is used for ceremonial occasions. Various food restrictions are used by different tribes for various rituals and ceremonies. There can be special foods and drink prepared for initiation ceremonies for boys and girls at puberty. Photography is a particularly sensitive issue, especially with the Pueblo Nations: Fees and restrictions vary from each pueblo and tribe and at times from activity to activity. Do not attempt to take photos, recordings or sketches if you have not gotten prior permission. The embarrassment of being caught is extreme. Alcohol & drugs are against the law on all reservations (*Native Americans*, New Mexico Magazine, Nov.2007) (Evans Craig, Navajo)

Native Americans do not meet in churches or temples but rather in sacred and ceremonial sites on their land. Although guests are not openly invited to religious ceremonies or observances, those who show a sincere interest in learning about various tribes may be invited. If you are invited, ask any questions about what will go on at the ceremony ahead of time and be prepared to sit, stand & stay a while for long periods of time and don't look at your watch. As my Navajo friend Evans Craig, says, "When it is an Indian ritual, you are on Indian time."

New Thought – Those in the New Thought faith act respectfully toward everyone they meet and expect the same will come back to them. There are no dietary rules or rules of interaction with others, assuming each person acts properly towards whomever they meet. New Thought services vary and usually include a meditation period before or during the service, a variety of group songs and an inspirational message from the minister. During meditation it is preferred for people not to walk in or out except for emergencies. Dress is usually casual to dressy casual, and the environments are very friendly and welcoming. A collection is made towards the end of the service, and a guest may give or not give depending how they are moved. There will usually be light refreshments after the service and visitors are always invited to stay. New Thought people may first shake hands, and then give each other a hug. If it is someone they do not know, they will ask if it is okay to hug.

New Thought philosophy does not forbid drinking yet definitely frowns upon drugs unless they are prescribed by a physician or are supplements prescribed by a wholistic practitioner. All are taught, "our bodies are the temple of the living God Spirit, and we are responsible to tend to the body and eat healthy foods and drink." The Law of Cause and Effect is taught to all ages and children are taught they will experience the consequences of their actions. Parents are encouraged to teach these laws in their home. (Rev. Abigail Albert)

Sikhism – Turbans for men are required for all Sikh men and must be worn at all times except when sleeping. The Sikh Gurus asked Sikhs not to cut their hair . It is proper to remove your shoes when entering a Sikh temple (Gurdwara). Then wash your hands, cover your head and think of the Guru. Fold both your hands and walk slowly as you enter the hall where the Guru Granth Sabib is present. Bow humbly and touch your forehead to the ground out of respect for the Guru Granth Sahib. Guests are asked to arrive any time due to the long service, enter during songs, not during prayers, take off their shoes, and put a head covering on. Men sit on the left, women on the right and they do not have to sit cross-legged. It is proper to sit and stand with the rest of the congregation. Regarding clothing, men wear a jacket and tie or more casual modest clothing while women wear a modest dress, skirt and blouse, or pants suit. LEGS need to be covered while sitting cross-legged. The Sikhs are very hospitable, and food is always available to everyone at all services and celebrations. If you choose to give an offering, you may offer money (into a box) or flowers to the Guru Granth Sahib, then bow before it.

Taoists –Most Taoists are vegetarian in their diet, but many are not. Even at some of the more severe Daoist monasteries in China monks farm fish in little ponds and eat wild game. Other no-no's include using religious figures such as Taoist monks in any manner. It is proper to remove your shoes when entering a Taoist religious space. Taoists have very few rules because they believe rules are made for those who would break them. Therefore if everyone lives a life flowing with the Tao, no rules need apply.

Rev. Dr. Stephen L. Albert

Generalities:

Drugs & Alcohol – Bahá'ís, Buddhists, Confucians, Hindus, Jains, Muslims, Sikhs and Taoists do not use drugs, drink alcohol or any intoxicating drink. All other faiths suggest moderation. Members of the Bahá'í faith are also forbidden to gamble.

General Greeting - In all the Eastern traditions, when greeting someone, especially someone from the clergy, do not extend your hand as in a traditional western handshake; it is a courtesy to put your palms together and lower your temple to your closed palms; this is called *gassho*. Although most religions accept shaking hands as a formal greeting between people, hugging someone you have just met is an insult to those in many religions. After being granted permission by a stranger, hugging that stranger is acceptable in the Baha'i faith and in New Thought. In all other faiths, hugging is permitted with acquaintances. Muslims say "Peace be with you," shake hands and embrace only those of the same sex. With folded hands (palms together) and a slight bow, 'Jai Jinendra' is how you greet someone from the Jain faith; it's like saying "hello and welcome." Touching others in general is not allowed for a Jain Holy man.

THE INTERFAITH MANUAL

"Those who merely perform rituals of worship are not pleasing to their Lord and Master."
Sri Guru Granth Sahib

Required Rituals & Observances

This section will discuss the "**liturgical**" rituals which emphasize standard traditional ceremonies in worship for each of the Faiths. A "Ritual" can be understood as the established form followed by a group as part of their regular coming together. It is "what they do" and the procedure of any ceremony is often set by customs or tradition. Despite the differences in the "what," the principles underlying ritual are often responses to primal or archetypal energies - an intuitive expression of something "beyond" the material world. Religion is an attempt to codify and explain the universe that we encounter, and the resulting rituals don't always have a clear or rational basis, especially in this age of logic and science. There are things that we are able to experience in common, as human beings (indeed with other living beings as well), but the nature of those experiences is ineffable. How do we talk about, or personify love - or peace? - or freedom? - or compassion? The varied use of objects, actions and voice can be developed to emulate aspects of a wide range of altruistic or spiritual qualities. It is not the things or the movements or the words in themselves that are holy but what they elicit in the human heart that gives them value - we create our own rituals. (buddahmind.info)

Bahá'í - The Bahá'í Faith places great importance on the relationship with God, but not on religious ritual. Bahá'ís have no priesthood or clergy, no initiation ceremonies, no sacraments, and no worship rituals. There are three different prayers from which a Bahá'í may choose to fulfill the requirement of daily obligatory prayer. One of those prayers is quite short, but it is not compulsory to use that particular obligatory prayer. Fasting is observed for nineteen days every spring from sunrise to sunset for purposes of spiritual cleansing. Divorce is strongly discouraged, and homosexuality and extramarital sex are forbidden. Bahá'ís must strive to maintain friendly relations with all other faiths, and avoid "worldly" behavior such as gossip, and materialism. (Lynne Yancy, Bahá'í National Center)

Buddhism - Buddhist tradition has developed many different customs and practices in different parts of the world. However, two customs are basic to all traditions: *Venerating the Buddha*, which may take the form of meditating on the qualities of Buddha and honoring the Buddha or Buddha-figure and *The exchange of gifts;* in the Theravada tradition, Buddhist laypersons often give gifts to Buddhist monks, but giving is also encouraged more generally, to one another and to good causes. In Theravada Buddhism, monks are considered to embody the fruits of Buddhist practice. Monks' responsibility is to share these with lay Buddhists through their example and teaching. Giving to monks is also thought to benefit lay people and to win them merit. Puja is a Pali word which means "*honor, worship and devotional attention.*" Puja can describe a variety of forms, but in the Buddhist monastery, it generally refers to the twice daily gathering of the community in the main meditation hall. The ritual of taking the Five Precepts is almost always accompanied by taking the Three Refuges. These two factors form the foundation of being a lay Buddhist. The Precepts and Refuges ceremony is probably the most common ritual seen in a Buddhist situation and will often precede most other rituals, ceremonies or celebrations. Perhaps for this reason it is relatively simple. Buddhists bow as an act of the heart; this is humility. Bowing is to the Buddha within us all, OUR Buddha-Nature. The image symbolizes the realization of the highest human potential, representing so much that is worthy of respect, worthy of bowing down to. (*Buddhist Customs*, experiencefestival.com)

Christianity - In Catholic Christianity, Penance ("reconciliation") is offered through Confessional booths inside the church where the local priest or minister grants forgiveness to its members for sins which may have been done. The Eucharist, It is also called The Lord's Supper, Communion, Catholic "Mass," or Divine Liturgy, is offered in the Catholic church. which is the partaking of bread and wine or juice as body and blood of Christ (Derived from "Last Supper"). Other Christian/Protestant denominations offer Baptism, which is the immersion or pouring of water over the head of the adult or infant church member by the priest so as to wash away sin in the person. Anointing the sick is also done by the priest to bless the congregant during a difficult period. In Mystical Christianity, it is believed the water currents quicken the connection with Guardian Angels. Not all sacraments are observed by all churches, though Baptism and Eucharist are accepted almost universally. (spiritualitytoday.org)

Confucianism - Confucianism does not contain all the elements of some other religions, like Christianity and Islam. It is primarily an ethical system to which rituals at important times during one's lifetime have been added. In the *Book of Rites*, Confucianism, two chief ceremonial observances are: 1). Capping, wherein a son is honored into manhood on reaching his twentieth year; and 2). Marriage at the age of thirty for a man and twenty for a woman, with the goal of having male children. (religioustolerance.com)

Hinduism - The Hindu culture is a culture of love, respect, honoring others and humbling one's own ego so the inner nature (the Atman), which is naturally pure and modest, will shine forth. Respect for elders is a keystone of Hindu culture. Younger people never use the proper name of their elders. In the Tamil tradition, a younger brother, for example, refers to his brother as annan, or periannan (older brother), not by name. The elder, however, may use the name of the younger. Children are trained to refer to all adults as auntie or uncle. Only people of the same age will address each other by first name. A Hindu wife never speaks the name of her husband. When referring to him, she uses terms such as "my husband," "him" or, for example, "Athan, Mama, etc." One touches the feet of holy men and women in recognition of their great humility and inner attainment. It is tradition to provide dakshina, a monetary fee or gift to a priest given at the completion of any rite. Dakshina is also given to gurus as a token of respect for their spiritual blessings. (himalayanacademy.com)

The daily ritual of **puja** is performed in a sacred corner in a worship room of the home. It is done to keep Hindus aware of their family gods and mindful of their duties as individuals. The ritual of puja has three steps. The first is seeing the family deity (**darshana**). A small statue or picture of the god is placed in the sacred corner. The second step is the worship of the god, or puja. The worshiper offers the god flowers, fruits, and cooked food (**bhog**). The third step is retrieving the blessed food (**prasada**) and consuming it. This practice is thought to bring the deity down to earth and brings the person closer to the Holy. There are special rituals that only the priests, or brahmin can perform. These are called the **shrauta** rituals and are very complex and involve offering elaborate sacrifices to the god Agni. These "fire-sacrifice" rituals are to bring out the central element of power of gods and nature through the fire. In some cases, the brahmins are paid by individuals to perform these sacrifices for the buyer's benefit. (asms.k12.ar.us)

Islam - The religious rituals of Islam are relatively few in number, but great in importance. The Five Pillars of Islam, as discussed earlier, are five practices regarded by all sects as essential to the Muslim faith. The pillars are acknowledged and observed by all sects of Muslims, although Shi'ites add further obligatory duties, including: jihad (inner negativity which all Muslims struggle to submit to), giving, the encouragement of good deeds and the prevention of evil. The Five Pillars of Islam are: 1). Confession of faith (*shahada*), 2). Daily ritual prayer (*salat*), 3). Giving (*zakat*), 4). Fasting during the month of Ramadan (*sawm*) and 5). Pilgrimmage to Mecca (*hajj*). A **Muslim** should greet his brethren by praying for them in the words: *"Assalaam Alaikum."* This is the greeting that was taught and promoted by the Prophet Mohammad (pbuh) in his *Sunnah*. As far as shaking hands or hugging or brushing cheeks or kissing the cheeks or kissing the forehead are concerned, none of these acts is a part of the Islamic *Shari`ah* or the *Sunnah* of the Prophet (pbuh). When verbally mentioning the Prophet (pbuh), the words "Peace Be Unto Him" (pbuh) should follow. The pronouncement of God's name before eating or drinking is with a twofold purpose. Firstly, it is a recognition of God's countless blessings upon us, and, secondly, it is a supplication for the continuation and abundance of these blessings in future. The Prophet (pbuh) is reported to have stressed strict adherence to this etiquette in a number of sayings ascribed to him. The Prophet (pbuh) is reported to have said: Whenever anyone of you eats, he should say: "[I begin] with the name of God." If he forgets, he should then say, "With the name of God, at the beginning as well as at the end." As part of the teachings related to physical cleansing, the Prophet (pbuh) directed the Muslims to trim their moustaches, remove the hair from their pubic area and that which grows under the armpits, clip their nails and circumcise their male offspring. These practices were approved, adopted and promoted by the Prophet (pbuh) as symbols of cleanness. (understanding-islam.com)

Jainism – Jains worship at stone temples or at home at wooden shrines resembling the temple. Spiritual practices and religious holidays are observed by celebrating the significant events of the lives of Tirthankars (Jinas), performing penances, reciting sacred texts, attending religious discourses, studying scriptures, taking certain vows to control senses, giving alms, and following other acts of compassion (*Jainism, Religion of Compassion and Ecology*, P. 28)

Worship rituals may include chanting mantras, (the Five Homages (*panka namaskarais*) are spoken by most Jains every morning), gazing at images of the gods (*puja*) or anointing such images. Although the prime focus of Jainism is self-discipline, adherents may call upon the deities for assistance on their journey. (religionfacts.com/Jainism) For a boy, a thread is bestowed at the coming of age (around twelve) to be worn around the waist as the symbol of being twice born. The equivalent of coming of age for girls is marriage. The bestowal of the thread is part of the wedding ceremony. That part of the wedding ritual is even preserved in Jainism.

Puja symbolizes various aspects of Jains' religion. One should reflect on such aspects while performing the puja rituals. There are different types of puja being performed for various religious and social ceremonies. The following eight types of materials are generally used for puja.

1. Jala Puja: (Water)

Water symbolizes the ocean and emotions. Every living being continuously travels through Life Ocean of birth, life, death, and misery. This puja reminds that one should live the life with honesty, truthfulness, love and compassion towards all living beings. This way one will be able to cross the Life Ocean and attain Moksha or liberation. The path of liberation is Samyak Darshan, Samyak Jnan and Samyak Charitra in Jain religion.

2. Chandan Puja: (Sandal wood)

Chandan symbolizes Knowledge (Jnan). During this puja one should reflect on Right Knowledge. Right knowledge means proper understanding of reality which includes soul, karma, and their relationship. Jainism believes that the Path of Knowledge is the main path to attain liberation. Bhakti or Devotion helps in the early stages of one's effort for liberation.

3. Pushpa Puja: (Flower)

Flower symbolizes conduct. Our conduct should be like a flower, which provides fragrance and beauty to all living beings without discrimination. We should live our life like flowers, full of love and compassion for all living beings.

4. Dhup Puja: (Incense)

Dhup symbolizes ascetic life. While burning itself, Dhup provides fragrance to others. Similarly true monks and nuns spend their entire life selflessly for the benefit of all living beings. This puja reminds us that one should thrive for a ascetic life which ultimately leads to liberation.

5. Deepak Puja: (Candle)

The flame of Deepak represents a Pure Consciousness or a Soul without any bondage or a Liberated Soul. In Jainism such a Soul is called Siddha or God. The ultimate goal of every living being is to become liberated from karma. By doing this puja one should thrive to follow five great Vows: Nonviolence, Truthfulness, Non stealing, Chastity and Non possession. Ultimately, these proper conducts, coupled with right faith and knowledge, will lead to liberation.

6. Akshat Puja: (Rice)

The household rice is the kind of grain seeds, which are non-fertile. One cannot grow rice plants by seeding the household rice. Symbolically, rice is the last birth. By doing this puja, one should strive to put all the efforts in the life in such a way that this life becomes one's last life, and after the end of this life, one will be liberated and will not be reborn on Earth.

7. Naivedya Puja: (Sweet)

Naivedya symbolizes a tasty food. By doing this puja, one should thrive to reduce or eliminate the attachment to tasty food. Healthy food is essential for survival, however, one should not live to eat a tasty food. Ultimate aim in one's life is to attain a life where no food is essential for our existence, and that is the life of a liberated Soul, who lives in Moksha forever in ultimate bliss.

8. Fal Puja: (Fruit)

Fruit symbolizes Moksha or Liberation. If we live our life without any attachment to worldly affairs, continue to perform our duty without any expectation and reward, be witness to all the incidents that occurred surrounding to and within us, truly follow an ascetic life, and have a love and compassion to all living beings, we will attain the fruit of Moksha or liberation. This is the last Puja symbolizing the ultimate achievement of our life. (jainuniversity.org)

Judaism - The religious rituals followed by Jews can be divided into two locations, at home and in the synagogue. Some of the rituals can be performed in either. On the first Sabbath after a child is born, the infant's father in an Orthodox synagogue or both parents in a Reform Synagogue, is/are called forward at the synagogue to recite the *aliyah,* the blessing before reading a part of the Torah, and ask blessings for the health of mother and child. If the child is a girl, she is named at this time. Boys, if healthy, will be named on the eighth day after birth, as part of the rite of circumcision.

An important life cycle event for a young Jewish boy or girl is the Bar Mitzvah or Bat Mitzvah respectively; both "Bar" and "Bat" (pronounced Ba<u>h</u>t) are Aramaic terms. A boy celebrates Bar Mitzvah when he reaches his thirteenth birthday, while Orthodox girls are Bat Mitzvah when they are twelve. However, the girl's ceremony can be postponed to their thirteenth birthday as well. The literal meaning of Bar/Bat Mitzvah is "son or daughter of the commandment" or age of majority. Historically, Bar Mitzvah and later Bat Mitzvah is the ceremonial occasion that marks the time when a young person is recognized as an adult in the Jewish community and is responsible for performing mitzvot. For example, before children are Bar/Bat Mitzvah, they do not need to fast on Yom Kippur. However, after the Bar/Bat Mitzvah, they are required to fulfill this mitzvah. At the Bar/Bat Mitzvah they are also counted in the minyon, a quorum of ten required to conduct a service. The Bar/Bat Mitzvah ceremony consists of the young person chanting the blessings, and his/her Torah portion which is the Torah portion of the week. One also reads the Haftorah portion. There are many traditions that accompany the Bar/Bat Mitzvah experience. While the actual day is important and memorable, the years of preparation before are enlightening and vital.

The *Shema* is the most central prayer in Jewish life. The first paragraph of the Shema is: Hear O Israel, the Lord is our G-d, the Lord is One. The fundamental difference between Judaism and Christianity is the belief in the Messiah, with most Jews believing that the Messiah is yet to come. (religionfacts.com)

Native American – The customs of the Native Americans are so many and vary so much from tribe to tribe, it would take a huge book dedicated to the Native American Faith to do it justice. However, there are some symbols which are similar from tribe to tribe. The Medicine Wheel is representative of American Indian Spirituality and symbolizes the individual journey we each must take to find our own path. The native people believe the medicine wheel is sacred because the Great Spirit caused everything in nature to be round. The Sun, Sky, Earth and Moon are round. Thus, man should look upon the Medicine Wheel (circle of life) as sacred. Within the Medicine Wheel are The Four Cardinal Directions and the Four Sacred Colors. The Circle represents the Circle of Life and the Center of the Circle, the Eternal Fire. The Eagle, flying toward the East, is a symbol of strength, endurance and vision. East signifies the renewal of life and rebirth as the sun rises in the East. The West, towards the completion of the sun's movement, represents the completion of life and a number of endings which are true of most of the tribes. Where North can represent defeat or trouble, South represents peace and happiness. Upward represents the Father (God) and downward equals Mother Earth. (users.ap.net/~chenae/spirit.html) The Center directions are always 'female' directions. In the Navajo way, there are two female centers, the first representing the female leader (being that all Tribes are matriarchal) & the second female direction representing "family." (Being that it is the female who bore more family onto our Mother Earth) (Evans Craig, Navajo)

New Thought - The customs of the New Thought faith are few due to the broad way each person defines his or her relationship with God and the Faith. The New Thought faith encourages, daily meditation and prayers, weekly attendance at worship services, responsible actions and interaction when dealing with other living things and the environment, tithing back to their source of inspiration, and constant learning, plus improvement and understanding as they go through life. At the same time, the faith teaches that each person has the free will to create the type of life they want. Marriage and Baptism are common ceremonies and vary depending on the church or center. New Thought followers observe Christmas, Palm Sunday and Easter. The idea of "Lent" is focused on throughout the year and not just the days before Easter. "Giving Up negative thoughts, feelings, ideas and actions" are focused on rather than a food. Fasting is a choice.

One common ritual between all New Thought divisions is the "Burning Bowl" ceremony, which usually occurs at the turn of the New Year. In the first part of the ceremony, participants write out a list of the mental, emotional and physical things they want to eliminate from the previous year and not bring with them into the next. Those lists are then burned in a controlled fire symbolically to eliminate their contents. During the second part of the ceremony, the participant gets to write a new list of things he or she wants to experience in the New Year. Many New Thought churches close the ceremony by giving every participant a "white stone," symbolizing their freedom from the past, similar to how prisoners in the Old Testament of the Bible were given a white stone when they were released to show they had served their time and were then free to start a new life (Rev:2:17). Another New Thought custom is to baptize a new baby by sprinkling rose petals instead of water over the baby's head to signify the beauty of God's spirit in this new life. The Association of Global New Thought has sponsored the "A Season for Nonviolence" program since 2001 which runs from January 30 - April 4, and is a national 64-day educational, media, and grass-roots campaign dedicated to demonstrating that nonviolence is a powerful way to heal, transform, and empower our lives and our communities. Their efforts towards bringing peace to the planet have been endorsed by His Holiness the Dalai Lama, UNESCO and the University for Peace. In 2007, AGNT has expanded the Seasons. From September-December, the "Season of Interfaith Celebration, 2007", April- June, the "Season for the Earth, 2008", and June-August the "Season for Humane Service, 2008" (Sandi Angotti, New Thought)

Sikhism - Sikhs are readily identifiable by their turbans. They take a vow not to cut their hair as well as not to smoke or drink alcoholic beverages. When Guru Gobind Singh founded (1699) the martial fraternity Khalsa, meaning *pure*, his followers vowed to keep the five K's: to wear long hair (kesh), a comb in the hair (kangha), a steel bracelet on the right wrist (kara), soldier's shorts (kachha), and a sword (kirpan). The tradition persists to the present day. Besides practicing meditating on God and uttering the Name, the disciples should follow the Guru's instructions, and chant his hymns. Sikhs believe truth is above everything, but higher still is true living; it is necessary to conquer the five deadly sins of lust, anger, greed, attachment, and egoism; we can love God only when we cease to love ourselves, but we must first destroy the ego, and righteous living and the destruction of egoism lead to the eternal bliss of merging into the divine. As water mingles with water, so the light merges with light.

There is great emphasis placed on daily devotion to the remembrance of God. This devotion can be accomplished by following the teachings of the Guru, meditating on the Holy Name and performing acts of service and charity. Members follow the admonition of the ten Sikh Gurus to rise before sunrise, bathe, and meditate upon God's Name. These individual practices are followed by the singing of hymns from the Holy Book. The Sikh Holy Book (Guru Sranth Sahib) is the perpetual Guru; there is no place in either groups for a living Guru. There is great emphasis placed on daily devotion to the remembrance of God. This can be accomplished by following the teachings of the Guru, meditation on the Holy Name and performance of acts of service and charity. (religiousmovements.lib.virginia.edu)

Taoism is an ancient tradition of philosophy and religious belief, deeply rooted in Chinese customs and worldview. Ritual was the primary expression of the religious needs and hopes of the community, and most Taoist rituals were developed in response to these needs. Rituals were performed for individuals at important transitional periods in their lives, such as birth and death. The significance of such moments, however, deeply affected their families. Taoism recognizes that physical actions have a spiritual effect and regards activities such as yoga, meditation, and martial arts as important. At the heart of Taoist ritual is the concept of bringing order and harmony to many layers of the cosmos: the cosmos as a whole (the world of nature), the world or human society, and the inner world of human individuals. Taoist rituals involve purification, meditation and offerings to deities. The details of Taoist rituals are often highly complex and technical and therefore left to the priests, with the congregation playing little part. The rituals involve the priest (and assistants) in chanting and playing instruments (particularly wind and percussion), and also dancing. One major Taoist ritual is the *chiao* (*jiao*), a rite of cosmic renewal, which is itself made up of several rituals. A shortened version of the chiao is a ritual in which each household in a village brings an offering for the local deities. In the ceremony a Taoist priest dedicates the offerings in the names of the families, performs a ritual to restore order to the universe, and asks the gods to bring peace and prosperity to the village. (*Taoism and The Arts of China*, artic.edu)

*"The first woman was created from the rib of a man.
She was not made from his head to top him,
nor from his feet to be trampled on by him,
but out of his side to be equal to him."*
Author Unknown

The Role of Men versus Women

Perhaps the one area of life which can stand the most improvement throughout the world is the relationships between men and women. Aside from their faith belief, I read of too many men disrespecting and harming women and too many women allowing this disrespect and harm to continue. As people and families developed over recorded time, the aggressive, more physically able males took an outside-the-home position to secure money or food to bring back to help the family survive. Child rearing was left to the woman who, obviously, was the only one who could bear children. Her life was being the keeper of the home and all which that entailed. Unfortunately, as government began to form in many countries, men demoted women to second class citizens devoid of making intelligent choices or even voicing an opinion. While in some places the abuse of women has changed, in many places women are still not given the equal rights for which they deserve from birth and have earned over the years. I am still amazed when a husband beats up his wife and feels it is okay to do because she is HIS property. There is a lot of educating which still must be done for people of all faiths.

Bahá'í - The equality of women and men is a fundamental Bahá'í principle. Bahá'u'lláh teaches that in the sight of God men and women are and always have been spiritually equal. In this day, equality is to be expressed in all areas. 'Abdu'l-Bahá explained, "And among the teachings of Bahá'u'lláh is the equality of women and men. The world of humanity has two wings, one is women and the other men. Not until both wings are equally developed can the bird fly. Should one wing remain weak, flight is impossible. Not until the world of women becomes equal to the world of men in the acquisition of virtues and perfections, can success and prosperity be attained as they ought to be." (*Selections from the Writings of 'Abdu'l-Bahá*, rev. ed. (Haifa: Bahá'í World Centre, 1982), p. 302.)

Buddhism - The Buddha discovered that gender is of no importance for the aim of freedom. A female saint, Arahat, or a female being striving after sainthood is in no way subordinate to a male saint or male follower of the Buddha. It is not possible to declare a higher or more important equality of the sexes. According to the teachings of the Buddha, there exists no practical difference between the sexes. Man and woman are equal in their dependence upon each other and in their clinging which must be overcome (Angutara-Nikaya I,1). Man and woman are equal in the rights and duties of their partnership.

Christianity – The Bible and Christianity historically have been interpreted as prescribing separate gender roles, with women often being excluded from church leadership. For the first 19 or 20 centuries after the Resurrection and Ascension of Christ (according to Christian belief), institutionalized Christianity was very unfavorable to women. A gender-based hierarchy, claimed by Complementarians to be biblical, has been constructed to place woman under the man's authority—in the church, in marriage, and elsewhere. (*Comment on God*, deviantart.com) Times have changed somewhat. Women in all sorts of Christian service are finding new avenues of ministry. Unprecedented numbers of women are entering seminaries today. Mary Kassian affirms that women are discovering and exercising their spiritual gifts in inspiring innovative ministries. However, both concur that ambivalence about women's roles still exists. Seminary-trained women don't always receive a call to a church; women gifted in leadership are not always encouraged to lead. (*Ministering Women*, Christianity Today, ctlibrary.com)

Confucianism - Throughout history, elite Chinese women were governed by Confucianism, and all Chinese women by shared folk social norms and rituals. When a female child was born, the Chinese girl was placed underneath her cradle as a symbol of lowliness and weakness. Women were regarded as vastly inferior to men and were treated accordingly. A daughter was also given a piece of pottery to play with, symbolizing the expectation placed on her to be industrious and to serve her family and her husband. Lastly, her birth was announced before the ancestors, symbolizing the fact it was the woman's job to continue worship in the home. Women were, as a rule, not allowed to learn to read, write, conduct business or anything else that was considered a man's job. However, from the Sung dynasty (960-1279) many educated families provided their daughters with fairly sophisticated educations that would fit them for being early teachers of the Confucian Way to their own children. When they were young, they obeyed their parents implicitly, and after they were married, they were expected to do the same to their husbands and parents-in-law. They did have control over many areas, including finances, on their homes and in the raising of their children. (Rev. Dr. John Berthrong) While four decades of reform have provided a constitutional and legislative framework that promotes equity between men and women, the underlying cultural beliefs and traditions emanating from Confucianism may remain influential. The Confucian tradition in the family places authority with the husband, and family relations are defined on the basis of duty, which supersedes individual legal rights. For a woman this means her duty is as a daughter to her father, as a wife to her husband and as a mother to her eldest son. (*Two Tugs of War*, arts.cornell.edu)

Hinduism - In ancient India, women occupied a very important position, in fact a position superior to, men. It is a culture whose only words for strength and power are feminine -"Shakti" means "power" and "strength." In Vedic times women and men were equal as far as education and religion were concerned. Women participated in the public sacrifices alongside men. (Women in Hinduism, hinduwisdom.info) "Women were held in higher respect in India than in other ancient countries, and the Epics and old literature of India assigned a higher position to them than did the epics and literature of ancient Greece. Hindu women enjoyed some rights of property from the Vedic Age, took a share in social and religious rites, and were sometimes distinguished by their learning. The absolute seclusion of women in India was unknown in ancient times." (*The Civilization of India* - R. C. Dutt, p. 21-22). According to tradition, women, more delicate than men, require and deserve protection. Hindu texts extol the virtues of womanhood and of the essential role women have in nurturing future generations. Though Hindus are themselves re-examining and restructuring the roles of women, there still remain powerful ideals, exemplified by ladies such as Sita, Gandhari, Draupadi, Mandodari, and Savitri. Such idealism is often at odds with many prevalent attitudes in the West and those now emerging in contemporary India. (*Woman's Dharma*, hinduism.iskon.com)

Islamic - The roles assigned to men and women in Islamic theology have often come under fire in the Judeo-Christian world, mostly due to misunderstandings of Islam's position on gender roles, or the interpretation of Qur'anic doctrine by present-day imams or leaders in Muslim countries. The Qur'an says that men and women are created equally before God, and that while they have different attributes and take on different roles, neither gender is superior. However, in a husband-and-wife relationship, the husband has been given the final decision making authority. Other than that, each party is obliged to treat the other with respect and work together to create a happy home with Islamic beliefs. Both men and women have souls and can go to Heaven if they lead a life without sin, contradicting early Christian doctrine that women do not possess souls and are inherently evil, because of Eve's original sin. Islam does not blame Eve for what it believes happened in the Garden of Eden; it maintains that both Adam and Eve were responsible, but they repented before God and were forgiven. Believing women descended from the sinful Eve colored Christian ideas of women's character for centuries - as untrustworthy, morally inferior, wicked beings - with menstruation, pregnancy, and childbirth believed to be punishment for all women after Eve. The Qur'an has no such images of women, who are not put on earth solely to bear children, but also to do good deeds the same as men. These basic tenets of gender roles are set out in the Qur'an, but as with many religions, the word of the holy scripture has not always been followed by those with political power. (*Islamic Beliefs and Practices*, ucalgary.ca)

Jainism – In Jainism women are treated as equals with men. Svetambara Jains believe that tirthankaras can be men or women, and say that Malli began her life as a Princess; but Digamber Jains believe that women cannot be tirthankaras and that Malli was a man. The Digambaras, who hold that an adherent should own nothing, not even clothes, say that women must be reborn as men before they can attain moksha (liberation from the life-death cycle). (Religion and Ethics, Jainism, bbc.co.uk)

Judaism - In Orthodox Judaism, women are for the most part seen as separate but equal. Women's obligations and responsibilities are different from men's, but no less important. Reform and conservative congregations now have equality between men and women, with reform synagogues accepting women who choose to become Rabbis. In 1972, Sally Priesand became the first ordained female Rabbi in the United States, ordained by Hebrew Union College-Jewish Institute of Religion in Cincinnati, Ohio. Even Orthodox synagogues are redefining women's roles and giving more equal power to women even as to the amount of study women can participate in. In the Orthodox synagogue Jewish men have an obligation to pray at three fixed times each day, while Jewish women on the other hand, don't have this obligation. In the area of study, women learned separately and were traditionally exempted from any study beyond a basic understanding of the Torah due to their being responsible for other activities in other places, such as being responsible for running a Jewish household. Women were discouraged from learning Talmud and other advanced Jewish texts. Women are exempt from having to follow most of the set daily prayer services, and most other positive time bound *mitzvot*, such as wearing tefillin (two small black boxes with black straps attached to them; while praying, Orthodox Jewish men are required to place one box on their forehead and tie the other one on their arm). (Judaism FAQ, groups.msn.com)

Native American - The statuses and roles for men and women vary considerably among Native Americans, depending on each tribe's cultural orientations. In matrilineal and matrilocal societies, women have considerable power because property, housing, land, and tools, belong to them. Because property usually passed from mother to daughter, and the husband joined his wife's family, he was more of a stranger and yielded authority to his wife's eldest brother. As a result, the husband was unlikely to become an authoritative, domineering figure. This is one of the Great Fallacies of Indian Peoples due to white beliefs; that there is a Chief (Male) that runs the Tribes. In actuality, the females ran the Tribe, usually collaboratively, and that is why one tribe did not obey the Treaty Rights of nearby Tribes, knowing that the Treaty was signed by an appointed Speaker, not the real 'Head of the Tribe.' (Evans Craig, Navajo) Moreover, among such peoples as the Cherokee, Iroquois, and Pueblo, a disgruntled wife, secure in her possessions, could simply divorce her husband by tossing his belongings out of their residence. (customessaymeister.com)

New Thought - All New Thought centers give equal authority and responsibility in all matters to both men and women. Women at this time hold the role of Minister or Assistant Minister at more than 50% of all New Thought centers in all of the denominations.

Sikhism - In the 15th century, Guru Nanak established Sikhism as the first religion to advocate emphatically the equality of all people, especially women. With this assertion, the Sikh Gurus invited women to join the sangat (congregation), work with men in the langar (common kitchen), and participate in all other religious, social, and cultural activities of the gurdwaras (Sikh places of worship). In marriage, the Guru's advocated the joining of two equal partners. Guru Amar Das, the third guru, wrote: "Only they are truly wedded who have one spirit in two bodies." (sikhwomen.com)

Taoism - Taoist followers believe the supreme power of the female is for creation and enlightened understanding. Therefore, it is no surprise that women are treated with reverence and respect. In Taoism, women could become ordained. They were equal with men for all ranks but the highest of Divine Lord. Goddesses populated the Taoist pantheon, including the well-worshipped Queen Mother of the West, who could grant immortality. The development of this unique religion in the heart of patriarchal China is amazing. Unfortunately, Taoism was never widespread. Like women, Taoism was viewed with suspicion and was given little credit in Chinese histories. As Confucianism grabbed hold through the centuries, its more conservative values took away much of the sexual freedom experienced by Taoist women. Taoism offers women positive body images and encourages them to see themselves as an important part of the cosmos. (gauntlet.ucalgary.com)

REV. DR. STEPHEN L. ALBERT

*Teamwork is the ability to work together
toward a common vision;
The ability to direct individual accomplishments
toward organizational objectives.
It is the fuel that allows common people
to attain uncommon results."*
Andrew Carnegie

Part III
How to "Do" Interfaith

Part 1
The Interfaith Environment

According to David Barrett et al, editors of the "*World Christian Encyclopedia: A comparative survey of churches and religions - AD 30 to 2200,*" there are 19 major world religions which are subdivided into a total of 270 large religious groups, and many smaller ones. 39,000+ separate Christian groups have been identified in the world. "*Over half of them are independent churches that are not interested in linking with the big denominations.*" This being said, how would a single church create a fully "Interfaith Environment" which would do justice for every faith; the obvious answer is... it cannot.

Remember, the goal of this Interfaith Manual is not to change your existing church or the way you worship. We honor whatever your faith is and what you believe. This manual is designed to give you information which you can insert into your services about other faiths so each participant can begin to understand how similar they are to others. Your church does not have to be redesigned or change its worship area. In fact we have found by just becoming aware of the various religious holidays and what they mean to worshipers of those faiths, and to add in the opinions and beliefs of one or two other faiths into each lesson the worship leader presents, congregants get the feeling of inclusion rather than exclusion about other people. Having occasional special classes about the different holidays can take away the misconceptions people have about other faiths being "bad" or about them believing "bad" things. Taking away the fear of the unknown is the essential goal of Interfaith.

The last part of this manual is dedicated to ideas which you may want to incorporate into your home discussions, faith environment, worship service or in other areas. The following calendar is for the year 2008, and it is important to be aware of when different faiths celebrate their holidays, especially those holidays which have different dates for their rituals every year. In this way you will never disrespect a faith by inviting them to participate in a program only to find that the date you have chosen for the program falls on one of their holy days.

Aztec Calendar

Holidays & Observances

The following information is from interfaithcalendar.org where you can purchase an Interfaith calendar each year. Trying to schedule an Interfaith event without an interfaith calendar in your hand, will cause you to change the date you have chosen for your program over and over and over again. With the calendar below, * means that Holy days begin at sundown the day before this date. ** Means regional customs, group preference or moon sightings may cause a variation of this date. Check your local calendar for the exact date(s).

JANUARY

Mary, Mother of God - **Catholic Christian**
Feast Day of St. Basil - **Orthodox Christian**
Gantan-sai (New Years) - **Shinto**

Twelfth Night - **Christian**
Gukru Gobindh Singh birthday – **Sikh**

Epiphany - **Christian**
Feast of the Theophany - **Orthodox Christian**
Dia de los Reyes (Three Kings Day - **Hispanic Christian**

Feast of the Nativity - **Orthodox Christian**

Muharram - (New Year) * - **Islam**

Baptism of the Lord Jesus - **Christian**
Maghi - **Sikh**

Maghi - **Sikh**

Blessing of the Animals - **Hispanic Christian**

Week of Prayer for Christian Unity - **Christian**
Ashura * - **Islam**

World Religion Day - **Bahá'í**

Tu B'shvat * - **Jewish**

Mahayana New Year ** - **Buddhist**
Conversion of Saint Paul - **Christian**

FEBRUARY

Lammas - **Christian** - Southern hemisphere

Candlemas - Presentation of Christ in the Temple - **Christian**
Imbolc * - **Wicca**- Northern Hemisphere
Lughanssad * - **Wicca**- Southern Hemisphere

Four Chaplains Sunday - **Interfaith**
Transfiguration Sunday - **Christian**

Shrove Tuesday - **Christian**

Ash Wednesday - Lent begins - **Christian**

Chinese New Year - **Confucian/Daoist/Buddhist**

Vasant Panchami ** - **Hindu**

St. Valentine's Day - **Christian**

Nirvana Day ** - **Buddhist**

Triodion - **Orthodox Christian**

MARCH

Intercalary Days * - **Bahá'í**
Saturday of Souls - **Orthodox Christian**
St. David of Wales - **Christian**

Meatfare Sunday - **Orthodox Christian**

New Thought Day – **New Thought**

Maha Shivaratri ** - **Hindu**

Cheesefare Sunday - **Orthodox Christian**
Passion Sunday ** - **Christian**

Lent begins - Clean Monday - **Orthodox Christian**

Palm/Passion Sunday - **Christian**
Orthodox Sunday - **Orthodox Christian**

St Patrick's Day - **Christian**
Mawlid an Nabi * - **Islam**
Ostara Vernal Equinox * - **Wicca** - Northern Hemisphere
Mabon * - **Wicca** - Southern Hemisphere
Maunday Thursday - **Christian**

Good Friday - **Christian**

Purim * - **Jewish**
Norouz (New Year) - **Persian/Zoroastrian**
Naw Ruz (New Year) * - **Bahá'í**
Magha Puja ** - **Buddhist**

Holi ** - **Hindu**
Hola Mohalla - **Sikh**

Easter - **Christian**

Annunciation of the Virgin Mary - **Christian**

Khordad Sal (Birth of Prophet Zaranhushtra) - **Zoroastrian**

APRIL

New Year ** - **Hindu**
Ramayana ** - **Hindu**

Baisakhi - **Sikh**

Ramanavami ** - **Hindu**
Baisakhi - **Sikh**

Lazarus Saturday - **Orthodox Christian**

Hanuman Jayanti ** - **Hindu**
Palm Sunday - **Orthodox Christian**

Theravadin New Year ** - **Buddhist**
Pesach (Passover) First two days * - **Jewish**

Ridvan begins * - **Bahá'í**

St. George's Day - **Christian**

Pesach (Passover) final two days * - **Jewish**

Holy Friday - **Orthodox Christian**
Easter/Pascha - **Orthodox Christian**
St. James the Great Day - **Orthodox Christian**

MAY

Ascension of Christ - **Christian**
Beltane * - **Wicca** Northern Hemisphere
Samhain * - **Wicca** Southern Hemisphere

Yom HaSho'ah * - **Jewish**

Yom Ha'Atzmaut * - **Jewish**
Pentecost - **Christian**
Trinity Sunday - **Christian**

Buddha Day - Visakha Puja ** - **Buddhist**
Corpus Christi - **Catholic Christian**

Declaration of the Báb * - **Bahá'í**

Ascension of Baha'u'llah * - **Bahá'í**

Sacred Heart of Jesus - **Catholic Christian**

Lag B'Omer * - **Jewish**

Rev. Dr. Stephen L. Albert

JUNE

Pentecost - **Christian**

Ascension of Jesus - **Orthodox Christian**

St. Columba of Iona - **Christian**

Shavuot * - **Jewish**

Trinity - **Christian**

Corpus Christi - **Catholic Christian**
Pentecost - **Orthodox Christian**

Guru Arjan Dev martyrdom - **Sikh**

New Church Day - **Swedenborgian Christian**

First Nations Day - **Canadian Native People**
Litha * - **Wicca** Northern Hemisphere
Yule * - **Wicca** Southern Hemisphere

All Saints - **Orthodox Christian**
Sacred Heart of Jesus - **Catholic Christian**

Feast Day of Saints Peter and Paul - **Christian**

JULY

Martyrdom of the Báb * - **Bahá'í**

St. Benedict Day - **Catholic Christian**

Ulambana - Obon ** - **Buddhist**

Asalha Puja Day - Dharma Day ** - **Buddhist**

Pioneer Day- **Mormon Christian**

St. James the Great Day - **Christian**

Lailat al Miraj * - **Islam**

AUGUST

Lammas - **Christian**
Fast in honor of Holy Mother of Lord Jesus - **Orthodox Christian**

Lughnassad * - **Wicca** Northern Hemisphere
Imbolc * - **Wicca** Southern Hemisphere

Transfiguration of Our Lord - **Orthodox Christian**

Interfaith Awareness Week -

Tisha B'Av * - **Jewish**

Assumption of Blessed Virgin Mary - **Catholic Christian**
Dormition of the Theotokos - **Orthodox Christian**

Raksha Bandhan ** - **Hindu**
Lailat al Bara'ah * - **Islam**

Assumption of the Virgin Mary - **Catholic Christian**

Krishna Janmashtami ** - **Hindu**

Beheading of John the Baptist - **Christian**
Lailat al Miraj * - **Islam**

SEPTEMBER

Church year begins - **Orthodox Christian**

Ramadan begins * - **Islam**

Ganesa Chaturthi ** - **Hindu**

Nativity of Mary - **Christian**

Holy Cross Day - **Christian**

Mabon * - **Wicca** Northern Hemisphere
Ostara * - **Wicca** Southern Hemisphere

Laylat al Kadar - **Islam**

Michael and All Angels - **Christian**

Rosh Hashanah * - **Jewish**

Navaratri ** - **Hindu**

OCTOBER

Eid al Fitr - Ramadan ends * - **Islam**

St Francis Day - **Catholic Chrisian**
Yom Kippur * - **Jewish**
Dasera ** - **Hindu**

Sukkot * - **Jewish**

Birth of the B'ab * - **Bahá'í**
Installation of Scriptures as Guru Granth - **Sikh**

Semini Atzeret * - **Jewish**

Simhat Torah * - **Jewish**

Reformation Day - **Protestant Christian**

Milvian Bridge Day - **Christian**
Diwali - Deepavali ** - **Hindu** - **Sikh** - **Jain**

All Hallows Eve - **Christian**
Reformation Day - **Protestant Christian**

NOVEMBER

All Saints' Day - **Christian**
Samhain * - **Wicca** Northern Hemisphere
Beltane * - **Wicca** Southern Hemisphere

All Souls' Day - **Christian**

Birth of Baha'u'llah * - **Bahá'í**

Birthday of Guru Nanak Dev Sahib - **Sikh**

Nativity Fast begins - **Orthodox Christian**

Christ the King - **Christian**

Guru Tegh Bahadur Martydrom - **Sikh**

Day of Covenant * - **Bahá'í**

Thanksgiving - **Interfaith USA**

Ascension of 'Abdu'l-Baha * - **Bahá'í**

First Sunday of Advent - **Christian**
St. Andrew's Day - **Christian**

DECEMBER

Bodhi Day (Rohatsu) ** - **Buddhism**
Immaculate Conception - **Catholic Christian**
Eid al Adha * - **Islam**

Feast day - Our Lady of Guadalupe - **Catholic Christian**
Advent Fast begins - **Orthodox Christian**

Posedas Novidenas - **Christian**

Yule * - **Wicca** Northern Hemisphere
Litha * - **Wicca** Southern Hemisphere
Yule - **Christian**

Hanukkah * - **Jewish**

Christmas * - **Christian**
Feast of the Nativity ** - **Orthodox Christian**

Zarathosht Diso (Death of Prophet Zarathushtra) - **Zoroastrian**

THE INTERFAITH MANUAL

Holy Innocents - **Christian**
Feast of the Holy Family - **Catholic Christian**

Muharram (first day of new year) * - **Islam**
Watch Night - **Christian**

Rev. Dr. Stephen L. Albert

*"We must all hang together,
or assuredly, we shall all hang separately."*
Benjamin Franklin

Part 2
Material for Interfaith Services
Interfaith Quotes

"Blessed and happy is he that ariseth to promote the best interests of the peoples and kindreds of the earth." *Bahá'u'lláh, Tablets of Bahá'u'lláh, p. 167*

"Cleanse ye your eyes, so that ye behold no man as different from yourselves. See ye no strangers; rather see all men as friends" *Abdul-Bahá, Selections from the Writings of 'Abdul-Bahá, p. 24*

"Love ye all religions and all races with a love that is true and sincere and show that love through deeds" *'Abdul-Bahá, Selections from the Writings of 'Abdul-Bahá, p. 69*

"Our inability to stand (accept) someone, results from our lack of cultivation. Having a wider heart and mind is more important than having a larger house. Happiness does not come from having much, but from being attached to little." *Venerable Cheng Yen*

"Your worst enemy cannot harm you as much as your own unguarded thoughts. Develop the mind of equilibrium. You will always be getting praise and blame, but do not let either affect the poise of the mind: follow the calmness, the absence of pride.
Sutta Nipata

"Conquer the angry man by love. Conquer the ill-natured man by goodness. Conquer the miser with generosity. Conquer the liar with truth. *The Dhammapada*

"We must feel toward our people as a father toward his children; yea, the most tender love of a mother must not surpass ours…" Richard Baxter

"If you can't feed a hundred people, then feed just one." Mother Teresa

"The Bible tells us to love our neighbors, and also to love our enemies: proBáb ly because they are generally the same people." G.K. Chesterton

"Forget injuries, never forget kindnesses." Confucius

"Men's natures are alike; it is their habits that carry them far apart." Confucius

"To be able under all circumstances to practice five things constitutes perfect virtue; these five things are gravity, generosity of soul, sincerity, earnestness and kindness." Confucius

"If you wish to experience peace, provide peace for another." The 14th Dalai Lama

"Compassion, forgiveness, these are the real, ultimate sources of power for peace and success in life." The 14th Dalai Lama

"I have come not to disturb or destroy any faith, but to confirm each in his own faith - so that the Christian becomes a better Christian, the Muslim, a better Muslim, and the Hindu, a better Hindu." Sri Sathya Sai Báb a

"It is lack of love for ourselves that inhibits our compassion toward others. If we make friends with ourselves, then there is no obstacle to opening our hearts and minds to others."
Karen Ravn

"A human being is part of a whole, called by us the Universe, a part limited in time and space. He experiences himself, his thoughts and feelings, as something separated from the rest a kind of optical delusion of his consciousness. This delusion is a kind of prison for us, restricting us to our personal desires and to affection for a few persons nearest us. Our task must be to free ourselves from this prison by widening our circles of compassion to embrace all living creatures and the whole of nature in its beauty."
Albert Einstein

"Without a love of humankind there is no love of God."
Asch, Sholem Novelist (1880-1957)

"Honor the sacred. Honor the Earth, our Mother. Honor the Elders. Honor all with whom we share the Earth:- Four-leggeds, two-leggeds, winged ones, Swimmers, crawlers, plant and rock people. Walk in balance and beauty."
Native American Elder

"When one sits in the Hoop Of The People, one must be responsible because all of Creation is related. And the hurt of one is the hurt of all. And the honor of one is the honor of all. And whatever we do affects everything in the universe."
White Buffalo Calf Woman

"When you were born, you cried and the world rejoiced. Live your life so that when you die, the world cries and you rejoice."
White Elk

Rev. Dr. Stephen L. Albert

"Every child born into the world is a new thought of God, an ever fresh and radiant possibility."
Kate Douglas Wiggins

If life is love, then all the physiological processes must be modified by our affection states. … The life of God is love. His love is an infinite desire to impart his own good to others (Evans 1869, 216).

"I awoke this morning with devout thanksgiving for my friends, the old and the new." Ralph Waldo Emerson

"Be not the slave of your own past. Plunge into the sublime seas, dive deep and swim far, so you shall come back with self-respect, with new power, with an advanced experience that shall explain and overlook the old."
Ralph Waldo Emerson

"You can have all the faith of God and take no faith from your neighbor, as you can have all the wisdom of God and take no wisdom from your neighbor. You can have all the riches of God and take no riches from your neighbor. There is always enough and to spare. The mere knowledge of this Principle will work out in your affairs in a new and different fashion. It is a knowledge that liberates a fine white light to sift itself through you and turn and overturn all your affairs, to give free way for a new set of affairs to settle themselves."
Emma Curtis Hopkins

"God is one, but he has innumerable forms. He is the creator of all and He himself takes the human form."
Guru Nanak

"A single God touch, from God's Compassion, can transform man's unimaginable and countless weaknesses into God's own infinite, Immortal and omnipotent Power." *Sri Chinmoy*
Peace we achieve when we do not expect anything from the world, but only give, give, and give unconditionally what we have and what we are.
Sri Chinmoy

"Get together, my brethren, and remove all misunderstandings through regard for each other." *Guru V, Basant Rag*

"The advantages of getting together, I cannot enumerate."
Guru I, Gujri Rag

"The rich and the poor are all brethren, this the Lord has ordained and none can gainsay it; Says Kabir, poor is he in whose heart, there is not the Name of the Lord."
(Kabirji, Bhairo Rag)

"Do not think about whatever service you may have done for others; think about what you may have done to offend them. Don't forget what others have done for you; forget what others have done to offend you."
Back to Beginnings, Reflections on the Tao by Huanchu Daoren

"Those who trust others will find that not everyone is necessarily sincere, but they will be sincere themselves. Those who suspect others will find that not everyone is necessarily deceiving them, but they have already become deceivers themselves.
Back to Beginnings, Reflections on the Tao by Huanchu Daoren

When your mind is empty of prejudices you can see the Tao. When your heart is empty of desires you can follow the Tao. *(From Master Lu Teachings)*

Rev. Dr. Stephen L. Albert

Don't be proud if you gain, nor be sorry when you lose. (Mahavira, Acaranga 2/4/114, 115)

"A living body is not merely an integration of limbs and flesh but it is the abode of the soul which potentially has infinite perception, infinite knowledge, infinite energy and power and infinite bliss."
Lord Mahavir

The Interfaith Manual

"Synergy is the highest activity of life; it creates new untapped alternatives; it values and exploits the mental, emotional, and psychological differences between people."
Stephen Covey

Miscellaneous Quotes

Taken from Culture of Peace.org
(cultureofpeace.org/quotes/interfaith-quotes)

Whenever a human being ceases to live for themselves and begins to care about that which is greater than themselves, the personality begins to experience ecstasy, joy and spontaneous liberation. And that's found through doing, through action, through giving, through deeply embracing the human experience. — **Andrew Cohen**

The problems we face today, violent conflicts, destruction of nature, poverty, hunger and so on, are human-created problems which can be resolved through human effort, understanding and the development of a sense of brotherhood and sisterhood. We need to cultivate a universal responsibility for one another and the planet we share.
— **The Dalai Lama**

What is faith if it is not translated into action? —
Mohandas Gandhi

Every breath we take, every step we make, can be filled with peace, joy, and serenity. We need only to be awake, alive in the present moment. — **Thich Nhat Hanh**

Rev. Dr. Stephen L. Albert

In the next 30 years we can destroy our world. With the very same powers — spiritual, social, scientific — we can evolve our world. Our mission is to serve as catalysts for a planetary awakening in our lifetime, to take a non-violent path to the next stage of our evolution. — **Barbara Marx Hubbard**

All things are bound together, all things connect. Whatever befalls the earth, befalls also the children of the earth." — **Chief Oren Lyons, Onandaga Nation**

"Be a sweet melody in the great orchestration, instead of a discordant note. The medicine this sick world needs is love. Hatred must be replaced by love, and fear by faith that love will prevail."- - **Peace Pilgrim**

Love is a fruit in season at all times and within the reach of every hand. Anyone may gather it and no limit is set. Everyone can reach this love through meditation, prayer, sacrifice, and an intense inner life. ~ **Mother Teresa**

We are not human beings having a spiritual experience; we are spiritual beings having a human experience. — **Pierre Teilhard De Chardin**

"My humanity is bound up in yours, for we can only be human together."
— **Desmond Tutu**

THE INTERFAITH MANUAL

"Slightly more than 2 in 10 (22.3%) congregations reported participating in an interfaith worship service in the past year (9/06). Nearly 4 in 10 (37.5%) congregations reported joining in interfaith community service activities."
Faith Communities Today 2005 (FACT2005)

Part 3
Interfaith Worship Lessons

"The key question isn't "What fosters creativity?" But it is why in God's name isn't everyone creative? Where was the human potential lost? How was it crippled? I think therefore a good question might be not why do people create? But why do people not create or innovate? We have got to abandon that sense of amazement in the face of creativity, as if it were a miracle if anybody created anything."
Abraham Maslow

On Creativity

When I began my schooling to be an architect in 1969, one of the first assignments given the students was to take a six-inch square piece of stiff cardboard and with ten ping pong balls and a number of three inch long wood dowels, make a sculpture on the cardboard. Of the fifty incoming freshmen that year only one student was commended for his sculpture. That student and his design taught the rest of us a powerful lesson because he had cantilevered his sculpture outside the boundaries of his six inch piece of cardboard. From that point on, creativity was judged by how far 'out of the box' you went while still maintaining structural integrity and obeying the rules.

Bahá'í - In the Bahá'í Writings, creativity is a continuous process, an on-going act of God, implying not only ongoing physical creativity but also the creation of new essences or ideas–in other words "the creation" is not a fixed environment within which we live but an ever-expanding world in both physical and intellectual senses. The creative process also implies ever-expanding *spiritual* capacities which is a fundamental idea within the Faith. (*Bahá'í Studies Review, Letters*, breacais.demon.co.uk)

Buddhism – Creativity is strongly linked to a receptiveness to life and what it has to offer us. It means being open to what is true about ourselves and about others. Creativity flourishes when the truth about things is admitted to oneself. For instance, it is always true that people are important. If I try to achieve my goals by neglecting the rights/feelings of others, I deceive myself, and my perception of reality is blurred. Since creativity depends on accurate information about one's environment, my lack of concern for others becomes a roadblock to creativity. It is believed that we cannot create adequately from the control and illusion of the mind. One must go beyond it, beyond its power, and just let the mind be free to express anything it wants. As soon as we try to create, i.e. "to do it," we start controlling. We have to learn to loosen control, to let the mind be. Instead of forcing anything, we let it come, or more appropriately, we give it a chance to come (although this does not work with everyone). (*What Can I Do To Increase My Creativity*, members.obtusenet.com)

Christianity – Many Christians believe man is wholly dependent upon God in human creativity because his creative ability, his very existence, and the pre-existing "raw materials" he uses all come to him from God. Therefore, man also "creates." However, God is Creator out of nothing ("ex nihilo"), while man can only "create" out of pre-existing things. Christians, as in all their work, exercise their literary or artistic creativity by "thinking God's thoughts after Him." (*Man's Creativity: Literature, Music, Fine Arts*, creationism.org)

Confucianism - According to Csikszentmihalyi (1988), creativity is a very complex interaction among a person, a field, and a culture. While people may vary in their native capacity for creativity, it is in the individual's interaction with the macrocosm where creative expression can be found. Confucius was perhaps the most individualistic of Chinese thinkers in this regard, as he accorded *li* much room for personal creativity, rebuking the ruler who merely copies his predecessor. (*Exploring the Interactions between Asian Culture (Confucianism) and Creativity*, The Journal of Creative Behavior, Kyung Hee Kim, Volume 41, Number 1 / First Quarter 2007)

Hinduism - One aspect of Hindu deities is they embody creativity, and Hinduism represents this quality by adorning statues &

pictures representing the gods in various ways. Goddess Saraswati (Sarasvati) is the wife (consort) of Lord Brahma and possesses the powers of speech, wisdom and learning. She is goddess of all the creative arts and in particular of poetry and music, learning and science. She is represented as a graceful woman with white skin, wearing a crescent moon on her brow; she rides a swan or peacock, or is seated on a lotus flower. In classical and medieval Hinduism, Saraswati is primarily a goddess of poetic inspiration and learning. She becomes associated with the creator god Brahma as his wife. In this role she is creative sound, which lends to reality a peculiar and distinctive human dimension. Her specific creative function in relation to the other saktis is to pervade reality with insight, knowledge, and learning. (*Hindu Gods*, mailerindia.com)

Islam –Islamic creativity has been directed to the pursuit of greater meaning rather than the creation of alternatives for greater control of the physical world around us. The Islamic world has not lacked philosophy or speculative creative thought in many instances of its evolution. It has lacked rationalist philosophers, simply because our philosophers have sought spiritual truth rather than material and preferred the metaphysical over the physical. This is again because of the recognition of man's mortality and belief in there being a greater reason for life than the apparent world around us. (*Why didn't the Scientific Revolution happen in Islam?* Tanoon Re: Saima Shah, chowk.com). Creativity in Islam is permitted as long as it does not change the basic beliefs or practices of Islam.

Jainism - Despite the huge amount of temple building that goes on among Jains in India today, there is very little in terms of quality creativity and imagination. At best, they try to replicate the old. Shanti has taken from the old and created something new, fresh and timeless at the same time. Genuine creativity cannot come out of insecurity but from inner security – we live in a world of insecurity and materialism, and that is why we are so starved of creativity (*Compassion and Creativity*, Dr. Atul K. Shah)

Judaism - In one of the greatest creative acts in history, Jews planted the seed of ethical monotheism, and from this fertile soil sprang both Christianity and Islam. In these kinds of situations, survival required adaptability, perseverance, and the capacity to see situations in new ways and to discover connections among seemingly disparate facts. All of these traits are at the heart of creativity, innovation, and for that matter survival itself. Jewish culture and the sacred writings of Judaism reflect and encourage these qualities. Throughout history, the relationship between man and God has been at the core of Jewish thinking and Jewish lifestyle. The way that Jews think about God and their relationship to Him is one that reflects the most basic principles of creativity. (*Creativity in Judaism*, Rabbi Philip Kranz and Jeffery Grossman, creativityinjudaism.com)

Native American – "Creative thinking styles emphasizing originality may be strengths aiding the teaching of Native American students." (Rhonda L Tannehill) No cultural or artistic expression is more central to Native American life than music and dance. Children are taught to respect the ways of their people through songs and dances. Indeed, Iroquois tradition maintains that children who can't dance well were born of mothers who didn't dance when they were pregnant. Perhaps no form of Native creativity is more enduring than music—the songs of the Aymara contain echoes of the beautiful Andean flute and ocarina music described by Spanish chroniclers, while the haunting synthesis of Baptist hymns and the Cherokee language captures one Native group's response to the challenge of contact with European culture. Nor is any art more diverse—Native American music encompasses social and ceremonial dances, oral histories and personal stories passed on in song, and traditional and Christian religious music. (*Creation's Journey*, Native American Music)

New Thought - In interpreting the creative process, New Thought draws on both the Western and Eastern philosophies and combines them into a complete way of life for its followers. God's creativity becomes the driving force to create the mental, emotional, physical and spiritual experiences available to the person. The Creative Essence of God is inherent in each individual. God, our Creator has given us the 'power of thought' to create our lives. "All Thought is creative, according to the impulse, emotion or conviction behind the thought." (*Science of Mind*, Holmes, p.94) All the beauty which is in God may be channeled through the individual and presented as an outer expression of good. Affirmations are often used to discover innate creative talents such as "Thank you, God, for Divine Ideas which I can understand and use to prosper me greatly and for a higher purpose." New Thought people encourage each others abilities knowing these are expressions of God, not to be repressed or depressed. (Rev. Abigail Albert)

Sikhism - Creativity is the core of Akal (The Timeless One Acting through Time, the Timeless One creates worlds and beings of the worlds. It is through creativity that the Timeless One transforms itself from a void to something, from the aphur state into saphur state, from the pre-creation sunn, or dormant essence, into cosmic existence. The creativity of Akal is not confined to the timeless and temporal aspects of the Supreme. From 'It' the Ultimate becomes 'God', the person with whom communication is sought and established. The Sikh greeting, *Sat Sri Akal,* sums up the concept that the timeless Being is the singular Eternal Reality. The phrase combines the concepts of Sat and Akal, implying that the Eternal and the Timeless are one; Sat, itself is the Everlasting Lord-beyond-Time. Thus, the creative essence turns the metaphysical Being into active principle of the world, into conscious Power involved in the cosmic process, into Hero or Master of the world, cherishing His creation with benign joy. Being the beneficent Lord, God lends some of God's creativity to the created beings. Humanity draws its creativity and creative energy from the Divine reservoir of creativity. (*Akal,* SikhiWiki Encyclopedia)

Taoism – Regarding creativity, Wu Zhen (1280-1354), a Taoist and one of the four most celebrated painters of the Yuan dynasty, described his experience in painting: "when I begin to paint, I do not know that I am painting; I entirely forget it is myself who holds the brush." Because of his freedom from the restrictions imposed by the medium and his intentional inattention to the particularities concerning the skills, he is able to identify himself with the object he is painting and reach a tacit agreement with it. His Taoist TK helps him move his brush at an unconscious level and concentrate on rendering the spirit of the image rather than portraying the form of it. (Tacit Knowledge in Taoism and Its Influence on Chinese Culture, Cheng Zhu, May, 2002)

The Interfaith Manual

*"In our every deliberation,
we must consider the impact of our decisions
on the next seven generations."*
From The Great Law of The Iroquois Confederacy

On The Environment

As a child, when we look around us we see endless expanse; the world looks so big and infinite in its vastness. As we grow and take trips away from home, we learn "around the globe" is only a few hours away. By traveling we gain an appreciation for the smallness of this planet and for the effect even our individual actions have on others. No matter what faith you choose to follow, the same rules about the universe and the environment holds true. Whether you believe gravity exists or not, you will fall when you jump off a cliff. The more pollutants we pump into our atmosphere, the less clean air we will have. We have a choice, to see our environment as a child or to take responsibility to find ways to reverse or minimize the damage.

Bahá'í – Bahá'ís recognize the world is undergoing rapid socio-economic transitions that make the protection of the environment and sustainable development both critical and challenging. Bahá'ís believe that only an integrated, balanced and comprehensive world view with a belief in a divine creator and unity of purpose will resolve environmental and development challenges. (bahai-library.com)

Buddhism - To live in harmony with nature is a crucial Buddhist practice. Buddhism exists to help us break out of the prison of isolated selfhood (centered on the self) and wake up to the true nature of reality, to help us become Enlightened. The Enlightened person is fully aware that everything in the universe is inter-connected, not just as an intellectual concept, but in every fiber of their being. Such a person will inevitably live in harmony with the world around them. They will no more willingly hurt another being or desecrate the environment, no matter how far away the damage takes place, than they will willingly hurt themselves. In a world of Enlightened beings there could be no environmental problem. (fwbo.org)

Christianity - Christians see themselves as stewards of the world which God created and believe it is their responsibility to care for it for future generations. They have to make their own decisions about how to do this. (asa3.org)

Confucianism - Confucian ethics in its most comprehensive form relies on a cosmological context of the entire triad of heaven, earth, and humans. Human actions complete this triad and are undertaken in relation to the natural world and its seasonal patterns and cosmic changes. In this context humans are biological-historical-ethical beings who live in a universe of complex correspondences and relationships. Cultivation of the land and of oneself are seen as analogous processes requiring attention, care, and constant vigilance. (*Confucianism and Ecology*: Potential and Limits by Mary Evelyn Tucker)

Hinduism - To Hindus, the concept of environment protection is not a modern phenomenon; they inherited it from their ancestors. During the earliest, formative period of their society, Hindus first perceived God's presence around them through nature. The natural forces that governed their daily lives were considered as manifestations of an almighty Creator they called the *Brahman* (not to be confused with the Brahmin caste). Ancient Hindus felt Brahman's presence in everything around them. Since these divine forces sustained all living creatures and organic things on this earth, to please God, they felt they must live in harmony with His creation including earth, rivers, forests, sun, air, and mountains. (boloji.com)

Islam - In the words of Allah, "There is not an animal on the earth, nor a creature flying on two wings, but they are nations like you." (6:38) Islamic cleric Mufty Imam Tajuddin H. Alhilaly, argues that all living things "are partners to man in existence and they deserve their own respect." "The earth is our first mother," says Imam Alhilaly. "Therefore, it has certain rights over us. One of these rights is making it come alive with green vegetation and other plant life. "The Prophet said he who is kind and merciful towards animals, Allah will be kind and merciful towards him.... We must deal with animals with utmost beneficence and compassion and strive to ensure the preservation of the different species," Imam Alhilaly instructs. "It is forbidden in Islam to kill an animal for mere play. Islam has forbidden wastage of animals and plants in peacetime and in wartime." (earthisland.org)

Jainism - Lord Mahāvir preached a universal truth for all times to come when he said, "One who neglects or disregards the existence of earth, air, fire, water and vegetation, disregards his own existence which is entwined with them." Not only did he preach on environmental and ecological issues, but his entire life was also an example of how to live in perfect harmony with the environment. The following ancient Jain aphorism is refreshingly contemporary in its promise and forms the basis of the modern-day science of ecology. "*Parasparopagraho Jivānām.*" All life is bound together by mutual support and interdependence. Environment is imbued (saturated) with living beings. Therefore if we harm "ONE," we harm "ALL" living beings. (*Jainism and Environment*, Pravin Shah, yjponline.org) The Jain faith advocates eating only what you need to survive, never killing anything for food and never wasting. Only fruits which have fallen from the tree may be eaten and the seeds may not be eaten because they may be planted and bring up more fruit. Rohak Vora from the Jain Society of San Diego says, "As much as possible, care about everyone and everything."

Judaism - "The framework for Judaism's teachings on the environment emerges from the dynamic tension between two verses at the beginning of Genesis. In Genesis 1:28, God blesses the newly created humans, "...Be fruitful and multiply and replenish the earth and subdue it; have dominion over...every living thing...." This apparent grant of absolute power was seized upon by Arnold Toynbee and some environmentalists as a basis for the extraordinary assertion that the Bible was at fault for human exploitation of nature. Toynbee and others, in their selective reading of the Bible, did not even bother to take note of its language just one chapter later. In Genesis 2:15, God takes the newly created human,"...and placed him in the garden of Eden, to cultivate it and to guard it." This verse imposes upon humans a stewardship relationship to the world in which they live." (Rabbi Saul Berman) Another point well made in this regard is that nature, the environment, does not take a sabbatical. We were given the world to cultivate and guard even on our Sabbath days. While man may rest on the Sabbath, animals do not; cows still need to be milked and all animals still need to be fed. A Jewish mother still feeds her family on the Sabbath even though it is considered her "day of rest." (Marilyn Clement)

Native American - The whole Native American Culture & Spirituality revolve around Mother Earth (Mother Nature) & the environment; they believe themselves to be "The Keepers of the Earth." An Ancient Indian Proverb states, "Treat the earth well. It was not given to you by your parents; it was lent to you by your children. We do not inherit the Earth from our Ancestors; we borrow it from our Children. (Evans Craig, Navajo)

New Thought - The teachings of New Thought regarding our environment, reflect back to the influence of Eastern philosophy. With the belief that "God is everything" and therefore "God is in everything," New Thought believers see each blade of grass as being holy as well as each person who comes before them. Followers of the faith allow their free will to dictate how much they want to get into the political and other areas of protecting the environment.

Sikhism - The Sikh scripture, Guru Granth Sahib, declares that the purpose of human beings is to achieve a blissful state and to be in harmony with the earth and all of God's creation. *"Air is the Guru, Water is the Father, and Earth is the Great Mother of all. Day and night are the two nurses, in whose lap all the world is at play. Good deeds and bad deeds-the record is read out in the Presence of the Lord of Dharma. According to their own actions, some are drawn closer, and some are driven farther away. Those who have meditated on the Naam, the Name of the Lord, and departed after having worked by the sweat of their brow - O Nanak, their faces are radiant in the Court of the Lord, and many others are saved along with them! (||2||"* SGGS page 146)

Taoism - Chinese Daoism rejects such ideas that humans have dominion over the earth and its other inhabitants (Richard and David, 1988). Nature in Daoism is something of great value in and for itself. In pursuing sustainable development and preserving environment, mankind must abandon the traditional development road that has overemphasized economic profit without considering the supporting capacity of the environment. As we attempt to satisfy the present generation, we should leave space for the development of future generations. Daoism considers that the orientation of life is to return to simplicity and go back to reality. One should live a simple, quiet and natural life. Daoism believes in a plain and simple lifestyle. It considers that one should not be selfish and have few desires, and one should live a life of plain tea and simple food. Daoism advocates frugality, thinking that contentment with what one has brings happiness, making one's mind peaceful with no troubles. (crvp.org/conf/Istanbul). Feng shui ("wind water") applies to the taming of any physical environment, home, work, ceremony, meditation cave and so on.

Rev. Dr. Stephen L. Albert

"When you hold resentment toward another,
you are bound to that person or condition
by an emotional link that is stronger than steel.
Forgiveness is the only way
to dissolve that link and get free."
Catherine Ponder

On Forgiveness

I was taught, and I believe forgiveness is one of the most valuable tools we have to remove the heavy weight of sorrow and pain which we might be carrying from a previous hurt. Similar to the ball and chain a prisoner's ankle is shackled to, when we hold on to a negative past event or a person who treated you wrongly, you become weighed down when trying to move forward with your life. True forgiveness, which includes honoring the person or event which caused you the pain, breaks the chain and sets you free. The visualization of seeing your directed love dissolving the chain or chains which are holding you back from experiencing a worthwhile, happy and abundant life, is one of the most freeing experiences a person can have. I pray you have many of them.

Bahá'í - In the Bahá'í Faith we are given more explicit divine instruction on living. 'Abdu'l-Bahá said, "There are imperfections in every human being, and you will always become unhappy if ye look toward the people themselves. But if ye look toward God, ye will love them and be kind to them, for the world of God is the world of perfection and complete mercy. Therefore, do not look at the shortcomings of anybody; see with the sight of forgiveness." (*The Promulgation of Universal Peace*, Wilmette: Bahá'í Publishing Trust, 1982. p. 92.)

Buddhism - Have forgiveness in your heart for anything you think you've done wrong. Forgive yourself for all the past omissions and commissions. They are long gone. Understand that you were a different person, and this one is more forgiving than one that you were. Feel that forgiveness filling you and enveloping you with a sense of warmth and ease. (geocities.com)

Christianity - All the prophets of God give us divine instruction on forgiveness. Jesus Christ taught his disciples the Lord's Prayer, wherein it says, "and forgive us our trespasses, as we forgive those who trespass against us." He commands us to return good for evil, so if a man is struck by another, and if he pardons and forgives him, if he acts in a manner contrary to that which has been used toward him, this response is praiseworthy. He has shown the greatest mercy and is worthy of admiration. (bahai.us)

Confucianism - Confucianism talks about "loyalty and forgiveness." Loyalty means being loyal in holding oneself to certain standards. "No matter what I do, I am loyal"— this is a basic criteria for developing one's character. Forgiveness means forgiving others. Be forgiving with other people's faults and be tolerant with other people's ideas. If you can be loyal to standards you set for yourself, your character becomes lofty; if you can forgive others, you will wish to help others rather than ask too much of them. Confucianism isn't separate from the mind. (thienlybuutoa.org)

Hinduism - First, we must learn to forgive ourselves, to accept ourselves as we are and proceed with confidence. New energy is released for a healthy future when we forgive ourselves. Yes, forgiveness is a powerful force. We must start with ourselves, for as long as we hold self-contempt, we are unable to forgive others, because everyone else is a reflection of ourselves. We react to what we see in them that we are not ready to face up to in ourselves. (hinduismtoday.com)

Islam - God in the Qur'an also gives Islamic people instruction on forgiveness. The Qur'an says, "He who forgiveth, and is reconciled unto his enemy, shall receive his reward from God; for he loveth not the unjust doers. (Sura 42)

Jainism - The Jain faith is relatively small in terms of numbers. Yet it has made a disproportionate contribution to the practice of forgiveness and peace. Of all major world faiths, it is perhaps the most consistent in rejecting all forms of violence and in promoting peaceful inter-personal relationships based on co-operation and forgiveness. Jains have this wonderful prayer in their hearts always asking for forgiveness for all living beings also seeking and receiving the forgiveness of all beings. Jainism may seem an abstract, unrealistic philosophy, but in fact it was a major source of inspiration for one of the great politicians of the twentieth century, Mohandas Gandhi. Gandhi was brought up as a Vaishnavite Hindu, but in a part of Gujarat where Jainism was strong. He liked to frequent Jain teachers and temples. In the 1890s he came to know one of the great Jain saints of modern India, Shrimad Rajchandra. Rajchandra settled many of Gandhi's spiritual doubts and was a significant personal inspiration for him: local people referred to Rajchandra as "Gandhi's Guru." So the ancient Jain ideals were transmitted to modern politics in India and beyond. (Forgiveness in Jainism, Alan Hunter, May 2003, corporate.coventry.ac.uk)

Judaism - Forgiveness is the lightening of our own hearts. The darkness of hatred, of rage and contempt which we harbor inside rarely injure the unforgiven as much as they do the one who will not forgive. We imagine our continued anger is so powerful it will bring sorrow and ruin on those against whom we hold a grudge. But its influence is far more dangerous for our own hearts. According to one rabbinic tradition, Rosh Hashannah and Yom Kippur (the Jewish New Year) celebrates the days of the creation of human beings and self-examination. That sixth day of creation, the same tradition goes on to teach, is the day on which Adam and Eve were placed in the garden, ate the fruit, were ejected from the garden, and were forgiven by God. (belief.net)

Native American - "We need a great healing, and we need a Great Forgiving. But healing cannot begin without forgiveness. We must forgive each other, Forgive our loved ones, Forgive our friends, Forgive our enemies, Forgive ourselves. We need to pray even for a person who has done wrong! In our Tiyospaye - our family, when two people fight they are made brothers or sisters. Forgiveness itself is a powerful medicine. We need forgiveness to create PEACE! (mail-archive.com)

New Thought - The benefits of forgiveness are: better health, cancer prevention, more energy, better relationships, more freedom, empowerment and spiritual growth. Collective benefits of forgiveness are it promotes open-hearted communication, transforms the energies of violence and abuse, and leads to the creation of world peace. As we eliminate the weight of un-forgiveness from our soul, we are freed up in all other areas of our life. (*Forgiveness and Health: An Unanswered Question,* Carl E. Thoresen Stanford) Doc Childre and Howard Martin of The HeartMath Solution says, "In the long run, it's not a question of whether they deserve to be forgiven. You're not forgiving them for their sake. You're doing it for yourself."

Sikhism - Forgiveness is viewed as the remedy to anger. You forgive an offender when aroused by compassion. Compassion generates peace, tranquility, humility and co-operation in human interactions. The act of forgiveness is considered a divine gift, not the work of a human agent. Otherwise, pride would increase when we take personal credit, which would impede our spiritual progress. Anger is often considered the result of unfulfilled desire. If a person fulfills our desires and wants, we feel love for them but when they impede our desires anger can well up. The ego can easily feel slighted, embarrassed, belittled or in some other way be offended. As we learn to discipline our mind through meditation on the Word, our ego and anger naturally turn to compassion and forgiveness. Since anger and forgiveness are considered opposites, the human mind can only contain one of them at a given time. Here are some verses from the Guru Granth Sahib, the Sikh scriptures, that capture the essence of forgiveness: "To practice forgiveness includes fasting, good conduct and contentment" (Guru Arjan Dev, page 223)

Taoism - On forgiveness, Taoists understand unforgiveness to be very toxic, and that alone is enough reason to forgive, but they also feel that true forgiveness comes with transcending the concept of self. If someone was wronged, then they must have a self to be injured. Also, from the point of view of ming/destiny/curriculum, if the challenge of our life is, for example, to experience war, then the circumstances and the people involved are only the instruments of that experience. (Michael Arnold, Taoist)

"When we are unable to forgive others, we carry negative feelings with us everywhere. That negativity becomes a burden to us and, after a while, it festers." "Yes, that is exactly what happens when one holds a grudge. So, how can we lighten the load?" "We must strive to forgive." (Taoism.net)

Rev. Dr. Stephen L. Albert

*"Gratitude unlocks the fullness of life.
It turns what we have into enough, and more."*
Melody Beattie

On Gratitude

Like forgiveness, gratitude is an amazing attribute. And to be grateful when there is no apparent reason for it makes life that much sweeter. Being grateful is linked with the faith that whatever we do and whatever we experience, it is all happening for our greatest good; this in turn causes us to realize our temporary lack or limitation is only a holding pattern for incredible good to come our way. By doing this we always are grateful to each event and each person who graces our life. Being grateful raises you high above hurt and anger and lowers you to a place of humility and peace.

Bahá'í - Baha'u'llah, founder of the Baha'i Faith said, "Were men to discover the motivating purpose of God's Revelation, they would assuredly cast away their fears, and, with hearts filled with gratitude, rejoice with exceeding gladness." (Bahá'u'lláh, *Gleanings from the Writings of Bahá'u'lláh*, Wilmette: US Bahá'í Publishing Trust, 1990 p. 175)

Buddhism - "Reverence, humility, contentment, gratitude and hearing the good Dharma, this is the best good luck." "Good men and bad men differ radically. Bad men never appreciate kindness shown them, but wise men appreciate and are grateful. Wise men try to express their appreciation and gratitude by some return of kindness, not only to their benefactor, but to each other." (Buddha)

Christianity – One of the core indications of being a Christian is being grateful to God regardless of any human action taken towards you... a combination of contentment and relational readiness with no desire to benefit yourself (Emmons, 2007).

Confucianism - "Act with kindness, but do not expect gratitude." (Confucius) Confucius invented a good model for the people, which he called junzi- a man of great moral quality or a gentleman, in the sense of a cultivated or a superior man. To be a junzi, one must first of all follow the principles of li and ren and then develop the following personalities: loyal to his ruler, loving his family, wise and brave, modest and humble, honest and sincere, kind and generous, having a heart of gratitude and a feeling of shame in doing something wrong. If all people were junzi and followed the principles of li and ren, society would be an ideal one. (*A Passage to China*, china-club.de)

Hinduism - Hindus believe life begins with an inbreath and ends with an outbreath. Appreciate your breath! Practice gratitude before you eat and sleep. Say "three things I am grateful for are..." every day. Practice expressing gratitude when you wake up in the morning. Say "thank you" for whatever inspires you in your life. Count your blessings daily. Every day, remind yourself of how lucky you are. Make a list of all the miracles in your life. To be able to see, feel, walk, talk, laugh, cry, eat, swim, go to the theatre, play with your children... The list will be endless. (*Your Personal Peace Formula*, Mansukh)

Islam - An Islamic saying goes, "Going against the call of whims and desires is patience, and responding to the call of Allah and the hereafter is gratitude." (Abdul Wali) In the Islamic story of Luqman, he tells his son, "Be grateful to God; this is the greatest wisdom."

Jainism – Jains believe a better form of prayer is a prayer of Gratitude and not Supplication. Here you visualize yourself enjoying what you deeply desire. If you want to be rich, you constantly imagine yourself riding the best cars, living in a luxurious bungalow, earning millions. You make that dream of richness a part of your conscious thought process even though you can't actually act that way at this moment. Then you thank God for making you rich, thank him for making richness a part of your reality, and the whole universe will conspire to make your subconscious reality your existential reality. (*From Supplication to Gratitude: A different Prayer*, Kamlesh Acharya, kamfucious.blogspot.com). Another Jain principle is to "Give until it hurts" meaning to sacrifice as much as you can for the happiness of others. Their goal is to purify their soul and be grateful for every minute and every person they meet. (Rohak Vora)

Judaism - No matter what, always affirm life. Live like the psalm writer who fervently declared: "This is the day the Lord has made. We will rejoice and be glad in it" (Psalm 118:24). Train your mind to count the blessings. Counting blessings, 100 times a day, builds faith, strengthens us emotionally, and produces contentment even in the most adverse of circumstances.

Native American - Every portion of a Native American's life is filled with gratitude. It is part of a Native American's belief that all he has is lent to him by Spirit, and at any moment it can change. All things are temporary and all things are permanent for the period of time it is part of one's life.

New Thought - "Gratitude unlocks the fullness of life. It turns what we have into enough, and more. It turns denial into acceptance, chaos to order, confusion to clarity. It can turn a meal into a feast, a house into a home, a stranger into a friend. Gratitude makes sense of our past, brings peace for today, and creates a vision for tomorrow." (Melody Beattie)

Sikhism – The belief in Sikhism is that it is important to be thankful for one's role and to have the opportunity to appreciate life. Also, being thankful with an attitude of gratitude is important.

Taoism - A lesson Lao Tzu often used is being modest and thankful, such as when he says, "The partial becomes complete; the crooked, straight; the empty, full; the worn out, new. He whose (desires) are few gets them; he whose (desires) are many goes astray. Therefore the sage holds in his embrace the one quality (of humility), and manifests it to the entire world. He is free from self-display, and therefore he shines; from self-assertion, and therefore he is distinguished; from self-boasting, and therefore his merit is acknowledged; from self-complacency, and therefore he acquires superiority. (wsu.edu)

> *"Love yourself—accept yourself—forgive yourself—and be good to yourself, because without you the rest of us are without a source of many wonderful things."*
> **Leo Buscaglia**

On Love

When God said to Abraham, "Be a blessing to the world," he opened the door of loving to compete with His own love for us. **WE** are the blessing! WE are the connection between whatever our belief is of a God and the person who is standing before us. God did not tell Abraham to go find a Priest or Rabbi or Minister and have that official bless the person. God said, "**BE** the blessing" and in this way all God's love can flow through each person and into everyone else. When this happens, we each receive the Love and accept the Love within ourselves and at the same time see that Love grow inside all others.

Bahá'í – The following is a brief but key example that sets the basic understanding the average Bahá'í has about love: "Know thou of a certainty that Love is the secret of God's holy Dispensation, the manifestation of the All-Merciful, the fountain of spiritual outpourings. Love is heaven's kindly light, the Holy Spirit's eternal breath that vivifieth the human soul. Love is the cause of God's revelation unto man, the vital bond inherent, in accordance with the divine creation, in the realities of things. Love is the one means that ensureth true felicity both in this world and the next. Love is the light that guideth in darkness, the living link that uniteth God with man, that assureth the progress of every illumined soul. Love is the most great law that ruleth this mighty and heavenly cycle, the unique power that bindeth together the divers elements of this material world, the supreme magnetic force that directeth the movements of the spheres in the celestial realms. Love revealeth with unfailing and limitless power the mysteries latent in the universe. Love is the spirit of life unto the adorned body of mankind, the establisher of true civilization in this mortal world, and the shedder of imperishable glory upon every high-aiming race and nation." (Abdu'l-Bahá, *Selections from the Writings of Abdu'l-Bahá*, p. 27)

Buddhism - Advesa and maitrī are benevolent love. This love is unconditional and requires considerable self-acceptance. This is quite different from the ordinary love, which is usually about attachment and sex, which rarely occur without self-interest. Instead, in Buddhism it refers to detachment and unselfish interest in others' welfare. (1000ventures.com)

Christianity - Christians believe that to love God and to love other people (God's creation, as they see it) are the two most important things in life. They are the first and greatest commandment of God, according to Jesus. In The Gospel of Mark, Jesus replied, 'Love the Lord your God with all your heart and strength and with all your soul and with all your mind.' This is the first and greatest commandment. And the second is like it: 'Love your neighbor as yourself.' All the Law and the Prophets hang on these two commandments" (Matthew 22:37-40 NIV).

Confucianism - Confucius himself had a simple moral and political teaching: to love others; to honor one's parents; to do what is right instead of what is of advantage; to practice "reciprocity," i.e. "don't do to others what you would not want yourself"; to rule by moral example instead of by force and violence. (friesian.com)

Hinduism - Bhakti is a Sanskrit term from Hinduism meaning loving devotion to the supreme God. A person who practices bhakti is called a bhakta. (mandalayoga.net)

Islam – Islam encourages Love for the sake of God. Muslims must love God and all God's creations. Muslims must not love God's creations more than God. (Imam Baseem Syed)

Jainism - Lord Mahavir, the twenty-fourth and the last Tirthankara, also preached the gospel of universal love, emphasizing that all living beings, irrespective of their size, shape, and form how spiritually developed or under-developed, are equal and we should love and respect them.

Judaism - The Torah states: "Love your neighbor like yourself" (Leviticus 19:18). As for the latter, one is commanded to love God "with all your heart, with all your soul and with all your might" (Deuteronomy 6:5).

Native American – All aspects of Native American life are characterized by love: love of nature, love of music (their cedar flute is called the "Love Flute"), love of all living things. Most of their songs are love songs, and today's concern about conservation and environmentalism is inspired by views which were first held holy by the Native American tribes.

New Thought - In New Thought it is taught that guidance and love surround us by the design of the Infinite which is all good and that God's Love is ALWAYS flowing in all, as all and is all. Love is the Highest Power. Jesus's Great Commandment is taught: "Love God with all your heart, mind and soul, and Love your neighbor as yourself." Like all major religions The Golden Rule is the most important. "Do unto others as you would have others do unto you." A Silver Rule was added recently. "Do unto others as they would like to be treated." This is very helpful when one meets people of different cultures and religions.

Sikhism - Sikhs believe in one true God, whose reality can be realized through two perspectives – intellect and love.

Taoism - Taoists would say that all things, the entire phenomenal world, all beings, arise from the Tao, so whatever we are looking upon, we are looking upon Dao, perfection. When our small thinking minds place judgment and reject, we have departed from Tao and lost touch with the fundamental Love of being. (Michael Arnold, Taoist)

Taoists believe the meaning of life is love and in Love, all is complete. The Tao itself does not judge, it does not condemn, it does not punish. Rather we ourselves, in our refusal to go along with its love and majestic flow, punish ourselves and cause ourselves all sorts of worries and problems. (*Taoism 101*, abodet.ao.com)

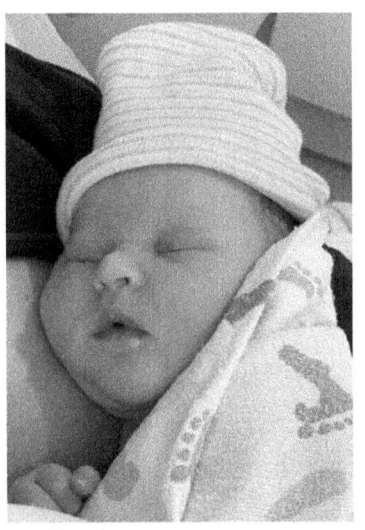

"I (Muaviyah b. Haidah) said, 'O Apostle of God! What is my duty to my wife?' He said, 'That you give her to eat as you eat yourself, and clothe her as you clothe yourself; and do not slap her in the face nor abuse her, nor separate yourself from her in displeasure."
Prophet Muhammad

ON MARRIAGE AND DIVORCE

With the divorce rate rising throughout the world among all of the faiths groups, there is no one source of advice to listen to when trying to learn the correct recipe with which to run a marriage. What is generally true though is, very few people go into a marriage *expecting* they will be divorced in the future. Having been a statistic of divorce myself, I make it my business to ask the advice of couples who have been married 40, 50 and 60 years or more, what seems to be their "secret." The best advice I have ever gotten came from a couple who were celebrating their 60th anniversary was, "No Secrets!"

Bahá'í - Bahá'ís believe marriage is a divine institution ordained by God and the foundation of a unified society. The key purpose of this union between a man and a woman — beyond physical, spiritual and intellectual companionship — is to procreate and rear children. Baha'u'llah called marriage **"a fortress for well-being and salvation."** Abdu'l-Baha said: "In a true Bahá'í marriage the two parties must become fully united both spiritually and physically, so they may attain eternal union throughout all the worlds of God and improve the spiritual life of each other." Bahá'ís believe marriage is a divine institution ordained by God and the foundation of a unified society. The key purpose of this union between a man and a woman - beyond physical, spiritual and intellectual companionship - is to procreate and rear children. Divorce is permitted but strongly discouraged. Bahá'í couples who seek a divorce must first observe a "year of patience" in which they live apart and attempt to resolve their problems. If they are unable to resolve their differences in that year, they are allowed to divorce. (bahai.us)

Buddhism - The Buddhist views on marriage are very liberal: in Buddhism, marriage is regarded entirely as a personal and individual concern, and not as a religious duty. There are no religious laws in Buddhism compelling a person to be married, to remain as a bachelor or to lead a life of total chastity. It is not laid down anywhere that Buddhists must produce children or regulate the number of children that they produce. Buddhism allows each individual the freedom to decide for himself all the issues pertaining to marriage. Separation or divorce is not prohibited in Buddhism though the necessity would scarcely arise if the Buddha's injunctions were strictly followed. Men and women must have the liberty to separate if they really cannot agree with each other. Separation is preferable to avoid a miserable family life for a long period of time. The Buddha further advises old men not to have young wives as the old and young are unlikely to be compatible, which can create undue problems, disharmony and downfall (Parabhava Sutta).

Christianity - In Christian law, marriage is a sacred institution. However, a variety of denominations have different approaches to divorce. The Church of England teaches that marriage is for life. It also recognizes that some marriages sadly do fail and, if this should happen, it seeks to be available for all involved. The Church of England accepts that, in exceptional circumstances, a divorced person may marry again in church during the lifetime of a former spouse.(*General Synod, 2002)* Most Protestant denominations allow a divorced person to marry again in their church although Orthodox Protestant and Roman Catholic churches do not allow/endorse divorce or remarriages.

Confucianism - Marriage is one of the five relationships of Confucianism. The master viewed the family as the undying structure of civilization. So, the harmonious partnership of husband/

wife is of utmost importance. Cheating on a spouse would be one of the greatest wrongs a person could ever commit. A man who is disloyal to his wife is unworthy of being called a man (and vice versa). However, divorce is NOT strictly forbidden. The master himself got a divorce in his early years. (historycooperative.org) Moreover, again though very difficult, women could initiate successful divorces as well. (Rev, Dr, John Berthrong)

Hinduism - Arranged marriages have been part of the Indian culture since the fourth century. "Marriage is treated as an alliance between two families rather than a union between two individuals" (Prakasa 15). Ninety-five percent of all current Indian marriages are arranged, either through child marriages or family / friend arrangement. Hindu civil codes permit divorce on certain grounds however the religion as such does not approve divorce. (english.emery.edu) In Bangladesh, Hindu marriages differ from caste to caste. Some Hindu marriage rituals have often no lawful ground. So, when Hindu women want to come out of bad marriages they are in trouble because there is no marriage registration system in the Hindu society in Bangladesh. It is surprising that there is also no Hindu marriage law or Hindu marriage register in the country. So, if any Hindu woman suffers in the hands of her in-laws, she does not get legal help. (*Bangladesh - Women in Marriage*, uninstraw.org)

Islam – For all men and women of Islam, it is recommended they should get married and each must honor the husband and wife relationship as Prophet Muhammad said. From the time of Prophet Mohammad, Muslim marriage became a civil contract in which a woman does not lose her individuality. Her personality is not merged into that of her husband. In this way a woman remains absolute owner of her property in any way she pleases without any extraneous control of her husband. After solemnization of marriage between parties, if some problems arise, the couple are encouraged to seek help in keeping the marriage together. If a woman asks for a divorce, she must seek a judge who will fairly decide on all matters including that the woman is financially taken care of. If a man asks his wife for a divorce, he pronounces "Talaq" meaning "I divorce you." This should begin a period of time in which the couple seek advice as to how to deal with their issues. After that period of time, if the man pronounces Talaq again, once again they should remain together doing all they can to save the marriage. Upon a third pronunciation of Talaq, the divorce is created. All efforts as provided in the Qur'an and Sunna should be made to avoid a breach of the marriage. (religioustolerance.org)

Jainism - In Jain wedding ceremonies, a grand public proclamation is made of the intention of the prospective bride and groom to live together for their entire life. Jainism advocates the peaceful co-existence and interaction of two different living organisms in mutual beneficence or mutual dependence. Life is regarded as a gift to be shared together, helping each other to exist and grow. Jains regard marriage as more or less a worldly affair mating two families together for life. Marriage and family raising are recommended for all the Jain Shravakas, because children born out of the wed lock would follow the Jain dharma only. The divorce in Jain society is very rare. Intercaste marriages within different Jain communities or other religious communities are not penalized; sometimes they are accepted and blessed by the community leaders. Widow marriages are permitted in some caste groups. Pre-marital relationships bring discredit to families and are discouraged. (Jainism: The World of Conquerors, Natubhai Shah, P.161)

Judaism - Marriage is highly revered and strongly encouraged in Judaism. Except in ascetic groups like the Essenes, the celibate life has never been considered more holy than the married life. In fact in Orthodox Judaism, one must be married in order to become a rabbi. Judaism's high view of marriage derives from its view of the home and family as the center of religious life. In Judaism, divorce is viewed as a great tragedy, but a sometimes necessary one. In the Torah, the prophet Malachi declared, "I hate divorce, says *Adonai*, the God of Israel." According to the Talmud, "When a man puts aside the wife of his youth, even the very altar weeps." Yet allowances for divorce have always been a part of Jewish law. To protect the woman, a man wanting a divorce had to put his request to her in writing with terms that protected her rights after the divorce. (religionfacts.com) The poetic line, "How goodly are your tents, O Jacob, your dwelling places, O Israel" which is sung when Jewish people enter the Synagogue, creates a parallel between tents and dwelling places, yet they are not exactly the same. The tents could be understood as the places where the individual, Jacob, lives, and the dwelling places, *mishk'notekha*, are the special places the people, Israel, dwell. Each tent also refers to each "family" as goodly. If we look closely at mishk'notekha we see that the Hebrew root *mishkan* (tabernacle) is at its core. The mishkan is the place where God dwelled while the Israelites wandered in the desert. Israel's dwelling places are not only those that the people inhabit, but they are God's dwelling place as well. So each family is being blessed by God. (*Sacred Spaces*, jewishjournal.com)

Native American - Native American courtship, wedding, and marriage customs and the possibility of divorce, differ from tribe to tribe. Marriage is considered sacred, and couples marry for the good of the family and tribe. Some tribes have a high divorce rate while others have almost none. This is due to the Matriarchal Tribe, since women own everything. Getting a divorce means the man turns over everything. Only a strong willed man divorces, knowing 'traditionally' he will turn over everything he owns to the woman's family.

New Thought – Marriage in New Thought is considered sacred and is the joining of two "whole" people to become a stronger "whole" for their spiritual growth. Their individual dedication to each other and to the newly formed family takes precedence over all other relationships. As a last resort in the case of not being able to work problems out, divorce is acceptable.

Sikhism - The Sikh marriage is not merely a physical and legal contract but is a holy union between two souls where physically they appear as two individual bodies but in fact are united as one. The Sikh marriage ceremony is also known as *Anand Karaj* meaning 'blissful union'. The Sikh marriage is monogamous. In the case of a broken marriage, divorce is not possible according to the Sikh religious tradition. The couple can, however, obtain a divorce under the Civil law of the land. (realsikhism.com)

Taoism - For Taoism, marriage is a public declaration of sharing as well as when a couple finds themselves wanting to follow the Way. As with Buddhism, the wedding rituals change for the individual but have the same general theme of sharing the invitation of the Way. Divorce is looked down upon only because the whole point for life is to seek balance and harmony, and poor marriage choices can derail this. (angelfire.com)

THE INTERFAITH MANUAL

*"Miracles are not contrary to nature,
but only contrary to what we know about nature."*
Saint Augustine *(354-430) Theologian.*

Rev. Dr. Stephen L. Albert

"The Prophet arrives
Veiled in the cloak of future thought,
'Mid people hid in ancient garb,
Who could not see the gift he brought.
He is a stranger to this life,
Stranger to those who praise or blame,
For he upholds the Torch of Truth,
Although devoured by the flame."
Khalil Gibran

ON MIRACLES

A miracle is an extraordinary event that cannot be explained logically, implying God's divine intervention and supernatural timing. The powers of nature, both great and small, are set in motion outside of man's control. Each faith has a different belief about this topic. My miracles occur every day. The fact that my body is no longer paralyzed as it was in 2003, the fact our home is standing while the one next door and across the street along with seven others on the block were destroyed in a fire, the fact that in 1999 my future wife came a few minutes late to the start of a spiritual conference and in a room of 1200+ people, could only find one vacant seat which happened to be next to me, these things and so much more all make me a believer and I am thankful.

Bahá'í - The Bahá'í writings describe the Messengers of God as Manifestations of God, persons who manifest divine attributes. In many of His Writings, Bahá'u'lláh elucidates the nature of the Manifestation and His relationship to God. He underlines the unique and transcendent nature of the Godhead. He explains that *"... since there can be no tie of direct intercourse to bind the one true God with His creation"*, God ordains that *"in every age and dispensation a pure and stainless Soul be made manifest in the kingdoms of earth and heaven."* (Bahá'u'lláh, *The Kitáb-i-Aqdas*: Notes 160, p. 233.) The purpose of the Manifestations of God is, thus, not to impress people with miracles that happen through them, but to educate them in divine virtues. However, most people forget the essentials and concentrate on that which is an outward sign of a deeper spiritual reality.

Buddhism – Buddhist texts frequently acknowledge the importance of the performance of miracles as a means to impress unbelievers of the greatness of the faith ... the Buddha subconscious. There are also numerous descriptions of Shamanism and related topics in the Native American, the Traditional Asian, Australian, Pacific, and African sections. (Internet Sacred Text Archive, sacred-text.com) Over tens of thousands of years, their ancient ancestors all over the world discovered how to maximize human abilities of mind and spirit for healing and problem-solving. The remarkable system of methods they developed is today known as "shamanism," a term that comes from a Siberian tribal word for its practitioners: "shaman" (pronounced SHAH-mahn). Shamans are a type of medicine man or woman especially distinguished by the use of journeys to hidden worlds otherwise mainly known through myth, dream, and near-death experiences. (The Foundation for Shamanic Studies, shamanism.org)

Christianity – The Christian Bible and the acts of Jesus tell the many stories of miracles performed by God working through Jesus. Jesus said, "It is not I but the Father within who does the work." This said, Christianity accepts the Divinity of Jesus and what has been written in the Bible. Christianity makes the claim that the events described in its adopted canon are verifiable (at least in principle), historical events. Christianity's validity thus rests in part upon the idea that these events happened in real time to real people.

Confucianism - The arguments for Confucius' *Anallects* do not rely on the actual occurrence of some historical event or miracle. Instead, each of those religions/philosophical systems appeals to what the reader/listener can confirm from their present, personal observations of the world and intelligent reflection on those observations. In the lives of Confucius and Lao-Tzu, there are no serious miracle claims. (*The Case for the Resurrection of Jesus*, Gary Habermas, 2004)

Hinduism - Bhagwan Mahavira stated he does not have the power to put life into someone ... neither it is possible for any other human being to do so. Neither could he perform even a single miracle. He repeatedly emphasized that every human being has the power within to invoke the positive energy of the cosmos. This event happens only when we develop a positive attitude towards life. (in. answers.yahoo.com)

Islam - "The following miracles were demanded of Mohammed by Qureish as proofs of his mission," (Sale. p. 281) whereupon this passage is said to have been revealed:- "And they say, We will by no means believe on thee, until thou cause a spring of water to gush forth for us out of the earth; or thou hast a garden of palm trees and vines, and thou cause rivers to spring forth from midst thereof in abundance; or thou cause the heaven to fall down upon us, as thou hast given out, in pieces; or thou bring down God and the angels to vouch (for thee); or thou hast a house of gold; or thou ascend by a ladder to heaven: neither will we believe thy ascending (thither alone); until thou cause a book to descend unto us, (bearing witness of thee), which we may read. Answer, My Lord be praised! Am I (other) than a man, sent (as an apostle)?" (XVII. p. 281). Mohammed insisted that the Qur'an was his only miracle. (*The Illustrated World's Religions,* Huston Smith, 1995)

Jainism - Jindattsuri was born in 1075 C.E. and was, above all, a great worker of miracles, as were all the Dadagurus. It is extremely important to emphasize that the hagiographies insist that these miracles always had a higher purpose than merely solving someone's worldly problems. From the standpoint of Jainism's highest ideals, ascetics are not supposed to be magicians. In the case of Chagansagar, the hagiographers must therefore legitimize this power by establishing a Jain context for it. One legitimizing strategy is to accentuate the point that the miraculous power is associated with its possessor's asceticism. Another strategy is to stress that the purpose of the miracles was always to glorify Jain teachings or to help Jainism flourish. The miracle-working ascetic protects Jain laity, defeats Jainism's enemies, and often aids non-Jains, who may become Jains as a result. (Magical Monks a Ritual, Scholarship Edition, content.cdlib.org)

Judaism - Israel's first Prime Minister, David Ben Gurion, once said that one who doesn't believe in miracles isn't a realist! The parting of the Reed Sea, (not Red Sea) which allowed the Israelites to escape their Egyptian pursuers, is a good example. After Nacsham took action and put his foot in the water (the first Israelite to do so), the sea divided. Someone had to take action first, IN FAITH, before the miracle could occur. Not only did the children of Israel cross safely over dry land, but the Lord also caused the waters to return, drowning the Egyptians. A miracle to one may prove to be a misfortune to another. Judaism accepts the biblical account of creation as evidence that even today, nothing is impossible for God. They believe the Burning Bush was a miracle, Isaac's birth to a mother who was in her nineties, and the fact that a small band of men won over the entire Syrian army to save the Temple where one days' worth of oil lasted eight days which is now celebrated as Chanukah. It is important to note that miracles rarely lead to true repentance, though they certainly get one's attention. Jesus of Nazareth saw this with the many miracles He performed. "Blessed be the Lord, the God of Israel, Who alone does wondrous things" (Psalm 72:18)

Native American – Native Americans believe everything which happens in life, including miracles, happens because it was supposed to be. They cherish the land, the sky and all which is on the earth and see a miracle in everything they encounter. Not to see miracles in everything would mean you are not completely thankful and accepting of all the gifts the universe has for you.

New Thought – New Thought followers believe experiencing miracles is the natural way of life and miracles happen when you believe they can happen. You attract miraculous things to you when you accept that you deserve those things and when your intent in any thought is for the good of all. It is then that the universe will respond in kind to those mental beliefs and others will call it "a miracle."

Sikhism - The Sikhs believe that every event in life is a miracle. They simply recognize that each sun rise, each birth of a child, each encounter we have with another person, is part of the miracle of life.

Taoism – Miracles are taken for granted throughout Taoism. Lao Tsu taught that all straining, all striving are not only vain but counterproductive. One should endeavor to do nothing (wu-wei) which is sometimes called the effortless effort. But what does this mean? It means not to literally do nothing, but to discern and follow the natural forces of nature, which includes the creation of miracles, to follow and shape the flow of events and not to pit oneself against the natural order of things. (*Father of Taoism*, chebucto.ns.ca) Taoists believe in the divinity, specialness and deep down holiness of each individual, including themselves. Everything is a miracle; it is all the Tao.

Rev. Dr. Stephen L. Albert

*"Just as in earthly life lovers long for the moment
when they are able to breathe forth their love for each other,
to let their souls blend in a soft whisper, so
the mystic longs for the moment
when in prayer he can, as it were, creep into God."*
Soren Kierkegaard

*" I am not a philosopher who is trying
to make a system of thought.
I am a mystic who is trying to convey the mysteries
that have become available to me. I will confuse you. "*
Bhagwan Shree Rajneesh

*"All that God asks you most pressingly is to go out of yourself
and let God be God in you'?
One could think that, in separating himself from creatures
the mystic leaves his brothers, humanity, behind.
On the contrary,
the mystic is marvelously present to them on the only level
where he can truly reach them, that is in God."*
Meister Eckhart

On Mysticism

If I were asked whether there was one area of this Interfaith manual which I most enjoyed, it would have to be this section on the Mysticism of Interfaith. This is due to my life experiences and my overall belief in, 'there is more if only we would choose to look deeper.' That deeper search is something I have felt driven to make in every area of my life. If the general definition of "a Mystic" is, someone who believes in the existence of realities beyond human comprehension, I feel certain my 'what if' mind would fall into the mystical range. Having said that, I also know I have only skimmed the surface of what true mystics understand in their quest to know and understand God better.

All cultures seem to have their own superstitions and mystical beliefs. They put the individual in touch with the spiritual side of their being. The term "mysticism" comes from the classical Greco-Roman mystery cults. Perhaps it came from *myein* meaning "to close the lips and eyes, and refers to the sacred oath of the initiates, the *mystes*, to keep secret about the inner workings of the religion." (themystica.com) Perhaps the most significant aspect of being a Mystic, which anyone of any faith faces, is the total elimination of the ego and of wanting material possessions. I am not there yet. Truthfully, I will most probably not be there during this life incarnation. That however, does not stop me from exploring the mystical side of all the faiths and, once again, recognizing the great similarities of the faiths and their relationship with God when looked at from an even deeper level through meditation and prayer.

Bahá'í - Most people have a fairly good idea of what it means to be religious. Most people probably also have a fair idea of what it means to be spiritual, although that concept can be a bit more (difficult to define). But what does it mean to be mystical? Mysticism deals in mystery. It treads the paths of the unknown and the unknowable. The very word conjures up images of haggard, unwashed hermits eating lichen in the wilds of the Himalayas while reciting incomprehensible Zen koans (parables).

Besides, quite a few people who call themselves mystics seem prone to speaking in flowery phrases that often make no sense to anyone else. So while religion may seem to be concrete and inflexible, and spirituality may seem to be less concrete but still comprehensible and even liberating, mysticism is often seen as confusing at best and an irrelevant flight of fancy at worst. But in reality, all three of these concepts are intimately related. Spirituality consists in developing the qualities of the human spirit, such as love, compassion, honesty, justice, and the like. That person is truly spiritual who displays these spiritual qualities. Religion consists (in one sense) of a set of teachings and practices that, when followed conscientiously, assists us to become spiritual. Any religion that does not serve the cause of spiritual development is worse than useless. Mysticism lies at the very heart of both religion and spirituality. Shoghi Effendi put it this way:

"For the core of religious faith is that mystical feeling which unites man with God. This state of spiritual communion can be brought about and maintained by means of meditation and prayer. And this is the reason why Bahá'u'lláh has so much stressed the importance of worship. It is not sufficient for a believer merely to accept and observe the teachings. He should, in addition, cultivate the sense of spirituality which he can acquire chiefly be means of prayer." (*Lights of Guidance*, p. 506) (The Mystery of Mysticism, planetbahai.org)

Buddhism - One of the central points of Zen Buddhism is *intuitive* understanding. As a result, words and sentences have no fixed meaning, and logic is often irrelevant. Words have meaning only in relation to who is using them, who they are talking to, and what situation they are used in. Zen and poetry have gone hand in hand for centuries. (ibiblio.org/zen) The way to gain self-knowledge is through meditation which is what the word "**zen**" means. The practice of Dzogchen, or 'Great Perfection', is the most ancient and direct stream of wisdom within the Buddhist tradition of Tibet. It is considered the very pinnacle of all teachings, and the most immediate path towards enlightenment. As a way in which to realize the innermost nature of mind, Dzogchen is the clearest, most effective, and most relevant to the modern world. A path at once simple and profound, it can be integrated with ordinary life and practiced anywhere. The origins of Dzogchen are traced to the primordial Buddha, Samantabhadra, from whom this remarkable heritage of wisdom has been transmitted from master to student in an unbroken lineage down to the present day. Sogyal Rinpoche, having been given the complete transmission and guided every step of the way, has been authorized by his masters as an authentic holder of these unique and precious teachings of Dzogchen. "Dzogchen is the primordial state, that state of total awakening that is the heart essence of all the Buddhas and all spiritual paths, and the summit of an individual's spiritual evolution. It is the final, ultimate and heart of the teaching of all the Buddhas, and brings precise experiences of the awakened state." (What is Dzogchen? Sogyal Rinpoche, rigpa.org)

Christianity - Gnosticism is the teaching based on Gnosis (the Greek word for knowledge), the knowledge of transcendence arrived at by way of interior, intuitive means. (They de-value the material world for inner knowledge thereby separating Spirit and matter.) Although Gnosticism thus rests on personal religious experience, it is a mistake to assume all such experience results in Gnostic recognitions. It is nearer the truth to say that Gnosticism expresses a specific religious experience, an experience that does not lend itself to the language of theology or philosophy, but which is instead closely [aligned] to, and expresses itself through, the medium of myth. Indeed, one finds that most Gnostic scriptures take the forms of myths. The term "myth" should not here be taken to mean "stories that are not true," but rather, that the truths embodied in these myths are of a different order from the dogmas of theology or the statements of philosophy. Gnosticism begins with the fundamental recognition that earthly life is filled with suffering. In order to nourish themselves, all forms of life consume each other, thereby visiting pain, fear, and death upon one another (even herbivorous animals live by destroying the life of plants). In addition, so-called natural catastrophes: earthquakes, floods, fires, drought, volcanic eruptions, bring further suffering and death in their wake. Human beings, with their complex physiology and psychology, are aware not only of these painful features of earthly existence, they also suffer from the frequent recognition that they are strangers living in a world that is flawed and absurd. (The Gnostic World View: A Brief Summary of Gnosticism, webcom.com)

Mysticism simply means the spirituality of the direct experience of God. It is the adventure of "the wild things of God." The direct experience of God is a kind of knowing, which goes beyond intellectual understanding. It is not just a matter of "belief." It is marked by love and joy, but it is not "emotional experience." In many ways, it is better described by what it is not. To describe what it is, we must use metaphors such as the marriage of the soul to Christ, the death of the "old man" and birth of the "new man," being the "body of Christ." Jesus proclaimed "I and the Father are one," (Jn. 10.30) showing the world what the union of God and man can be. Christian mysticism is about nothing else but this transforming union. Christ is the sole end of Christian mysticism. Whereas all Christians have Christ, call on Christ, and can (or should) know Christ, the goal for the Christian mystic is to become fully Christ-like, to become as fully permeated with God as Christ is, thus becoming like him, fully human, and by the grace of God, also fully divine. (It is having the Divinity speaking and expressing through us.) In Christian teaching this doctrine is known by various names—theosis, divinization, deification, and transforming union. (What is Christian Mysticism? frimin.com)

Confucianism - Confucian mysticism, especially in its second great phase, Neo-Confucianism, leans more and more in the direction of pantheism (the view that everything is of an all-encompassing immanent abstract God; or that the Universe or nature and God are equivalent). This teaching is borne out by the later philosopher, Chang Tsai (1020-77). It is here that Confucian religion and mysticism show the imprint of Taoist-and Buddhist- influences. Yet Chang Tsai still shows a profoundly Confucian bent to his mystical vision of the unity of the world, by expressing this as one of a perfected family. In this vision, the entire world becomes related to him as his own family. The note of inter-subjective concern sounded by Confucius and Mencius is reaffirmed. (Sages and Immortals, Chinese Religions, Rev. Dr. John Berthrong)

Hinduism - The Indian mystical philosophies and religions are concerned not so much with the manifest reality we see about us, but with the un-manifest Absolute Transcendent. What matters is simply the practical attainment of a state of this universal, transcendent, transpersonal existence. In that state, there is no difference between individual Self (Jiva) and God (Ishwara); there is only the quality-less Absolute (*Nirguna Brahman*). In short, they are not a mental or analytical philosophy as we understand the term in the West, but rather a conceptual system for guiding yogic practice, with the goal being the complete transcendence of embodied existence. Perhaps the most important school of Indian spiritual philosophy is Advaita Vedanta which originates from the writings of Gaudapada and Sankaracharya, who in turn were commentators on earlier scriptures such as the *Brahma Sutra*, the Bhagavad Gita, and the Upanishads. As with all Indian systems of thought, Advaita Vedanta is at the same time a school of philosophy, a religion, a theology and a doctrine of salvation. Its basic premise is all that ultimately exists is the Absolute Reality, *Nirguna Brahman* ("Brahman without qualities"). The phenomenal world has empirical validity; but it has no absolute reality. It is ultimately *maya,* a magical show, and *mithya,* false (neither real nor unreal). All that exists is nothing but Brahman. One's individual self is ultimately no different from Brahman, hence the importance given to the Upanishadic sayings "I am Brahman" and "that thou art." It is only a sort of metaphysical ignorance (*avidya*) that prevents us from realizing our true nature as one with the Absolute, as in fact The Absolute Itself. Once avidya is removed there arises the experience of the Atman's identity with Brahman. One becomes *jivanmukti,* liberated while in the body, and after death attains Moksha (being fully liberated), identity with the Absolute. (kheper.net)

Islam - Sufism is Islamic Mysticism. As such, it has the special distinction of being found in the Sunnite as well as the Shiite traditions of Islam. It is extremely difficult to attempt a description of Sufism. Like all forms of mysticism, it is, above all, the search for God and this search may be expressed in many different ways, taking various forms. On the other hand, by reason of its esoteric aspects, it introduces secret practices, initiation rites that vary depending on the masters who teach them. The most original aspect of Sufism is its spirituality. In the Sufi view, God is approached by degrees. Firstly, the law of the Koran must be respected; but this is only a first step which does not lead to the understanding of the nature of the world. The rituals are of no use if one doesn't know their hidden meaning. It is only through an initiation that one is enabled to see behind the appearance of things. For example, Man is a microcosm, a world in miniature, in which the image of the universe is to be found, the macrocosm. So it is quite natural that in deepening one's knowledge of man one should arrive at an understanding of the world which is already a step towards God. According to the Sufis, all existence comes from God and God alone is real. The created world is but a reflection of the Divine; "The universe is the Shadow of the Absolute." The ability to discern God behind the screen of things implies purity of soul. It is only through an effort to withdraw from the world that one can approach God. The God that the Sufis discover is a God of love and the way to him is through Love: "whoever knows God, loves him; whoever knows the world turns away from him." "If you wish to be free, become a prisoner of Love." (What is Sufism? 1000 questions.net)

Jainism - "In Jainism fourteen stages are indicated through which the soul progresses from impurifying matter on to final liberation. The psychical condition of the soul due to the rising (Udaya), settling down and partly perishing of Karma matter (Kshyopasham) is called "Gunasthan." However, there is more depth and meaning involved in this subject which has been called occult Jainism or Jain Mysticism. Just as Mysticism elsewhere e.g. Sufism involves the union of the being with God, in Jainism the Gunasthans describe the path, modalities and pre-requisites for the bonded soul-Bahiratama to become liberated soul or Paramatma through the path of internal progress or by becoming Antaratma. The process begins with the soul which is at the lowest stage from times immemorial circulating in the whirlpool of births and deaths due to lack of true knowledge and true conduct. Since there is a divine spark in every soul (without which it will not be a living being), it is struggling to find its true identity and the potential of becoming liberated. Thus a constant struggle is going on between forces of darkness of unbelief (mithyatva) which try to keep the soul tied down to the Sansar (worldly existence) on the one hand, and forces of light or true belief (Samyaktva) which try for its liberation on the other. In the long run there comes a chance when by reducing its Karma load, the forces of light (Samyaktva) prevail and the soul is able to break the shackles of Mithyatva (Unbelief), just like a piece of straw or paper is able to escape out of a whirlpool. This is like cutting the Gordian knot and is also called *Granthi bhed* in Jain terminology. Once this happens, the soul is set on the road of rising Gunasthans. In other words the pilgrim has found his path and the Pilgrim's Progress has begun which may ultimately lead to the liberation of the soul though it may take many millenniums. During this progress through different Gunasthans the soul has to encounter ups and downs and also very unusual and unprecedented experiences known as *Sreni*. (jainworld.com)

Judaism - The Hasidic movement started in the 1700's (CE) in Eastern Europe in response to a void felt by many average observant Jews of the day. The founder of Hasidism, Rabbi Israel Baal Shem Tov (referred to as the "Besht," an acronym of his name) was a great scholar and mystic, devoted to both the revealed, outer aspect, and hidden, inner aspect of Torah. He and his followers, without veering from a commitment to Torah, created a way of Jewish life that emphasized the ability of all Jews to grow closer to God via everything they do, say, and think. In contrast to the somewhat intellectual style of the mainstream Jewish leaders of his day and their emphasis on the primacy of Torah study, the Besht emphasized a constant focus on attachment to God and Torah no matter what one is involved with.

Early on, a schism developed between the Hasidic and non-Hasidic (i.e., *Misnagdim*, lit. "opponents") Jewish movements, primarily over real or imagined issues of halachic observance. The opposition was based on the concern that the Hasidim were neglecting the laws regarding appropriate times for prayer, and perhaps concern about the exuberance of Hasidic worship, or a concern that it might be an offshoot of false messiahs Shabbtai Zvi or Jacob Frank. Within a generation or two, the rift was closed. Since then, many Hasidic practices have influenced the Misnagdim, while the Misnagdim, in turn, moderated some of the extremes of early Hasidism. Nevertheless, the dispute between particular groups of Hasidim and Misnagdim continues to this day, especially in Israel. Today, Hasidim are differentiated from other Orthodox Jews by their devotion to a dynastic leader (referred to as a "Rebbe"), their wearing of distinctive clothing and a greater than average study of the inner aspects of Torah. (Hasidism, jewishvirtual libray.com)

"While Hasidism flourished in Eastern Europe, different forms took root in the oriental Jewish Communities, Yemen, Syria and the Mediterranean countries of north-west Africa. Here there were no significant sects or large-scale movements, but mysticism became an important part of most communities. The Hebrew word Kabbalah simply means "to receive" or "tradition." "It is a body of esoteric literature which emerged in medieval Spain and France and looked deeply into biblical texts to discover secrets of how to harness divine energy and establish direct contact with God." Many Rabbis and Jewish scholars looked beyond the mainstream Jewish religious teachings which were based out of the Talmud and sought ideas which were *nistar* (hidden) referring to the 'hidden aspect of God.' These were the hidden teachings, believed to be handed down to the Jewish people orally by Moses when he received the Ten Commandments from God and then it was orally translated from one generation to the next. Rabbi Shimon Ben Yochai, who wrote the *Zohar* (brightness) in the 13th century, which is a central work of the Kabbalah, became the undisputed person of Judaic Mysticism. The more the Jewish people were persecuted by neighboring forces, the more they began to reassure themselves of their heritage by studying Kabbalistic thinking and philosophy so as to live a fuller and more spiritual life. (Kabalah Inspirations, Jeremy Rosen, Duncan Baird Publishers) In Kabbalah, every letter of every word has meaning which the individual can link back to God. All life forms from plants to animals have the essence of God and therefore should be respected as God. Kabbalists believe through deep meditation and life-long study, a person can learn to know God more closely and enjoy a more fulfilled life.

Native American - Shamanism and Animism are traditional belief systems which consider the entire universe to be alive and interconnected. Shamanism in practice is used to heal and enlighten, using ceremonials which can include rhythmic music, mind altering drugs and mythic journeys into the subconscious. There are also numerous descriptions of Shamanism and related topics in the Native American, the Traditional Asian, Australian, Pacific, and African sections. (Internet Sacred Text Archive, sacredtext.com)

Over tens of thousands of years, their ancient ancestors all over the world discovered how to maximize human abilities of mind and spirit for healing and problem-solving. The remarkable system of methods they developed is today known as "shamanism," a term that comes from a Siberian tribal word for its practitioners: "shaman" (pronounced SHAH-mahn). Shamans are a type of medicine man or woman especially distinguished by the use of journeys to hidden worlds otherwise mainly known through myth, dream, and near-death experiences. (The Foundation for Shamanic Studies, shamanism.org)

New Thought - The goal of mysticism in New Thought is union with the divine or sacred. We all know that when we experience Love within us, we are somehow more grounded, more at peace with who we know ourselves to be, more at ease in the world, less ruffled by that which we may not understand. Though we may find it all very difficult to discuss why this is so, we intuitively know that there is something not visible and we wish to gain access to its secrets, if only out of curiosity. (emersononlinestudies.org) "The knower and the known are one. God and I, we are one in knowledge" and "There is no distinction between us." (Meister Eckhart) "The secret of spiritual power is a consciousness of one's union with the whole and the availability of good. We are one with a universal creativeness which is the God of theology, the Spirit of mysticism, the Reality of philosophy, and the Principle of science. God is accessible to all people." (Ernest Holmes, Can We Talk to God?) Emma Curtis Hopkins wrote *High Mysticism and Scientific Christian Mental Practice* and founded the Emma Hopkins College of Metaphysical Science. Mrs. Hopkins was herself a Mystic, a Mystic of a new type. She sang the song of the Life triumphant over loss, pain, sickness, poverty, sin and death, and the joy that comes from living the Christ Life. "The Mystical Science is the oldest Science in the world. It concerns that swift, subtle faculty possessed by us all, whereby we look whithersoever we will; to the Deity ever beholding us, or to the dust beneath, without the aid of our physical eyes."

Sikh - As opposed to religion, that which binds one to a set of beliefs, Mysticism is boundless; it is the direct experience of "religious" truth. Mysticism is nearly universal and unites most religions in the quest for divinity. (sikh-mysticism.com) Sikh Mysticism aims at the complete denial of self and the vehicle of God's Will. Sikh Mysticism focuses more on what Sikhs themselves call *'gurmat'* (lit. the central teachings or religious philosophy of Nanak who is both the founder of Sikhism and the epithet adopted by the nine spiritual masters who succeeded him). Expressions of Sikh mysticism as found in the writings of the Sikh Gurus shows how Sikh mystics, far from dwelling on theological issues, draw attention to the way in which we construct ourselves and notions of reality. "Unless you can see Christ in me, you are failing as a Christian. Unless I see Guru in you I am failing as a Sikh. Jesus says that as you have treated the least of people, so you have treated me (Matthew 25:40). Guru Gobind Singh asked the disciple Bhai Kannaya why he was providing water to the enemy troops in a battle. He answered that he could only see the Guru's Face. The Guru then asked him to apply ointment as well as provide water!" (*Gurmat and Jesus*, Dr. Kanwar Ranvir Singh, sikhwomen.com)

Taoist - The goal of Nei-Yeh, which is a collection of poetic verses on the nature of the way (Tao), means inward training to achieve tranquility and harmony by bringing oneself into a direct apprehension of this all-pervading cosmic force. Taoism is interested in intuitive wisdom, rather than in rational knowledge. Acknowledging the limitations and the relativity of the world of rational thinking, Taoism is, basically, a way of liberation from this world and is, in this respect, comparable to the ways of Yoga or Vedanta in Hinduism, or to the Eightfold Path of the Buddha. In the context of Chinese culture, the Taoist liberation meant, more specifically, liberation from the strict rules of convention. Mistrust of conventional knowledge and reasoning is stronger in Taoism than in any other school of Eastern philosophy. It is based on the firm belief that the human intellect can never comprehend the Tao. In the words of Chuang

Tzu, "*The most extensive knowledge does not necessarily know it; reasoning will not make men wise in it. The sages have decided against both these methods.*" Logical reasoning was considered by the Taoists as part of the artificial world of man, together with social etiquette and moral standards. They were not interested in this world at all but concentrated their attention fully on the observation of nature in order to discern the characteristics of the Tao. Thus, they developed an attitude which was essentially scientific and only their deep mistrust in the analytic method prevented them from constructing proper scientific theories. Nevertheless, the careful observation of nature, combined with a strong mystical intuition, led the Taoist sages to profound insights which are confirmed by modern scientific theories. One of the most important insights of the Taoists was the realization that transformation and change are essential features of nature. A passage in the Chuang-tzu shows clearly how the fundamental importance of change was discerned by observing the organic world: *(The Way of Eastern Mysticism*, An excerpt from *The Tao of Physics* by Fritjof Capra).

The Interfaith Manual

*"Peace will not come out of a clash of arms
but out of justice lived and done
by unarmed nations in the face of odds."*
Mahatma Gandhi

International Day of Peace

ON PEACE
("THE GOLDEN RULE")

Did you know a form of "The Golden Rule" appears in <u>every</u> religion's holy texts? For this fact alone we begin to appreciate the similarities rather than look at the differences. Imagine, we are all supposed to live in peace; why not!

Bahá'í - The idea of the familiar "Golden Rule" appears in the Bahá'í Writings several ways. The quote closest to the wording of the Golden Rule probably is this one:
   "And if thine eyes be turned towards justice, choose thou for thy neighbor that which thou choosest for thyself." (Bahá'u'lláh, *Epistle to the Son of the Wolf,* Wilmette: Bahá'í Publishing Trust, 1988, p. 29)

Buddhism - "...a state that is not pleasing or delightful to me, how could I inflict that upon another?" *Samyutta NIkaya v. 353*
   Hurt not others in ways that you yourself would find hurtful." *Udana-Varga 5:18*

Christianity - "Therefore all things whatsoever ye would that men should do to you, do ye even so to them: for this is the law and the prophets." *Matthew 7:12, King James Version.*
   "And as ye would that men should do to you, do ye also to them likewise." *Luke 6:31, King James Version.*

"... and don't do what you hate ... ", *Gospel of Thomas 6*. The Gospel of Thomas is one of about 40 gospels that were widely accepted among early Christians, but which never made it into the Christian Scriptures (New Testament).

Confucianism - "Do not do to others what you do not want them to do to you" *Analects 15:23*

"Tse-kung asked, 'Is there one word that can serve as a principle of conduct for life?' Confucius replied, 'It is the word *'shu'* which means reciprocity. Do not impose on others what you yourself do not desire.'" *Doctrine of the Mean 13.3*

"Try your best to treat others as you would wish to be treated yourself, and you will find that this is the shortest way to benevolence." *Mencius VII.A.4*

Hinduism - This is the sum of duty: do not do to others what would cause pain if done to you. *Mahabharata 5:1517*

Islam: "None of you [truly] believes until he wishes for his brother what he wishes for himself." *Number 13 of Imam "Al-Nawawi's Forty Hadiths."*

Jainism - According to Jainism, one can attain real peace and happiness by having a rational outlook towards life, and by leading a life of self-discipline and austerity. Meditation & reflecting on one's life and one's place in one's environment, is an important means of developing self-discipline and a life of austerity. (*Jainism At A Glance*, Mrs. Sushila Singhvi, jainstudy.org) Everyone has their own pain and suffering and there is no use planning for the next life since we have no control on anything other than our own non-violent actions.

"In happiness and suffering, in joy and grief, we should regard all creatures as we regard our own self." "A man should wander about treating all creatures as he himself would be treated."

Sutrakritanga 1.11.33 "One should treat all beings as he himself would be treated." Agamas Sutrakritanga 1.10.13

Judaism: "...thou shalt love thy neighbor as thyself.", Leviticus 19:18 "What is hateful to you, do not to your fellow man. This is the law: all the rest is commentary." *Talmud, Shabbat 31a.* "And what you hate, do not do to any one." *Tobit 4:15*

Native American: "Respect for all life is the foundation." The Great Law of Peace. "All things are our relatives; what we do to everything, we do to ourselves. All is really One." *Black Elk*

"Do not wrong or hate your neighbor. For it is not he who you wrong, but yourself." *Pima proverb.*

New Thought - "What we do unto others will be done also to us – The Law of Cause and effect." (*The 10 Core Concepts of Science of Mind, Ernest Holmes, Pg.2*)

Sikhism - Compassion-mercy and religion are the support of the entire world." (Japji Sahib) "Don't create enmity with anyone as God is within everyone." (Guru Arjan Devji 259) "No one is my enemy, none a stranger and everyone is my friend." (Guru Arjan Dev : AG 1299)

Taoism - "Regard your neighbor's gain as your own gain, and your neighbor's loss as your own loss." *T'ai Shang Kan Ying P'ien.*

"The sage has no interest of his own, but takes the interests of the people as his own. He is kind to the kind; he is also kind to the unkind: for Virtue is kind. He is faithful to the faithful; he is also faithful to the unfaithful: for Virtue is faithful." *Tao Teh Ching, Chapter 49*

"Prosperity is only an instrument to be used, not a deity to be worshiped."
Calvin Coolidge

ON PROSPERITY

I believe every person of faith you speak with will tell you, prosperity is a state of mind and one which every person can obtain by his or her consciousness. I have read, almost every multi-millionaire today was once poor and by being so, chose not to be in that financial condition again. Most of the richest people in the world are also the biggest givers and as such understand, "What goes around comes around." Those who share their prosperity receive more; this is a spiritual truth talked about by every faith. The more you give, with the intent of helping others, the more you receive. You can never out-give God.

Bahá'í – The Bahá'í faith has presented papers to the United Nations seeking a Prosperity of Humankind philosophy for the people of the world. This "world vision" of prosperity discusses that with the science and technology emerging, no person on this planet should be without the essentials many in the Western world take for granted. (*Prosperity of Humankind*, statements.bahai.org)

Buddhism - Limiting wants and restraining consumption lead to contentment according to Buddhism. What contributes to man's happiness in the long run is not the philosophy 'to have', but the philosophy 'to be'. (*Buddha*, thinkexist.com)

Christianity - That truth is, God loves us all and has blessed us. When Jesus said in Luke 17:6, *"If you have faith as small as a mustard seed, you can say to this mulberry tree, 'Be uprooted and planted in the sea,'* *and it will obey you."* He was speaking of the smallest seed that could be seen in His time. If He were here today, He might say "If you had faith as an atom..." or even smaller, "If you had a quark (which is a subatomic particle)...". The point he was making was that small things that cannot be easily seen manifest themselves and affect things in the larger world where we live. (Kenneth Copeland)

Confucianism - Confucius said, "the concept of creating harmony in the world will bring the prosperity we seek." Prosperity was not and still is not the goal of someone following the Confucian faith.

Hinduism - Prosperity is not for the envious, nor is greatness for men of impure conduct. (*Tirukkural 14:135*) Artha is prosperity or success in worldly pursuits. Although the ultimate goal of Hinduism is enlightenment, the pursuit of wealth and prosperity is regarded as an appropriate pursuit for the householder (the second of four life stages). It also ensures social order, for there would be no society if everyone renunciated worldly life to meditate. But while Hindus are encouraged to make money, it must be within the bounds of dharma. (religionfacts.com)

Islam - Islam guarantees prosperity and abundance: "If only the people of the various communities believed and maintained a righteous life, we would have showered them with blessings from the heaven and the earth." (Qu'ran 7:96, 41:30-31). God is the One who controls your happiness, or misery.

Jainism - The Jain community's prosperity has long enabled them to be generous patrons. Many Jains are affluent and well educated and there are many professional women. Almost 50% of the breadwinners in North American Jain families are engineers or medical doctors, or work in finance and private enterprise. (Jain Society of San Diego) "Prosperity comes from how much time we spend on our soul versus on our physical body." (Rohak Vora)

Judaism - The Abrahamic covenant provided physical healing, material prosperity and family well-being for Old Testament Judaism and Jews today feel they continue to receive the material prosperity and well-being from God if they follow the Laws. Jews are philanthropic because they believe they have to "pay back" and share with those less fortunate. The Mission of the Jews is "they are required to fix the world." (Marilyn Clement)

Native American - Native Americans understand and accept that health includes not just physical and mental well-being, but also prosperity (of self and community), harmonious relationships with family and lasting friendships.

New Thought - New Thought followers are taught, 'ALL is CONSCIOUSNESS!' Whatever beliefs (consciously and unconsciously) you have within you, are experienced and manifested in your life. The Law of Mind, spoken by Christ Jesus states, "It is done unto you as you believe." Believe in prosperity and it unfolds for you. Believe in lack and limitation and that unfolds as experiences in your life. This includes health, love, success and PROSPERITY. *We believe "The Creative Mind (God) surrounds us and receives the direct impress of our thoughts then acts upon it."*(Ernest Holmes) What we THINK about we BRING about. They believe there is a warehouse of GOOD in God and as we become more aware of our Spiritual Nature, as Beings and Expressions of God, we realize we have unlimited potential to create more good in our lives, which can also mean more money, better love relationships, a successful job, and better health.. Financial and all other types of prosperity begin when we keep our minds positive and pure in consciousness, free from doubt and feelings of unworthiness in order to accept the GOOD God is always willing to give us. If we are ready and able to accept a "thimble" of good, it will be given to us. If we are able to accept a "Barrel" of good, it will be given to us. What we BELIEVE is what we have, will gain and experience.

To develop prosperity in your life says New Thought Minister and author Edwene Gaines, in her book <u>The Four Spiritual Laws of Prosperity</u>, writes: 1. Put God first in your life and tithe 10% of all income to the place or person you have received spiritual nourishment. 2. Set clear goals and intentions. 3. Forgive yourself and everyone for anything. 4. Discover your Divine Purpose and follow it! Catherine Ponder from her book <u>Open Your Mind to Prosperity</u> states: 1. Cleanse your mind of negative thoughts and FORGIVE others. She also suggests cleaning out closets is the first step in releasing the old to let in the new. We need to release old habits, old negative thoughts and things that do not serve us anymore before we can bring in new and more good in our lives. 2. Write three lists, what you want to eliminate from your life, what you want to bring into your life and what you are THANKFUL for. 3. Visualize your desire. "You can picture your way to increased prosperity, health, family harmony and even world travel." Create a "Treasure Map" of your goals and the things you desire, by cutting out pictures and displaying them on a poster board. Look at it each day. A picture is worth a 1,000 words. 4. SPEAK your word out-loud and in writing with positive and specific AFFIRMATIONS, 5. TITHE 10% to your church, temple, mosque or place of spiritual nourishment. GIVING is the first step to receiving. Other ways to increase ones prosperity are to declare and affirm:

"The Divine Plan for my life is unfolding quickly and in peace. New doors of good now open to me." "I invite Divine Wisdom into every phase of my life and into this situation now. I know it is opening ways where to human sense there is no way."

"Divine Love is now working through me to adjust all the details of my life. Love transforms my life now." "I call upon the power of Divine Restoration. My good of past and present is now divinely restored to me.... and now pours forth into my life as rich blessings. This is a time of Divine Fulfillment and I give thanks for divine restoration in mind, body and affairs." (Rev. Abigail Albert)

Sikhism - Sikhism believes every Sikh is a member of the universal brotherhood and every member should live in prosperity. A Sikh is required to care for others and share their grief when they are emotionally hurting. The Sikh should feel pleasure in sharing the honest earnings with less fortunate and the poor so it should not create Haumai for charity but it should inculcate a spirit of responsibility towards needy, sick and poor. This is the reason Sikhs are never seen as beggars. Wherever they live, they live in prosperity under *Hukam*, the command, of the Guru. (globalsikhstudies.net)

Taoism - In the realm of health, all Taoists idealize a simple and harmonious lifestyle which seeks to achieve holism through the balancing of yin and yang. Meditation on the symbols of yin and yang increase the balance and thereby the amount of prosperity realized.

Rev. Dr. Stephen L. Albert

*"Although the act of nurturing another's spiritual growth
has the effect of nurturing one's own,
a major characteristic of genuine love is that
the distinction between oneself and the other
is always maintained and preserved."*
M. Scott Peck

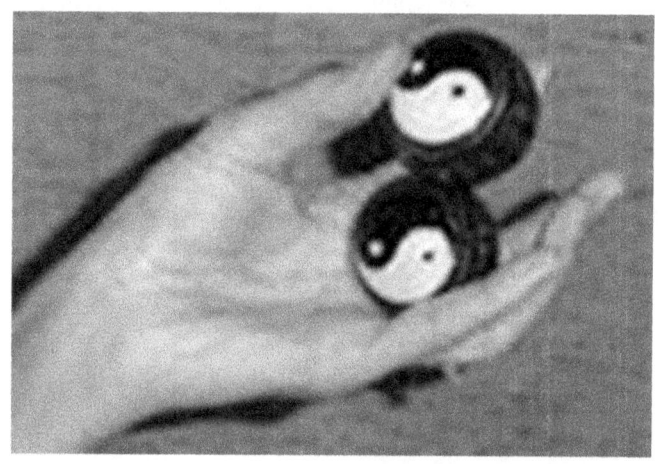

On Spiritual Growth

You may remember in the 1977 movie Star Wars, Master Yoda told his young apprentice Luke Skywalker, who was disappointed at his inability to correctly complete the tests his master was giving him, not "to try" but "to do!" Developing your spiritual growth is the same thing. Although one might voluntarily choose to return to help humanity as some believe, no matter what your faith, nobody is born a Guru, Master or Saint. We do not emerge on this plane of existence with the ability to be peaceful in all situations and to forgive all those who try to hurt or control us. Developing one's spiritual growth in a particular faith is a path which we can choose the degree of immersion we wish to have, and we DO IT until we learn a different way to complete the same learning but at an accelerated pace. Learning self-awareness, studying our faith and having a relationship with God is a lifetime endeavor. Spiritual growth can be the most frustrating and yet the most rewarding experience we will ever have.

Bahá'í - The ultimate aim in life of every human soul, the Bahá'í writings state, should be to attain moral and spiritual excellence, to align one's inner being and outward behavior with the will of an all-loving Creator. That each individual has been bestowed with a unique destiny by God, a destiny which unfolds in accordance with the free exercise of the choices and opportunities presented in life, lies at the center of Bahá'í belief . (info.bahai.org)

Buddhism - Practicing step by step, one gradually fulfills all Buddha teachings. It is like first setting up a foundation then building the room: Generosity and self-control, like this, are bases of enlightened beings' practices. (Garland Sutra 10)

Christianity – In Christianity, Four Steps to Spiritual Growth are: 1). Read your Bible daily, 2). Attend church services regularly, 3). Get involved in a ministry group and 4). Pray daily. Other churches use the Six "C's" which ask the adherent to develop: Character, Creativity, Caring, Community, a Connection with Christ and a Connection with God.

Confucianism - Spiritual Growth comes through Love, Truth, Relationships & Knowledge. Each and every person comes from a divine lineage as well as a human one. Each person is responsible for their own spiritual growth, for their own choices and produce the vines that through divine love bear flowers and fruit in his or her behalf. (*Spiritual Growth*, divinehumanity.com)

Hinduism - `Spiritual growth is more important in life than material benefits, and anyone can achieve it.' (K. Satyamurty)

Islam - The spirituality of Islam not only transcends the dualism of spirit and matter but is the nucleus of its integrated and unified concept of life. The first necessity for progression along the path of spiritual development is *Iman* which is generally rendered as religious belief or faith. The mind and heart of a man should always be aware: *Allah* alone is His Master, Sovereign and Deity; seeking His pleasure is the aim of all his endeavors; and His commands alone are the commands that are to be obeyed. The second stage is that of obedience (*it~ 'at*), meaning that man gives up his independence and accepts subservience to *Allah*. This subservience is called *slam* (submission) in the language of the Qur'an. The third stage is that of *taqwa* (*Allah*-consciousness). It consists in a practical manifestation of one's faith in *Allah* in one's daily life. *Taqwa* also means desisting from everything which *Allah* has forbidden or has disapproved of; man must be in a state of readiness to undertake all that *Allah* has commanded and to observe the distinctions between lawful and unlawful, right and wrong, and good and bad in life. The last and the highest stage is that of *ihsn* (godliness) It signifies that man has attained highest excellence in words, deeds and thoughts, identifying his will with the will of *Allah* and harmonizing it, to the best of his knowledge and ability, with the Divine will. (*The Spiritual Path in Islam*, islam101.com)

Jainism - The Jains believe in reincarnation. To free themselves of the cycle of birth and death, they practice asceticism that is stringent in nature. They basically struggle to make their present birth the last one. Their professions are chosen carefully and revolve around the protection of lives or doing good deeds for others. The ethical code followed by the Jains is very strict in nature and the ethics are followed with much dedication and sincerity. Jains believe in not stealing from others. They believe in being content with whatever they have. According to the Jains, nothing is permanent, not even one's body. Materialistic pleasures only hamper spiritual growth and create only a temporary sense of satisfaction. (History of India, Jainism, iloveindia.com) The Jain symbol of the palm of an open hand reminds them to "stop" and think before they act in any situation. When you believe you are always in the presence of thinking and doing good you experience no stress in life.

Judaism - Orthodox Jews daven (pray) in formal worship services three times a day, every day: at evening (Ma'ariv), in the morning (Shacharit), and in the afternoon (Minchah). Daily prayers are collected in a book called a siddur, which derives from the Hebrew root meaning "order," because the siddur shows the order of prayers. Becoming spiritual is about relinquishing your ego, cutting down on negative thoughts and channeling positive light through every action in life so you have a moment to moment relationship with G-d. (jewfaq.org)

Native American – Seeking spiritual growth is at the heart of Native Americans. The Sweat Lodge is a place of spiritual refuge and mental and physical healing, a place to get answers and guidance by asking spiritual entities, totem helpers, the Creator and Mother Earth for the needed wisdom and power to get through the day and personal challenges.

New Thought - New Thought believes spiritual growth is the result of a perpetually advancing mind. The mind is not content with the past or its achievements and it is not satisfied with studying only the systems of philosophy or religion. Continually evolving spiritual consciousness to achieve Christ Consciousness is what these adherents seek and through worship services, group and personal meditation they are constantly seeking to know and understand God more deeply and internalize the oneness of all.

Sikhism - A Sikh with firm faith in the Guru finds the Guru always stays with him/her to help and guide him/her towards spiritual growth. He/She depends on the Guru's inner guidance for each breath and activity, and does not do anything without the Guru being present. This nurtures a spiritual link between the Sikh and the Guru. Among other things, it also assures clean thoughts and action. A Sanmukh Sikh sees his/her Guru in everyone. (sikhs.org)

Taoism - "Spiritual Growth happens at a subtle level... not gross levels." Life is a journey with growth coming at unexpected times and during unexpected surroundings. Sometimes it is thrust upon you and if you are ready to accept it comes naturally. Other times, growth opportunities embody themselves in terms of a struggle or obstacle. The question is who are we fighting with. Often times, we find it is ourselves. The bigger battles are within us. Once we "conquer" ourselves, the rest is easy by comparison. Knowing and taming yourself requires great self discipline and work ethic. It does not come easy. (taoinstitute.org)

Rev. Dr. Stephen L. Albert

"If all the misfortunes of mankind were cast into a public stack in order to be equally distributed among the whole species, those who now think themselves the most unhappy would prefer the share they are already possessed of before that which would fall to them by such a division."
Socrates

On Unhappiness/Renewal

I tell people I have gone through divorce, bankruptcy, work problems, major medical issues and challenges for over sixty years, yet I feel I am the happiest person I know because I have been renewed by my spiritual faith in God. My so-called 'bad' experiences have led me to be more compassionate to those going through life issues. As an example, I usually get a very surprised look from someone who has just told me he was fired from his job, and I respond with, "Congratulations!" The more we refrain from want and building up our ego, the more God can work in our lives to bring about a renewal more grand than we can ever imagine.

Bahá'í - To the Bahá'í, the ideal life is both physical and spiritual development and happiness. Perhaps the most important source of unhappiness is spiritual degeneration, which causes the greatest unhappiness. Bahá'u'lláh advises us, "Disencumber yourselves of all attachment to this world and the vanities thereof." (Lynne Yancy, Bahá'í National Center)

Buddhism - Siddhartha developed the basic ideas of Buddhism, that "unhappiness is the result of desire and attachment to material items. That is when he became known as the Buddha. The understanding of this led to the enlightenment of Prince Siddhartha, and that enlightenment is the path to breaking free from samsara, or "material existence." This breaking free is called "Nirvana" meaning "cooling the fires of desire." Buddhism teaches us that everything changes in the world, yet desire makes us crave for eternal material pleasures. When the pleasures wither away, we are unhappy. True happiness arrives when one accepts that change is the ultimate reality of the material world, and that nothing lasts forever. (geocities.com)

Christianity - Unhappiness is perhaps the most obvious and pervasive feature of the life experience. We each have various degrees of unhappiness and depending upon our degree of guilt and self-worth, we can choose to be happy now or wait until we have left this physical reality.

Confucianism – Unhappiness is caused by selfish cravings. Unhappiness ends when selfish cravings can be destroyed. Controlling the ego and helping others find success reduces the unhappiness in our lives. (*The Way of the Bowl*, thebowl.limyanko.com)

Hinduism - The main reason for unhappiness in life is that we look for comfort in the exterior ... in the outside world. We should be looking for it inside us, explains guru Sri Sri Ravishankar. "How often do we say, "I will be happy if I get this?" Even if we achieve it, we only feel satisfied for a moment, until we set our eyes on a bigger attraction. So we make most of our lives miserable in search of momentary happiness." (thedaily.washington.edu)

Islam - Islam is a very realistic religion and the Qur'an itself recognizes the reality of human weakness. Those who are injured are permitted to take retaliation, but they are reminded at every turn that it is better to forgive and to seek reconciliation. Muslims are commanded to return good for evil, thus breaking the vicious circle of animosity; "to do good to those who have injured us" in the words of one of the classical commentators on the Qur'an, but this requires human qualities which are by no means universal although they were characteristic of Muhammad. (Charles Le Gai

Eaton) Muslims are taught to worship God as if He is seeing you and to worship God as if you are seeing Him.

Jainism - Jains believe that time is infinite, without any beginning or end. Time is divided into infinite equal time cycles (*Kalchakras*). Every time cycle is further sub-divided into two equal halves. The first half is the progressive cycle or ascending order, called *Utsarpini*. The other half is the regressive cycle or the descending order, called *Avasarpini*. Every Utsarpini and Avasarpini is divided into six unequal periods called *Äräs*. During the Utsarpini half cycle, progress, development, happiness, strength, age, body, religious trends, etc., go from the worst conditions to the best. During the Avasarpini half cycle, progress, development, happiness, strength, age, body, religious trends, etc. go from the best conditions to the worst. Presently, we are in the fifth Ara of the Avasarpini phase. When the Avasarpini phase ends the Utsarpini phase begins. This kälchakra repeats again and continues forever. (jainworld.com)

Judaism – No single moment of pleasure, according to Jewish tradition, is worth the pain of guilt, tragedy or even simple unhappiness that it might cause or afflict upon another. Unhappiness comes from seeking momentary happiness from someone or something rather than seeking true happiness from your relationship with God.

Native American - "The Native American understands the pain, the unhappiness, the addictions, the abuse...and he doesn't judge it because he knows why it's there; it comes from hundreds of years of others controlling your life. Native Americans today say, "Let's step beyond it." (coehs.uwash.edu)

New Thought – New Thought teaches that every person has free will in all things including whether or not to be happy. Unhappiness is a choice, and those who want to change their thinking towards being happy, are offered techniques including meditation, affirmations and self-awareness techniques. Ernest Holmes said, "Change your thinking, change your life."

Sikhism – "Be content within yourself" is the basic philosophy of Sikhism, suggesting that happiness comes from within." When we are content within, we are on our way to bliss or ultimate happiness. When we blame others for our unhappiness, we are actually misdiagnosing the cause of it. *"Be compassionate (daya) to others; Be satisfied (santokh) within yourself!"* (sikhmarg.com)

Taoism – Taoists say you are supposed to exist in keeping with the Way of Heaven, which in other words means doing what is right and moral. According to Lao Tsu the Way of Heaven is being engaged in a lively ethical life. According to Taoism the Way of life is to not interfere and not to strive to lead a moral life; just do it. Acting this way will help to make you happy. (Zhou Dynasty, ccds.charlotte.nc.us)

*"Violence is not merely killing another.
It is violence when we use a sharp word,
when we make a gesture to brush away a person,
when we obey because there is fear.
So violence isn't merely organized butchery in the
name of God, in the name of society or country.*

*Violence is much more subtle, much deeper,
and we are inquiring into the very depths of violence."*
Jiddu Krishnamurti

ON VIOLENCE

Of all the subjects in this interfaith manual, violence was the one I feared the most in talking about. I do not understand the 'wanting' to be violent. I was not raised with violence, and it was only the school bully who made me aware it existed at all. Different from war where one faction is defending his life and property from someone who wants to control him, violence has the factor of 'intent' in it, and I do not understand why someone would wake up one morning and INTEND to be violent against others. I have been told that people who are violent toward others are just seeking love which they never received while growing up. Yet I have no desire to put my arms around a violent person and hug him. I believe this is one of the areas where I need to grow more completely in my spiritual learning. I know an intently violent person will probably never pick up an interfaith manual like this because of his predisposed hatred against certain people. A rational person would at least argue the point however; most violent people are rarely rational. However, if you meet a violent person who is willing to read about the similarities in the faiths, please feel free to pass on this book to him and pray he is at least a little open to the possibility of peace.

Bahá'í - The Bahá'í Faith recognizes the economic problems which cause violence are spiritual in nature and cannot be solved by better technology or a set of well devised rules. "Any agency whatever, though it be the instrument of mankind's greatest good, is capable of misuse which can move others to violence. Its proper use or abuse depends on the varying degrees of enlightenment, capacity, faith, honesty, devotion and high-mindedness of the leaders of public opinion." Thus, the happiness and wealth of mankind depend upon our collective willingness to improve the way we think and act, hopefully without violence. (*Conservation of The Earth's Resources*, bcca.org)

Buddhism - The Buddha describes his sense of dismay at the violence in the world, together with his important discovery; that the only escape from violence is to remove the causes of violence from one's own heart. To remove these causes, one must first refrain from violence on the external level so as to create the proper karmic context, more peaceful and honest, for extracting the causes of violence on the internal level. (Thanissaro Bhikkhu)

Christianity – Despite the historic Christian violence of the crusades, the multiple blessings of wars, warrior popes, etc., when speaking about non-violence Christians look at Jesus, the beginning point of Christian faith, who is worshiped as 'Wonderful Counselor, Mighty God, Everlasting Father, Prince of Peace' (Isa. 9:6); whose Sermon on the Mount taught nonviolence and love of enemies; who faced his accusers nonviolently and then died a nonviolent death; whose nonviolent teaching inspired the first centuries of pacifist Christian history and was subsequently preserved in the justifiable war doctrine that declares all war as sin even when declaring it occasionally a necessary evil, and in the prohibition of fighting by monastic and clergy as well as in a persistent tradition of Christian pacifism." (*Violence In Christian Theology*, J. Denny Weaver, crosscurrents .org)

Confucian - As a Confucian, Mencius based his entire system of thought on the concept of *jen*: "humaneness," "humanity," "benevolence," etc. To this basic doctrine he added the concept of *i*: "righteousness," or "duty." What does this mean? Mencius believed the "humaneness" or "benevolence" you show to individuals should in some way be influenced by the type of personal relationship you have to that person. One displayed *jen* to a person based on that person's position (as well as your own) and the obligations you owe to that person, so that you owe more jen to your immediate family than you do, say, to the Prime Minister of Canada. This, then, means we have obligations to people who arise from social relations and social organization, not because there is some divine law mandating these obligations. Mencius several times throughout Chinese history has been regarded as a potentially "dangerous" author, leading at times to outright banning of his book. This is because Mencius developed a very early form of what was to be called in modern times the "social contract." Mencius, like Confucius, believed that rulers were divinely placed in order to guarantee peace and order among the people they rule. Unlike Confucius, Mencius believed if a ruler failed to bring peace and order about, then the people could be absolved of all loyalty to that ruler and could, if they felt strongly enough about the matter, revolt. (*Mencius*, Richard Hooker, wsu.edu)

Hinduism - Hindus believe in the existence of God everywhere, as an all-pervasive, self-effulgent energy and consciousness. This basic belief creates the attitude of sublime tolerance and acceptance toward others. Even tolerance is insufficient to describe the compassion and reverence the Hindu holds for the intrinsic sacredness within all things. Therefore, the actions of all Hindus are rendered benign or ahimsa. One would not want to hurt something which one revered. On the other hand, when the fundamentalists of any religion teach an unrelenting duality based on good and evil, man and nature or God and Devil, this creates friends and enemies. This belief is a sacrilege to Hindus because they know the attitudes which are the by-product are totally dualistic, and for good to triumph over that which is alien or evil, it must kill out that which is considered to be evil. (hinduismtoday.com)

Islam – Violence is not permitted in Islam. Prophet Muhammad hated violence and war. However, self defense is allowed and defending your faith or family is permitted. Violence occurs due to unsolved political conflicts, frustration and, above all, ignorance causing terrorism and hatred; nothing that was born out of a theological conflict causes violence.

Jainism – For Jainism non-violence is its main core. Jains believe every being has life, and this also includes stones, sand, trees and every other thing. The fact that trees breathe came to be known to the science world only from the 20th century. Mahavira, who believed everything has life and also believed in non-violence, actually didn't eat anything causing his self-starvation to death. Mahavira was also extremely ascetic and walked around completely naked because of his renouncement of life. (adaniel.tripod.com/jainism) Jains take their shoes off when walking in the grass so that they will not be responsible for killing an ant or other insects with their hard shoes. They believe animals can live without humans. However, humans believe we need the animals as food sources to survive. (Rohak Vora)

Judaism - Hector Avalos argues that most violence in the world is due to scarce resources, real or imagined and when religion causes violence, it is often because it has created new scarce resources. He argues that enscripturation, sacred space, group privileging and salvation create exclusive, scarce resources which are available to some and denied to others, leading to the creation of causes for violence. Marilyn Clement points out that Jews talk about how to stay sensitive in battle so you do not become a killing machine. If you are a soldier you must do whatever is needed in battle to stay alive and protect your home. However, when the battle is over, you should no longer be seeking to do violence.

Native American - Group violence in America is viewed as a "response" to changing economic, political, social, cultural, demographic or religious conditions. Thus, however violent the episodes were, historians could see larger "reasons" for these group behaviors; somehow, these actions reflected a "cause." From 1622 through 1900 Americans and Native Americans fought for power and control. (informationclearinghouse.info)

New Thought – New Thought followers first seek peace within themselves and believe the world cannot change unless their heart and mind are at peace. They focus on the good, and their attention is on curbing violence with programs such as The Association of Global New Thought's "Season for Non-Violence," which is a national 64-day educational, media, and grassroots campaign dedicated to demonstrating that nonviolence is a powerful way to heal, transform, and empower our lives and our communities. This organization (AGNT) has also set up a number of international dialogs with the Dalai Lama and other world leaders. A person's thoughts about Peace are always a 365 day-a-year choice.

Sikhism – The history of Sikhism has many violent encounters, usually in the defense of the right to practice one's religion whether as Sikh, Hindu or otherwise. Sikhism seeks peace; when all other means have been exhausted, then they find it justifiable to use other means to defend those being oppressed.

Taoism – Taoists believe that on the individual and local level, violence can be reduced to a minimum by good education, good health and psychological care, social control and adequate recreational facilities. On all levels one may try to prevent violence by not threatening with violence. (*Causes of Violence*, tue.nl/redesintrum/debate/eykhof) Daoists believe that by our own vibrations we draw things to ourselves, so if we are confronted with violence it may well be because we are emanating violence. So we seek to calm our own violence. (Michael Arnold, Taoist)

REV. DR. STEPHEN L. ALBERT

*"Besides the noble art of getting things done,
there is the noble art of leaving things undone.
The wisdom of life consists in the elimination of non-essentials."*
Lin Yutang

ON WISDOM

Wisdom is the ability to use the information you have been given for an even greater purpose than for what it was initially intended. When a student learns a concept from a teacher and then goes out and uses that concept towards a more positive end, he or she is being wise. Someone may come out with a new invention, but it is the wise man who knows how to get that new idea into the hands of the people who can further develop it. So that is what this manual is about. Take the information in this interfaith manual and mix it with what you already know about the various faiths and spread the word that it is okay to associate with people who think differently than you. Let people know there is wisdom in every faith and through further interaction we can bring about a deeper peace. Use your wisdom and watch an Interfaith World of peace grow for everyone.

Bahá'í – For the Bahá'í the essence of wisdom is the fear of God, the dread of His scourge and punishment, and the apprehension of His justice and decree. (Bahá'u'lláh, *Tablets of Bahá'u'lláh revealed after the Kitáb-i-Aqdas*, Wilmette: Bahá'í Publishing Trust, 1988, p. 155)

Buddhism – The highest wisdom according to Buddha is seeing that in reality all phenomena are incomplete, impermanent, and not lasting self. This understanding is totally freeing and leads to the great security and happiness which is called Nirvana. True wisdom is to see and understand directly for us. At this level then, wisdom is to keep an open mind rather than being closed-minded, listening to other points of view rather than being bigoted; to carefully examine facts that contradict our beliefs. (buddha.net)

Christianity – Christians believe wisdom comes from knowing God and knowing yourself first. That was what Jesus Christ meant when he said, "Seek You The 'Kingdom Of God' First (*The Inner World*, 'Consciousness', 'Know Yourself', 'Infinity') And Everything Will Be Added To You." Being wise for Christians, or for anyone for that matter, goes beyond our human understanding of what we know and believe. It instead matches Abraham's willingness to sacrifice his son, Isaac, because God asked him to. Isaac was Abraham's greatest gift given to him by God when Abraham was very old. Yet when Abraham followed God's directions to sacrifice Isaac, Abraham was trusting the giver more than the gift. (Rev. Glen Larsen)

Confucianism – Confucius systematized and taught much of the accumulated social wisdom and ideals of his day and culture. His name is synonymous with wisdom. "If a man withdraws his mind from the love of beauty, and applies it as sincerely to the love of the virtuous if, in serving his parents, he can exert his utmost strength if, in serving his prince, he can devote his life if in his intercourse with his friends, his words are sincere - although men say that he has not learned, I will certainly say that he has." (Confucius, Analects of Confucius, Chapter VII)

Hinduism – Hindu philosophy is a practical answer for solving the planet's psychological and physical ills. The Hindu belief system alleviates the neuroses which plague our Western world by eliminating self-destructive tendencies and rewarding disciplined behavior. Believing that we are part of the earth, heavens, and one another, lights the fires of intuition, altruism, and deep love. By appreciating the presence of Brahman, the self, in all things, one is compelled to celebrate all living things as vessels of one eternal soul. (*The Wisdom of Hinduism*, Paula Vaughan)

Islamic – The Qur'an and Sayings of Prophet Muhammad are the source of Islamic law, values and traditions. They offer timeless wisdom for lasting community throughout the world. In Islamic teachings, the wise ones always had three wisdom principles: to help all living beings, to distribute the benefits of God in the places where people meet to mention and remember Him, to awaken people to God by words of wisdom.

Jainism - The treasury of Jain wisdom has provided many tools. Universal Friendship, Appreciation, Compassion and Equanimity are foundational qualities for our spirituality. We must cultivate Upsham, calming the passions. We have been given the powerful psychological insights that Forgiveness overcomes Anger; Humility, Ego; Sincerity, Deceit; and Contentment, Greed. Of course, we must look for their ultimate cause of these passions. (Institute of Jainology, *Ashik Shah,* jainology.org)

Judaism – While the Hebrew Bible is the cornerstone of Judaism, it is the Talmud (Jewish Lights) that provides many central values for living. The Talmud sets out specific guidelines and lyrical admonitions regarding many of life's ordinary events and offers profound words of advice and wisdom for life's most intractable dilemmas. Dov Peretz Elkins in his book "THE WISDOM OF JUDAISM" makes it clear from the outset that according to the ancient Rabbis, the ethical takes precedence over everything else in Judaism: "Helping a neighbor, providing food for the hungry, giving clothes for the needy, and offering assistance with a life-cycle event such as a birth, a wedding or a burial, are the mark of the religious person in Judaism." The seat of moral behavior is the heart, and it is a good thing to "lead a life that sparkles with sweetness, compassion, integrity, and honor." (*The Wisdom of Judaism*, Elkins)

Native American – Native American sayings, quotes and words of wisdom reflecting the beliefs and philosophy of the Native Americans have been quoted since recorded history in America. "Humankind has not woven the web of life. We are but one thread within it. Whatever we do to the web we do to ourselves. All things are bound together. All things connect." (Chief Seattle)

New Thought – The New Thought faith has impacted millions of people throughout the world with its searching for spiritual truth and ancient wisdom in world faiths and modern science. God's Divine Wisdom dwelling within each person, helps position the soul for ways of coping with daily living, New Thought wisdom sets up guiding principles to use. These include the centrality of mind, a focus on the immanence of the Divine within and the practice of metaphysical healing. Various programs help the followers to develop spiritual wisdom which can then be used in practical applications each day to bring about peace, love and prosperity in all areas of life.

Sikhism – The source of wisdom for Sikhs is Guru Granth Sahib. It contains the verses of the six of the ten Sikh Gurus and of 15 holy men from different social backgrounds (among others Kabir, Namdev, Shekh Farid, Ravidas, Pipa, and Trilochan). Sikhs believe "without the true wisdom (*Satgur*), no one has obtained the one. (The creator) Has placed herself within the true wisdom; revealing herself, she declares this openly. Internalize the true wisdom, eternal liberation is obtained, and attachment banished from within. The highest thought is when one's consciousness is attached to the one. Thus, the creator of the universe, the great giver is obtained (while living)." (GGS, p. 466, M. 1)

Taoism – Taoism is interested in intuitive wisdom, rather than in rational knowledge. Acknowledging the limitations and the relativity of the world of mere rational thinking, Taoism is, basically, a way of liberation from this world and is, in this respect, comparable to the ways of Yoga or Vedanta in Hinduism, or to the Eightfold Path of the Buddha. The Taoist sage does not strive for the good but rather tries to maintain a dynamic balance between good and bad. (*Taoism*, Fritjof Capra)

Rev. Dr. Stephen L. Albert

*"Give thanks unto the LORD with harp,
sing praises unto Him with the psaltery of ten strings.
Sing unto Him a new song; play skilfully amid shouts of joy."*
(Ketuvim [Writings], Tehillim [Psalms] 33:2-3)

*"O sing unto the LORD a new song;
sing unto the LORD, all the earth.
Sing unto the LORD, bless His name;
proclaim His salvation from day to day."*
(Ketuvim [Writings], Tehillim [Psalms] 96:1-2)

PART 4
INTERFAITH SONGS

I am a minister who cannot sing without dogs howling or people leaving the room, so I leave any musical choices and decisions to my wife and others who truly understand and feel comfortable with music. However, I am a person who appreciates inspiring lyrics and heart-felt words which make me tear-up as I (quietly) sing. The allure of music is universal, and I believe every faith uses music to enhance the message they are trying to get across in a worship environment. Whether it is a repetitive mantram or a Halleluiah choir, music has the ability to bring diverse people together with a common feeling. The following American songs are a few of those special verses which sing about Interfaith and about the One God which binds us together. I hope some of these become your favorites which you can use during your faith worship services. I also suggest you look into *"One World, Many Voices – An Interfaith Songbook"* published by the Interfaith Center at the Presidio in San Francisco. Their website is www.internet-presidio.org .

Weave"
by Rosemary Crow

Weave, weave, weave us together,
Weave us together in unity and love.
Weave, weave, weave us together,
Weave us together, together in love.

Rev. Dr. Stephen L. Albert

We are many textures, we are many colors,
Each one different from the other.
But we are entwined in one another,
in one great tapestry -

Weave, weave, weave us together,
Weave us together in unity and love.
Weave, weave, weave us together,
Weave us together, together in love.

We are different instruments playing our own melodies,
Each one tuning to a different key,
But we are all playing in harmony, in one great symphony.

Weave, weave, weave us together,
Weave us together in unity and love.
Weave, weave, weave us together,
Weave us together, together in love.

A moment ago still we did not know
Our unity, only diversity.
Now the Spirit in me greets the Spirit in thee in one great family.

Weave, weave, weave us together,
Weave us together in unity and love.
Weave, weave, weave us together,
Weave us together, together in love.

'No Man Is An Island'
Words by Joan Baez

No man is an island, no man stands alone.
Each man's joy is joy to me,
Each man's grief is my own.

We need one another, so I will defend,
Each man as my brother, each man as my friend.

No man is an island, far out in the blue.
We all look to One above, Who our strength doth renew.
When I help my brother,
Then I know that I, plant the seeds
Of friends that will never die.

I saw the people gather, I heard the music start,
The song that they were singing,
Is ringing in my heart.

No man is an island, no man stands alone,
Each man's joy is joy to me,
Each man's grief is my own.
We need one another, so I will defend,
Each man as my brother, Each man as my friend.

'One Voice'
Lyrics by Barry Manilow

Just one voice, singing in the darkness,
all it takes is one voice,
singing so they hear what's on your mind
and when you look around you'll find
there's more than

One voice, singing in the darkness,
joining with your one voice,
each and every note another rock
and hands are joined and fears unlock
If only one voice would start it on it's own,
You need just one voice

Rev. Dr. Stephen L. Albert

facing the unknown,
and then that one voice would never be alone
it takes that one voice.

It takes that one voice, just one voice
singing in the darkness
all it takes just one voice
shout it out and let it ring
just one voice
it takes that one voice and everyone will sing.

'One God'
Words by Ervin Drake

Millions of stars placed in the sky by one God,
Millions of men lift up their eyes to one God.
So many people calling to Him, by many a different name,
One Father, calling each the same.

Many the ways all of us pray to one God,
Many the paths winding their ways to one God.
Walk with me partner, there are no strangers
after the work is done,
For your God, and my God, are one.

'What A Wonderful World'
Words by Louis Armstrong

I see trees of green, red roses too
I see them bloom for me and you.
And I think to myself what a wonderful world.

I see skies of blue and clouds of white,

The bright blessed day, the dark sacred night.
And I think to myself what a wonderful world.

The colors of the rainbow so pretty in the sky,
Are also on the faces of people going by.
I see friends shaking hands saying how do you do,
They're really saying, I love you.

I hear babies cry, I watch them grow,
They'll learn much more than I'll never know.
And I think to myself what a wonderful world
Yes I think to myself what a wonderful world.

'Simple Gifts'
Words by Shaker Elder Joseph Brackett, Jr

'Tis the gift to be simple,
'tis the gift to be free,
'tis the gift to come down where you ought to be,
And when we find ourselves in the place just right,
It will be in the valley of love and delight.
Refrain:
When true simplicity is gained,
To bow and to bend we shan't be ashamed.
To turn, turn will be our delight,
'Til by turning, turning we come round right
'Tis the gift to be loved and that love to return,
'Tis the gift to be taught and a richer gift to learn,
And when we expect of others what we try to live
each day,
Then we'll all live together and we'll all learn to say,
Refrain:
'Tis the gift to have friends and a true friend to be,
'Tis the gift to think of others not to only think of "me",

And when we hear what others really think and really feel,
Then we'll all live together with a love that is real.

'Day By Day, Oh dear Lord'
Words by Sammy Cahn

Day by day, day by day,
Oh dear Lord, three things I pray.
To see thee more clearly,
Love thee more dearly,
Follow thee more nearly,
Day by day by day by day.

'I Believe'
Written by Ervin M. Drake, Jimmy Shirl and Al Stillman

I believe for every drop of rain that falls,
A flower grows.
I believe that somewhere in the darkest night,
A candle glows.
I believe for everyone who goes astray, someone will come
to show the way. I believe, I believe.

I believe above a storm the smallest prayer,
Can still be heard.
I believe that someone in the great somewhere,
Hears every word.

Every time I hear a new born baby cry,
Or touch a leaf or see the sky,
Then I know why, I believe.

THE INTERFAITH MANUAL

'On Holy Ground'
Words by Barbara Streisand

When I walked through the doors I sensed his presence.
And I knew this was a place where love abounds.
For this is a temple the God we love abides here
And we are standing in his presence,
On holy ground.

We are standing on holy ground.
And I know there are angels all around.
Let us praise, praise God now, praise him anyhow
For we are standing in his sweet presence
On holy ground.

In his presence I know there is joy beyond all measure
And at his feet sweet peace of mind can still be found
For when we have a need he is still the answer
Reach out and claim it for we are standing
On holy ground.

We are standing on holy ground
And I know there are angels all around
Let us praise, praise God now, praise him anyhow
For we are standing in his sweet presence
On holy ground.

'Surely The Presence'
Lyricist unknown

Surely the presence of the Lord is in this place,
I can feel his mighty power and his grace,
I can see the brush of Angel's wings

Rev. Dr. Stephen L. Albert

I see glory on each face
Surely the presence of the Lord is in this place.

There's a holy hush around us
As God's glory fills this place,
I've touched the hem of his garment; I can almost see his face
And my heart is overflowing with the fullness of his joy,
I know without a doubt, that I've been with my Lord.

Surely the presence of the Lord is in this place,
I can feel his mighty power and his grace,
I can see the brush of Angel's wings
I see glory on each face
Surely the presence of the Lord is in this place.

'In This Very Room'
Words by Ron Harris

In this very room there's quite enough love for one like me,
And in this very room there's quite enough joy for one like me,
And there's quite enough hope and quite
enough power to chase away any gloom,
For Spirit, God's Spirit... is in this very room.
And in this very room there's quite enough love for all of us,
And in this very room there's quite enough joy for all of us,
And there's quite enough hope and quite
enough power to chase away any gloom,
For Spirit, God's Spirit... is in this very room.
In this very room there's quite enough love for all the world,
And in this very room there's quite enough joy for all the world,
And there's quite enough hope and quite
enough power to chase away any gloom,
For Spirit, God's Spirit... is in this very room.

'Let There Be Peace On Earth'
Words by Jill Jackson and Sy Miller

Let there be peace on earth,
And let it begin with me.
Let there be peace on earth,
The peace that was meant to be.
With God as Creator,
Family all are we.
Let me walk with my Family,
In perfect harmony.

Let peace begin with me
Let this be the moment now.
With every step I take
Let this be my joyous vow.
To take each moment
And live each moment
With peace eternally,
Let there be peace on earth,
And let it begin with me.

REV. DR. STEPHEN L. ALBERT

The Boniuk Center
For The Study and Advancement of Religious Tolerance
Rice University, Houston, Texas
phone : 713-348-2269
quillen@rice.edu

REFERENCES

1000ventures.com
aaanativearts.com/article1143
Abdu'l-Baha, PUP
Abdul-Bahá, Selections from the Writings of 'Abdul-Bahá

Abdul-Lateef Abdullah
Adam & His Sin, readingislam.com
adaniel.tripod.com/jainism
Akal, SikhiWiki Encyclopedia
Albert Einstein, Einstein 1940
alislam.org
alkhidmat.no/artikler/ghusl
American Baptist Churches
Among Native Americans, infoplease.com
An Introduction to Islam, bbc.co.uk/Birmingham/faith/islam
angelfire.com
Angutara-Nikaya I,1
Apache tribes, native languages.com
A Passage to China, china-club.de
asa3.org
asms.k12.ar.us
Ayurveda, educ.uvic.ca

Báb a Narinder Singh
Back to Beginnings, Reflections on the Tao by Huanchu Daoren
Bahá'í International Community
Bahá'í Prayers, Bahá'í Publishing Trust
baha'i-library.org
Bahá'íNet
Bahá'u'lláh, Tablets of Bahá'u'lláh
Bahá'u'lláh, *The Kitáb-i-Aqdas*: Notes 160

Bahá'í Studies Review, Letters, breacais.demon.co.uk
bahai.us.node/91
bahai-library.com
(Bangladesh - Women in Marriage, uninstraw.org)
Baptist vs. Roman Catholic, baptistcatholic.com
Be Converted To The Buddhism, bouddha.ch
beliefnet.com
Beliefs about the Bahá'í Faith, allaboutreligion.org
Be Converted To The Buddhism, bouddha.ch
beliefnet.com
Beliefs about the Bahá'í Faith, allaboutreligion.org
Blackfoot, Martin 1996
Bob Sam-Tlingit Storykeeper, sitcatribal.com
boloji.com
Book of Ritual 21.2.1 from *Readings from World Scriptures* - by Prof Andrew Wilson
Book of the Supreme Venerable Sovereign's Opening of the Heavens
Bridging Our Faiths, The Interreligious Council of San Diego, Paulist Press 1997
buddahmind.info
Buddha, thinkexist.com
buddha.net
buddhism.kalachakranet.org/anger
Buddhist Customs, experiencefestival.com
Buddhist Prayer Explained, buddhistfaith.tripod.com

Causes of Violence, tue.nl/redesintrum/debate/eykhof
ccrs.org/FAQs
chabad.org
china-sd.net/eng/qiluculture/Confucius
Choctaw Nation, rootsweb.com
Christian History Institute
Christian Reformed Church
Christian Science, Encyclopedia.com
Citizen Potawatomi Nation, potawatomi.org
Code of Conduct, Sikh Missionary Society, gurmat.info
coehs.uwash.edu
Comanche Indians, Indians.org
Compassion and Creativity, Dr. Atul K. Shah
Confucian Analects, Confucius 1971
Confucianism and Ecology: Potential and Limits by Mary Evelyn Tucker

Confucianism Precepts, healpastlives.com
Confucianism, alislam.org
Confucianism, nvcc.edu
Confucius, Probe Ministries, leaderu.com
Conservation of The Earth's Resources, bcca.org
Conservative Judaism, Jewish Virtual Library
Creation's Journey, Native American Music
Creativity in Judaism, Rabbi Philip Kranz and Jeffery Grossman,
creativityinjudaism.com
crvp.org/conf/Istanbul
cultureofpeace.org/quotes/interfaith-quotes
customessaymeister.com
cyberessays.com/History/7

dailybahai.com/archives/category/spiritual-growth
Doctrine of the Mean 13.3

earthisland.org
Eastern Beliefs, ksuweb.kennsew.edu
Educational Cyber Playground, edu-cyberpg.com
Emmons, 2007
Encyclopedia of The Orient, Sunni
english.emery.edu
Epistle to the Son of the Wolf, Wilmette: Bahá'í Publishing Trust, 1988
Essays on Sikh Values, gurmat.info
evangelicaloutpost.com
Exploring the Interactions between Asian Culture (Confucianism) and Creativity, The Journal of Creative Behavior, Kyung Hee Kim, Volume 41, Number 1 / First Quarter 2007
Eye on Religion, ccat.sas.upenn.edu

Faith Communities Today 2005
Father of Taoism, chebucto.ns.ca
First Aid and Healing, reading islam.com
Forgiveness and Health: An Unanswered Question Carl E. Thoresen Stanford University Alex HS Harris Stanford University
Forgiveness in Jainism, Alan Hunter, May 2003, corporate.coventry.ac.uk
friesian.com
From Supplication to Gratitude: A different Prayer, Kamlesh Acharya, kamfucious.blogspot.com
fwbo.org

Rev. Dr. Stephen L. Albert

Garland Sutra 10
gauntlet.ucalgary.com
General Synod, 2002
geocities.com
geocities.com/Tokyo/Courtyard/1652/God
Gleanings from the Writings of Bahá'u'lláh, Wilmette: US Bahá'í Publishing Trust, 1990
globalsikhstudies.net
God and Human Suffering, irfi.org
Gods, Ghosts, and Ancestors, Arthur P. Wolf,
gratefulness.org
Gratitude as Viewed in Hinduism, Una Mysorekar, yale.edu
gurjari.net
Guru Arjan Dev

Hazrat Inayat Khan
Healing, Prosperity and Family Well-Being, jaysnell.org
helium.com
himalayanacademy.com
himalayanacademy.com
Hindu Gods, maileridia.com
Hindu Perspective of Life, shaivam.org
hinduwebsite.com/Jainism
hindugateway.com/library/prayer
Hinduism and Prayer, experiencefestival.com
Hinduism: Hindu Religion, All About Hinduism, Sri Swami Sivananda
hinduismtoday.com
hinduismtoday.com
history.com/minisite
historycooperative.org
History of India, Jainism, iloveindia.com
How American Values Have Overshadowed our Values and Beliefs, helium.com
How to Be a Perfect Stranger, Stuart Matlins, Sunlight Paths Publishing, 2006

I Ching
in.answers.yahoo.com
informationclearinghouse.info
innovationslearning.co.uk/subjects/re/information/creation/chinese_creation

innovationslearning.co.uk/subjects/re/information/creation/muslim_creation
interfaithcalendar.org
Islam The Modern Religion, themodernreligion.com
islamawareness.net
Islamic Beliefs and Practices, ucalgary.ca
Institute of Jainology, *Ashik Shah,* jainology.org

Jainism, Annie Besant, theosophical.ca
Jainism, Religion of Compassion and Ecology, Pravin K. Shah, 2001
Jainism and Environment, Pravin Shah, yjponline.org
Jainism At A Glance, Mrs. Sushila Singhvi, jainstudy.org
Jainism: Let Truth Prevail, experiencefestival.com
Jainism: The World of Conquerors, Natubhai Shah, P.161
Jainism, Religion of Compassion and Ecology
Jainism Simplified, Chapter 14, umich.edu
Jain Society of San Diego, Ronak Vora
jainuniversity.org
jainworld.com
jannah.org/articles/names
Japji
jewfaq.org
John Noss, *Man's Religion*
Judaism FAQ, groups.msn.com

Kabbalah: The Misunderstood Doctrine, Judaism 101
Karmic Law, geocities.com
Kharijite, Encyclopedia Britannica
kheper.net/topics/bardo

Lao Tsu, wsu.edu
lds.org
Lessons in Sarva Dharma, books4saikids.com
Lumbee Indian Nation, hunterbear.org
Luther, Martin. *Concerning the Ministry* (1523), tr. Conrad Bergendoff, in Bergendoff, Conrad (ed.) Luther's Works. Philadelphia: Fortress Press,

mail-archive.com
Magical Monks a Ritual, Scholarship Edition, content.cdlib.org
Making Sense out of Suffering, Peter Kreeft
mandalayoga.net

Rev. Dr. Stephen L. Albert

Man's Creativity: Literature, Music, Fine Arts, creationism.org
MarcoGram, marcopolo.mci.com
Mencius VII.A.4
Ministering Women, Christianity Today, ctlibrary.com
muslim-canada.org

nativeamericans.com
Native Americans, New Mexico Magazine, Nov.2007
Native American Spirituality, Donna Ladkin, greenspirit.org
native-languages.org
Natural Theology, William Paley, philosophy.tamu.edu
near-death.com/experiences/judaism06
New Advent Encyclopedia
New Advent Encyclopedia, Lutherans
New Advent Encyclopedia, Methodists
New JPS
ngfl.ac.uk/docs/DraftTeachingMaterial/2KS1-OurWorld
Number 13 of Imam "Al-Nawawi's Forty Hadiths
Numinous Treasure's Lofty and Sublime Book of the Limitless Salvation of Mankind

On Good and Evil, bahai.org
On The Absolute Tao, tao.org
Orange Pages, Protestantism
Original Sin, sullivancounty.com
Orthodox Judaism, Jewish Virtual Library
Osage Nation
Our Beliefs, Reform Taoist Congregation

painsley.org.uk/re/signposts/y8/1-1creationandenvironment/c-hindu
Pāli; Sanskrit: anātman
Parabhava Sutta
Pentecostalism and the Christian Right in America, About.com

Power of Prayer, nierica.com
Prayer and Devotion, Bahai.us
Prayer of Abundance, 1stwholistic.com
Prayer, christianfaith.com
Presbyterian Church USA

Prophets and Prophecy, jewfaq.org
Prosperity of Humankind, statements.bahai.org
Pueblo Indians, esortment.com
Pushpayurveda; The science of healing and way to happiness, Dr. Job Thomas, Kerala Caling, Sept. 2004
Purpose of Life, islamtommorrow.com

realsikhism.com
Reconstructioist, Jewish Virtual Library
Religion and Ethics, Jainism, bbc.co.uk
religion-cults.com
Religionfacts.com
Religions of the Axial Age, Mark Muesse, teach 12.com
Religious Tolerance.org
religiousmovements.lib.virginia.edu
religioustolerance.org/nataspir
religioustolerance.org/unity
rsintl.org/rstbelieve

Sabdavali, himalayanacademy.com
sagchip.org
Sanatana Dharma, ansatana-dharma.tripod.com
San Xavier del Bac Mission
Seeking Prosperity, asp.usatoday.com
<u>*Selections from the Writings of 'Abdu'l-Bahá*, rev. ed. (Haifa: Bahá'í World Centre, 1982)</u>
Seminole, Native Americans.com
Seventh Day Adventist Church
Shamanism, wellbeing.com
Shao-king
Sikh Missionary Society U.K
Sikh.net
Sikhism, members.tripod.com
sikhism.com/intro/itwo
sikhmarg.com
sikhs.org/transl
sikhwomen.com
simpletoremember.com/vitals/Kaddish
Smoky Mountain Mall, Cherokee

Rev. Dr. Stephen L. Albert

Some Answered Questions 'Abdu'l-Bahá
Spiritual Growth, *divinehumanity.com*
spiritualitytoday.org

Tablets of Bahá'u'lláh,
Tacit Knowledge in Taoism and Its Influence on Chinese Culture, Cheng Zhu, May, 2002
Tao Te Ching
tao-tsm-en.siutao.com
taoinstitute.org
Taoism and The Arts of China, artic.edu
Taoism and The Job Market, B. Ho, chronicle.com
Taoism, Fritjof Capra
Taoism.net
Taoist Healings, authentic breathing.com
Taoists, The Chaplaincy and Pastoral Care Department, West Suffolk Hospital, wsh.nhs.uk
Terror in the Mind of God, Mark Juergensmeyer
The 10 Core Concepts of Science of Mind, Ernest Holmes
The Anglican Church, re-xs.ucsm.ac.uk
The Baha'is,
The Bahá'í Faith, United Communities of Spirit, Dr. Robert Stockman
The Baptist Start Page, baptiststart.com
The Book of Common Prayer (1979)
The Book of Pillow Secrets, Ge Hong
The Buddhist Attitude to God, buddhist information.com
The Case for the Resurrection of Jesus, Gary Habermas, 2004
The Chickasaw Nation, Indian Health Services
The Christian Bible
The Contemporary Taoist
The Flathead Nation of the Salish & Kootenai Tribes
The Four Spiritual Laws of Prosperity, Edwene Gaines
 The Gleaning by Baha'u'lah

The Goodness of Pain, planetbahai.org
The Gospel of Thomas 6
The Great Sioux Nation, Native American People Tribes
The Holy Scripture of Sikhs
The Influence of Zoroastrianism, everything2.com
The Illustrated World's Religions, Huston Smith, 1995
The Inner World, 'Consciousness'

The Iroquois Today, iroquoismuseum.org
The Meaning of Life, members.tripod.com
The Meaning of Life, Rabbi Noah Weinberg, simple to remember.com
The Metaphysical Bible Dictionary
The Muscogee (Creek) Nation Today, nps.gov
The Name of God, jewishencyclopedia.com
The Pima Indians, Pathfinders for Health
The Promulgation of Universal Peace, Wilmette: Bahá'í Publishing Trust, 1982
The Prosperity of Humankind, statements.baha'i.org
The Purpose of Life in Hinduism, religionfacts.com
The Quoran
The Science of Mind, Ernest Holmes, 1933
The Secret of the Golden Flower, Cary Baynes, ed.; Richard Wilhelm and C. G. Jung, (Harcourte Brace Jovanovich, 1962)
The Spiritual Path in Islam, islam101.com
The Spiritual Seeker's Guide, Steven Sadlier, Allwon Publishing, 1992
The Sutra of Hundred Parables
The Tanach
The Tao-te-Ching, Leo- Tsu
The Victorian Web, The Congregationalists

The Way of the Bowl, thebowl.limyanko.com
The Wisdom of Hinduism, Paula Vaughan
The Wisdom of Judaism, Elkins
thedaily.washington.edu
thienlybuutoa.org
Tobit 4:15
To Walk in God's Ways: Jewish Pastoral Perspectives on Illness and Bereavement (Jason Aronson, 1995).
Tricycle: The Buddhist Review, Stephen Butterfield, Vol. I,
Two Tugs of War, arts.cornell.edu

Udana-Varga 5:18
understanding-islam.com
Ultra-Orthodox Judaism, about.com
Unity, Melton:1015
users.ap.net/~chenae/spirit.html

Violence In Christian Theology, J. Denny Weaver

Watchtower.org
Welcome To The Navajo Nation, navajo.org
What Becomes Of The Soul After Death, Sri Swami Sivananda
What Can I Do To Increase My Creativity, members.obtusenet.com
What Is "Religion"? Gerald A. Larue
What Is the Difference Between Sunni and Shiite Muslims, History News Network
What Reform Jews Believe, Beliefnet
What the Buddha Taught, Walpola Rahula
When Bad Things Happen To Good People, Rabbi Harold Kushner
Why didn't the Scientific Revolution happen in Islam? Tanoon Re: Saima Shah, chowk.com
Woman's Dharma, hinduism.iskon.com
World Christian Encyclopedia
worldandi.com/public/1998/cljul98
wps.prenhall.com
wsu.edu

Yaqui: A Short History, lasculturas.com
yesmagazine.org/article.asp?ID=1040
Your Personal Peace Formula, Mansukh

Zhou Dynasty, ccds.charlotte.nc.us
Zion National Park Profile, infowest.com

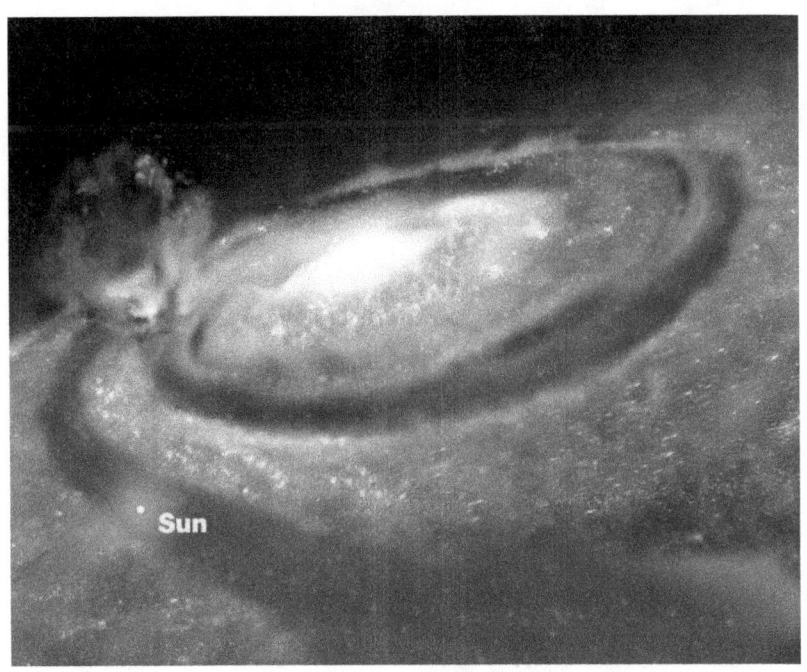

INTERFAITH GROUPS AROUND THE WORLD

(from ReligiousTolerance.org)
(Edited for accuracy)

Arizona Interfaith Movement at http://www.interfaitharizona.com
Center for Global Ethics at: http://astro.temple.edu/ **Grace**, at: http://www.grcmc.org/
North American Academy of Ecumenists, at: http://naae.net/
Interfaith/ Religions in Renewal at: http://www.usao.edu/
North America: The **North American Interfaith Network** http://www.nain.org/
United Kingdom: The **Inter Faith Network for the United Kingdom** http://www.interfaith.org.uk/
United Kingdom: The **Interfaith Alliance UK** http://www.interfaithalliance.org.uk/
Parliament of the World's Religions http://www.cpwr.org See: http://www.parliamentofreligions2009.org/
The World Council of Churches' interreligious relations and dialogue team : http://www.oikoumene.org/
Afterhours Inspirational Stories See: http://www.inspirationalstories.com/
All Religions http://www.all-religions.com/
Areopagus Revisited http://www.teo.au.dk/cms/
Biblaridion : http://www.biblaridion-online.net/
Common Ground http://www.cg.org/
Comparative-Religion.com http://www.comparative-religion.com
CoNexus Multifaith Media http://www.conexuspress.com/
Council for a Parliament of the World's Religions http://www.cpwr.org/
Encounter World Religions Centre http://www.worldreligions.ca

Rev. Dr. Stephen L. Albert

DruidsFoot http://www.druidsfoot.com/
Dharma, The Cat http://www.dharmathecat.com/
Discussion group: http://www.delphiforums.com/
The European Association for World Religions in Education ttp://www.eawre.org/
The Global Dialog Institute http://astro.temple.edu/~dialogue/
The Golden Rule Creative/Meditative Workshop www.carrot.com/events/joiedevivre/
The Harmony Project http://www.theharmonyproject.org/
The Institute for Interreligious Studies //www.interrel.de/
Interfaith Action's http://www.ifaction.org/
The Interfaith Alliance http://www.tialliance.org/
The Interfaith Encounter Association http://interfaith-encounter.org/
InterfaithForums http://www.interfaithforums.com/
Interfaith Fellowship http://www.interfaithfellowship.org/
Interfaith.org http://www.interfaith.org/
Jewish-Christian Relations http://www.jcrelations.net/
Miracle Minds http://www.miracleminds.org/
Multifaith Works http://www.multifaith.org/
MultiFaithNet at http://www.multifaithnet.org/
Ontario Multifaith Council on Spiritual and Religious Care http://www.omc.ca/
The Origin Network http://www.origin.org/
OurFaiths.org: The religion community: http://forums.prospero.com/faithtofaith/start
The Oxaty web directory http://oxaty.com/religion.html
Poway Interfaith Team http://www.powayinterfaithteam.org
Questhaven http:www.questhaven.org
The Religion Depot http://www.edepot.com/
Religion and Life http://reel.utsc.utoronto.ca/religionandlife/
Sisters of Embracement http://www.sistersofembracement.org
Spiritual and Religious Alliance for Hope http://www.sarah4hope.org/
Spiritual Traditions http://spiritualtraditions.net/
The Temple of love http://www.thetempleoflove.com/
The Temple of Understanding http://www.templeofunderstanding.org/
The True Light Project http://www.thetruelight.net/
For the United Kingdom http://www.interfaith.org.uk/

For additional interfaith information, go to
https://world-interfaith.com

About the Author

Rev. Dr. Stephen Albert was born in Philadelphia and lived and worked in St. Louis and Phoenix before he settled in San Diego, California in 1989. He began teaching college classes and creating seminars to bring people of diverse backgrounds together in 1975. Steve has 4 college degrees including the Doctor of Religious Studies from Emerson Theological Institute.

Rev, Steve discovered the New Thought religion in 1989 and took over his first religious center in 1995. He met his wife, Rev. Dr. Abigail in 1999 and they led New Thought services in their center before embracing Interfaith in 2005. Since that time they have devoted their efforts towards helping people realize the commonalities of all faiths and the need to honor and respect people of all backgrounds. In 2008 Steve authored the book, *The Interfaith Manual* which compares the New Thought faith with eleven other world faiths. In 2010, together with Abigail they co-authored *The Interfaith Workbook* which offers 40 weekly lessons to teach from for interfaith schools, religious centers and community classes.

Since his first book, **PEOPLEism** in 1986, Steve has authored 20 books and has taught in colleges since 1975. He created **'New Thought Day'** in 2012 which united the New Thought organizations throughout the world, and he did the ground work to have New Thought elevated to a 'World Faith' by the Multifaith Action Society. In 2010 Steve authored the E-Book, *From Religious to Spiritual; The New Thought Experience* and he and Abigail were asked to join the Advisory Board of the Association for Global New Thought. They also facilitated discussion groups at the 2012 AGNT Awakened World conference in Rome and Florence Italy. Steve designed the New Thought convention booth at the 2009 Parliament of the World's Religions conference in Melbourne Australia and at the PWR in Salt Lake City in 2015. He designed the 2018 New Thought Space at the PWR in Toronto, Canada.

In 2015, Steve took on the 2-year task of designing and developing the 'Connect' conference for the North American Interfaith Network and in 2017, over 250 people from over 20 different faiths attended the 5-day conference at UCSD in San Diego. The conference was so successful that it included a county celebration, **Interfaith Awareness Week,** which has now become a Global annual event the second week in August every year. Information can be obtained at their website:

https://world-interfaith.com

Many of Steve's books can be found on Amazon at:
https://www.amazon.com/Rev.-Albert/e/B088P7F8DG

Steve is a 2003 stroke survivor and has written about and counsels stroke victims and their families. He survived a 5-way, open-heart by-pass in 2012, gall bladder removal in 2016 and he received a replacement shoulder in 2020. Until COVID hit, Steve had been volunteering once a week in the Rehabilitation Center of Palomar Hospital since 2004.

Presently Steve is the Director of the World Interfaith Network which contains a database of Interfaith groups around the world. Over 36 presentations by interfaith groups and individuals are archived on the website **https://world-interfaith.com** and can be freely and easily accessed by the public.

www.ingramcontent.com/pod-product-compliance
Lightning Source LLC
Chambersburg PA
CBHW071645090426
42738CB00009B/1432